# Problems of Educational Administration

# Problems of Educational Administration

T.K. Hemchand

CRESCENT
PUBLISHING CORPORATION

*[The responsibility for the facts stated, conclusions reached and plagiarism, if any, in this book is entirely that of the Author. And the Publisher bears no responsibility for them, whatsoever.]*

**Problems of Educational Administration**



First Published : 2009

ISBN 978-81-8342-139-3

*Published by* :

**CRESCENT PUBLISHING CORPORATION**
4831/24, Prahlad Street,
Ansari Road, Darya Ganj,
New Delhi - 110002
Ph. : 23272541, 23257835
Fax : 91- 011- 23257835
e-mail : campusbooks@hotmail.com

*Printed at* :
**Roshan Offset Printers**
Delhi

# Preface

Education today encompasses a whole range of objectives—equipping people with the skills for making goods and providing services, help them respond creatively to their environment, satiate their aesthetic impulses or simply stretch their abilities to the best. As the needs of contemporary social, economic and political contexts widen, education has also enlarges in its goals, making it a complex process demanding a plethora of managerial actions. It is within this context that education administration has proved to be one of the most crucial elements which make the educational process more fulfilling and rewarding.

This book in the series on educational problems has been designed to serve as a manual which concentrates its focus on to the issue of education as a whole and its persistent problems. It effectively explores and delineates what entails the problems of education, both contemporary as well as those which are perennial. Taking into account such factors as educational planning, infrastructure teachers, social demands, etc., the book demystifies the rigmarole of the matter, providing an incisive analysis of the problems which plague the administration of education. In addition, the book brings under cover critiques of numerous educational programmes, fostering an understanding of the issue which is more encompassing, and also providing a model for solving local educational issues. Further, it also takes into consideration current trends in the field.

It is hoped that the book's erudition and insight serve well for the readers.

***Prof. T.K. Hemchand***

# Contents

# 1

# Indian Education System

India has a long history of organized education. The Gurukul system of education is one of the oldest on earth but before that the guru shishya system was extant, in which students were taught orally and the data would be passed from one generation to the next. Gurukuls were traditional Hindu residential schools of learning; typically the teacher's house or a monastery. Education was free, but students from well-to-do families payed Gurudakshina, a voluntary contribution after the completion of their studies. At the Gurukuls, the teacher imparted knowledge of Religion, Scriptures, Philosophy, Literature, Warfare, Statecraft, Medicine Astrology and "History". Only students belonging to Brahmin and Kshatriya communities were taught in these Gurukuls. However, the advent of Buddhism and Jainism brought fundamental changes in access to education with their democratic character.

The first millennium and the few centuries preceding it saw the flourishing of higher education at Nalanda, Takshashila University, Ujjain, & Vikramshila Universities. Art, Architecture, Painting, Logic, Grammar, Philosophy, Astronomy, Literature, Buddhism, Hinduism, Arthashastra (Economics & Politics), Law, and Medicine were among the subjects taught and each university specialized in a particular field of study. Takshila specialized in the study of medicine, while Ujjain laid emphasis on astronomy. Nalanda, being the biggest centre, handled all branches of knowledge, and housed up to 10,000 students at its peak. British records show that education was widespread in the 18th century, with a school for every temple, mosque or village in most regions of the country. The subjects taught included Reading, Writing, Arithmetic, Theology, Law, Astronomy, Metaphysics, Ethics, Medical Science and Religion. The schools were attended by students representative of all classes of society. Traditional structures were not recognized by the British government and have been on the decline since. Gandhi is said to have described the traditional educational system as a beautiful tree that was destroyed during the British rule.

But scholars have questioned the validity of such an argument. The village pathshalas were often housed in shabby dwellings and taught by ill-qualified teachers. Instruction was limited mainly to the three Rs and the native mahajanilzamindari accounts. Printed books were not used, and most writing was done on palm leaf, plantain leaf, or on sand. There was no fixed class routine, timetable, or school calendar. There was no annual examination, pupils being promoted whenever the guru was satisfied of the scholar's attainments. There were no desks, benches,blackboards, or fixed seating arrangements. The decline probably started in the mid-1700s.

By the 1820s neither the village schools nor the tols or madrasas were the vital centers of learning. In 1823, Raja Rammohan Roy wrote to the governor-general, Lord Amherst, requesting that he not spend government funds on starting a Sanskrit College in Calcutta but rather employ "European Gentlemen of talent and education to instruct the natives of India in Mathematics, Natural Philosophy, Chemistry, Anatomy and other useful sciences."The current system of education, with its western style and content, was introduced & founded by the British in the 20th century, following recommendations by Macaulay.

The first millennium and the few centuries preceding it saw the flourishing of higher education at Nalanda, Takshila, Ujjain, & Vikramshila Universities. Art, Architecture, Painting, Logic, Grammar, Philosophy, Astronomy, Literature, Buddhism, Hinduism, Arthashastra (Economics & Politics), Law, and Medicine were among the subjects taught and each university specialized in a particular field of study. Takshila specialized in the study of medicine, while Ujjain laid emphasis on astronomy. Nalanda, being the biggest centre, handled all branches of knowledge, and housed up to 10,000 students at its peak.this is

## Education under British Rule

British records show that indigenous education was widespread in the 18th century, with a school for every temple, mosque or village in most regions of the country. The subjects taught included Reading, Writing, Arithmetic, Theology, Law, Astronomy, Metaphysics, Ethics, Medical Science and Religion. The schools were attended by students representative of all classes of society. But scholars have questioned the validity of such an argument. They argue that proponents of indigenous education fail to recognize the importance of the widespread use of printed books in the West since the sixteenth century, which led to a remarkable advancement of knowledge. Printed books were not used in Indian schools till the 1820s or even later. There were institutions such as Gresham's college in London that encouraged scientific learning. In fact, there were a number of such academic and scientific societies in

England, often supported by Puritan and non-Conformist merchants, the like of which probably did not exist in India. The entire claim of indigenous education proponents is based on the thesis advocated by Dharampal which says that there was a general decline in Indian society and economy with the coming of British rule. In the process, indigenous education suffered. This, however, is too broad a generalization, and the exact impact of British rule on different regions at different times has to be studied more carefully before we conclude that the curve everywhere steadily declined. He argues that pre-British schools and colleges were maintained by grants of revenue-free land. The East India Company, with its policy of maximizing land revenue, stopped this and thus starved the Indian education system of its financial resources. Again, we need more detailed evidence to show how far inam lands were taken over by the government. More often, military officers, zamindar.~,and talukdars were deprived of revenue-free land rather than temples, mosques, madrasas. Recent research has revealed that inam lands continued to exist well into the nineteenth century, much more than was previously suspected.

The current system of education, with its western style and content, was introduced & funded by the British in the 19th century, following recommendations by Macaulay. Traditional structures were not recognized by the British government and have been on the decline since. Gandhi is said to have described the traditional educational system as a beautiful tree that was destroyed during British rule.

The British established many colleges like St. Xavier's College, Sydenham College, Wilson College and Elphinstone College in India.

According to Prof. Emeritus M.G. Sahadevan, F.R.C.P. (London), the first medical college of Kerala was started at Calicut, in 1942-43, during World War II. Due to shortage of doctors to serve the military, the British Government decided to open a branch of Madras Medical College in Malabar, which was under Madras Presidency then. After the war, the medical school at Calicut was closed and the students continued their studies at Madras Medical College.

## Education After Independence

After independence, education became the responsibility of the states. The Central Government's only obligation was to co-ordinate in technical and higher education and specify standards. This continued till 1976, when the education became a joint responsibility of the state and the Centre.

The Education Commission under the Chairmanship of Dr. D. S. Kothari, the then Chairman, University Grants Commission, began its task on October 2,1964. It consisted of sixteen members, eleven being Indians and five foreign experts. In addition, the Commission had the benefit of discussion with a number of internationally known as consultants in the educational as well as scientific field.

In 1976, education was made a joint responsibility of the states and the Centre, through a constitutional amendment. The center is represented by Ministry of Human Resource Development's Department of Education and together with the states, it is jointly responsible for the formulation of education policy and planning.

NPE 1986 and revised PoA 1992 envisioned that free and compulsory education should be provided for all children up to 14 years of age before the commencement of 21st century. Government of India made a commitment that by 2000, 6% of the Gross Domestic Product (GDP) will be spent on education, out of which half would be spent on the Primary education.

In November 1998, Prime Minister Atal Behari Vajpayee announced setting up of Vidya Vahini Network to link up universities, UGC and CSIR.

## Recent Developments

The Indian Education System is generally marks-based. However, some experiments have been made to do away with the marks-based system which has led to cases of depression and suicides among students. In 2005, the Kerala government introduced a grades-based system in the hope that it will help students to move away from the cut-throat competition and rote-learning and will be able to focus on creative aspects and personality development as well. iDiscoveri education started by Alumni of Harvard, XLRI is a pioneer in this field. This organization has already developed 5 model schools.

India has been a major seat of learning for thousands of years. While some of the country's universities (BITS, NSIT, ISB, IITs,BHU,IIITs, NITs, IISc, TIFR, ISI, IIMs, AIIMS) are among the world's well-renowned, it is also dealing with challenges in its primary education and strives to reach 100% literacy. Universal Compulsory Primary Education, with its challenges of keeping poor children in school and maintaining quality of education in rural areas, has been difficult to achieve (Kerala is the only Indian state to reach this goal so far). All levels of education, from primary to higher education, are overseen by Department of Higher Education (India) and Department of School Education and Literacy, and heavily subsidized by the Indian government, though there is a move to make higher education partially self-financing. Indian Government is considering to allow 100% foreign direct investment in Higher Education.

The system is divided into preprimary, primary, middle, secondary and higher levels. Preprimary is usually composed of Lower Kindergarten and Higher Kindergarten, where primary reading and writing skills are developed. Primary school includes children of ages six to eleven, organized into classes one through five. Secondary school pupils aged eleven through fifteen are organized into classes six through ten, and higher secondary school students ages sixteen through seventeen are enrolled in classes Eleven through twelve. In some places there is a concept called Middle schools for classes between six to eight. In such cases classes nine to twelve are classified under high school category. Higher Education in India provides an opportunity to specialize in a field and includes technical schools, colleges, and universities.

In India, the main types of schools are those controlled by:

— The state government boards like SSLC, in which the vast majority of Indian school-children are enrolled,
— The Central Board of Secondary Education (CBSE) board,
— The Council for the Indian School Certificate Examinations (CISCE) board,
— National Open School and
— "International schools."

These schools mimic the schools in the West in pattern and syllabi and are considerably more expensive than regular schools. The exams conducted have the syllabus of anyone of the above-mentioned Councils or Boards.

## Preprimary Education

In India, kindergarten is divided into two stages- lower kindergarten (LKG) and upper kindergarten (UKG).

Typically, an LKG class would comprise children 3 to 4 years of age, and the UKG class would comprise children 4 to 5 years of age. After finishing upper kindergarten, a child enters Class 1 (or, Standard 1) of primary school. Often kindergarten is an integral part of regular schools. In most cases the kindergarten is run as a private school. Younger Children are also put into a special Toddler/ Nursery group at the age of 2–2½. It is run as part of the kindergarten. There are some organized players with standardized curriculums such as the Shemrock Preschools.

## Elementary Education System

The Constitution of India directs that the State shall endeavour to provide free and compulsory education for all children until they complete the age of 14 years within a period of 10 years from the commencement of the Constitution. For various reasons, this goal has not yet been realised. For its developmental effort, India has adopted Five-Year Plans. So far, the country has gone through the process of 5 Five-Year Plans. Currently, the Sixth Five-Year Plan (1980-85) is in progress. According to the Policy frame of the Sixth Five-Year Plan, the main objective of educational development will be to ensure essential minimum education to all children up to the age of 14 years within the next 10 years. This objective has been reinforced by the 20-Point Programme announced by the Prime Minister of India on the 14th January, 1982.

Spread Universal elementary education for the age-group 6-14 with special emphasis on girls, and simultaneously involve students and Voluntary agencies in programmes for the removal of adult illiteracy.

Elementary Education has been accorded a very high priority in the Sixth Five-Year Plan with a total plan outlay of Rs. 905 crores (Rs. 851 crores in the State Sector and Rs. 54 crores in the Central sector) or 36% of the total outlay of Rs. 2,524 crores for education. Besides, elementary education as a whole constitutes an essential component of the Minimum Needs Programme (MNP) of the Plan.

Universalisation of elementary education requires that education be made relevant and meaningful to specific communities. In context, experimental projects being implemented are providing worthwhile experiences. It is hoped that the approaches being developed will go a long way in reaching the goal of providing relevant and meaningful education on a universal basis. These Projects include the following :

(i) Comprehensive Access to Primary Education which aims at meeting the minimum educational needs of a large number of out-of-school children in the agegroup 6-14. The main objective of the project is to develop and try out relevant and problemoriented learning materials for use in the non-formal education centres. The programme is being implemented in almost all the States.

(ii) Primary Education Curriculum Renewal Project aims at decentralising the formulation of syllabus for 6-11 age-group with special reference to educational needs of children of rural, tribal and urban poverty areas. The main aim of this Projects to experiment with (a) the decentralisation of the process of curriculum development through involvement of teachers, (b) to evolve diversified curriculum through a detailed socio- economic survey of the community leading to the attainment of a common core of competencies, (c) use of environment for meaningful learning, (d) involving local community in educational programmes and use of local resources for socially useful productive work.

(iii) Community Education and Participation Project aims at developing a package of educational programmes of encompassing the entire community drawing in the process on the resources already available in the community (such as the expertise and resources available with other development departments).

(iv) In the area of Early Childhood Education, various research and developmental projects have been undertaken for strengthening pre-school education as an important support to elementary education by strengthening motivation of students for schooling and by developing school readiness. It has been demonstrated that early childhood education helps in reducing the incidence of stagnation and drop-outs.

(v) Another Project which is being implemented is Nutrition Education, Health and Environmental Sanitation. Under this project textual materials are being developed on nutrition, health and environmental sanitation which are important concerns in all communities. Further, teachers and the communities are being trained in improved practices the adoption of which depends more on knowledge than on resources.

Education, particularly school education, continues to be the responsibility primarily of States/Union Territories. At present, education in classes I-VIII, in all the Government, local bodies, and aided schools in all States/ Union Territories of the country, is free.

In the base year of the Sixth Plan i.e. 1979-80, the enrolment at the primary stage stood at 710.2 lakhs or 83.72% of 6-11 age-group Population and 194.01 lakhs at the middle stage or 40.16% of 11-14 age-group population. The targets of additional enrolment during the Sixth Plan are 180 lakhs of 6-14 age-group population-

117 lakhs at the primary stage and 63 lakhs at the middle stage. If achieved, enrolment at the end of 1984-85 would rise to 95% and 50% respectively at the primary and middle stages based on the age-group population projections according to 1971 Census figures.

In addition to the enrolment position through the formal system indicated above, it is estimated that, for the country as a whole, coverage under the non-formal system is likely to be about 35 lakhs by the end of the current plan period. If achieved, the total additional coverage at the elementary stage is likely to be of the order of 240 lakhs.

The elementary age-group out-of-school children, more parti- cularly primary age-group, belong to weaker sections including Scheduled Castes and Scheduled Tribes. Such children are concentrated in the educationally backward States and backward areas/ pockets of each State. Further, about 70 per cent of the out-of-school children are girls including Scheduled Caste and Scheduled Tribe girls. The programme of Universalisation is, therefore, target-group-oriented with concentrated efforts in the educationally backward States and backward areas/pockets in a State. In this backdrop, the following steps have been, taken as part of the basic strategy :

(i) In the country as a whole, nine States have been identified as being educationally backward. They are: Andhra Pradesh, Assam, Bihar, Jammu & Kashmir, Madhya Pradesh, Orissa, Rajasthan, Uttar Pradesh and West Bengal.

(ii) Most of States/Union Territories have identified the backward areas/pockets for concentrated attention and have quantified the Sizes of non-enrolled scheduled caste and scheduled tribe children and fixed year-wise targets for enrolment.

(iii) Special efforts are being made by the States/Union Territories for accelerated coverage of girls including Scheduled Caste and Scheduled Tribe girls.

(iv) Efforts are also being made by the States to increase the coverage under the incentive programme like provision of free textbooks and stationery, free supply of uniforms particularly for girls, attendance scholarships particularly for girls and mid-day meals programme for the benefit of children of the weaker sections.

All the States and five Union Territories are having nonformal education programmes for out-of-school children including non-starters and drop-outs. Non-formal education is being developed as a massive alternate supportive system 'to, formal schooling. The main thrust and maximum extent of coverage is in the nine educationally backward States, which are receiving special Central assistance since 1979-80 under a centrally sponsored scheme of non-formal education for elementary agegroup children.

Voluntary organisations in the nine educationally backward States running non-formal education centres on the State Government pattern and academic institutions, Government or private, in any State/Union Territory taking up innovative and experimental non-formal education projects are given Central assistance.

In order to increase enrolment of girls in the Non-formal Education centres, enhanced (90%) Central assistance is being given for the establishment of NFE Centres exclusively for girls in the nine educationally backward States.

For production of teaching-learning materials, guide books etc. for the massive non-formal education, programme for elementary age- group children in all the

States/Union Territories, commodity assistance in the form of paper has been given.

To provide a further boost to the programme of universalisation of elementary education, and to give recognition for excellence in performance for the spread of girls' education, a scheme of incentives/awards is being implemented.

With a view to increasing enrolment of girls which is a critical target group, a scheme of Central financial assistance for appointment of women teachers in primary schools in the educationally backward States has been formulated and put into operation.

In the context of universalisation of elementary education, Early Childhood (Pre-school) Education has assumed importance. While the pre-school child receives care in ECE Centre, his young caretaker, usually a girl, is free to join and attend school, thus removing one basic cause of drop-outs, particularly in the first two or three years of the primary stage. Realising the importance of the role of voluntary agencies in this area, the Union Ministry of Education has formulated and put into operation a scheme of financial assistance to voluntary agencies to run Early Childhood (Pre-school) Education Centres as adjuncts of primary/middle schools run' either by Government, local body or private management, particularly for the disadvantaged sections in rural/tribal/backward areas in the 9 educa- tionally backward States.

Prior to the inception of Integrated Child Development Service Programme, Balwadis were being used for the Preschool education of children in the age-group 3 to 5 years. The Balwadis were located in the rural areas and were being run by voluntary organisations. The importance of pre-school education for the social and mental development of the Child has been recognised by the social scientists. When ICDS was formulated, informal pre-school education was introduced as one of its components.

Non-formal pre-school education implies· the Organisation of pre- school activities for children in the age-group 3 to 5 years in Angawadis, which stimulate the children to learn from the environment and through play and creative activities,

## Improvements in School Education

Apart from quantitative expansion of education as envisaged in the constitutional directives, the education policy has emphasised the need for bringing about qualitative improvement in education. The effort includes renewal and upgrading of curricula of elementary and secondary schools, environmental approach to teaching of different subjects, physical and moral education, art education including creativity and aesthetics.

For bringing about improvement of pre-service and inservice teacher education in the country both at the elementary and the secondary levels, the National Council of Teacher Educaton (NCTE) has been set up. Efforts are made to remodel teacher education on the curricular framework that NCTE has developed. Further, the other efforts undertaken by NCERT for improving teacher education include:

(i) implementation of innovative programmes of pre-service and in-service education of teachers including extension work of the centres of continuing education;

(ii) preparation of curricula and instructional material;

(iii) research into the problems of teacher education; and

(iv) collaboration with State Governments to improve teacher education programmes.

Centres for continuing education for elementary teacher educators and secondary school teachers have been set up in different States to provide facilities for in-service education on a continuous basis.

In the ten-year school curriculum, greater emphasis has been laid on science education to develop scientific attitude among the students. The curriculum content, textbooks, methods and techniques are not only up-dated but are related to the socioeconomic and cultural development of the country. Many more efforts are still needed so as to relate science education with agriculture, economic, cultural and scientific development in collaboration with the States. Several aids, gadgets and kits have been designed, fabricated and used for effective teaching-learning process. NCERT has organised various workshop-cum- training programmes to develop different training modules in collaboration with other developing countries. Publication of School Science Journal is a step towards the development and renewal of science education to improve cultural and technological standards of the masses.

In the field of school education, many programmes for improving the quality and content of education have been introduced. These include programmes for increasing the employability of students by programmes of Socially Useful Productive Work. Education for agriculture and industry and increasing the facilities for technical and vocational education at the secondary school stage are also included in these programmes. Socially Useful Productive Work has been recommended as an integral part of the 10-year school curriculum with the objective of familiarisation of children with the world of work. National Council of Educational Research and Training which is the apex body in India to advise the Government in matters relating to school education has formulated a comprehensive curriculum for the 10- year school which has been accepted by and large by all the State Governments. One of the highlights of this programme is the introduction of 10+2 System together with vocationalisation at the secondary stage which is also recommended by the National Policy on Education.

For the education of disabled children, a scheme of Integrated Education was launched in 1974 by the Department of Social Welfare as a Centrally Sponsored Scheme where handicapped children were sought to be integrated in the normal school system. For this purpose, certain resource facilities were made available and some financial incentives were given to the teachers and also to the children. These were mainly in terms of funding of salary of staff, special pay for teachers, allowance for books and stationery and initial equipment allowance.

The Scheme was revised in consultation with the experts and Planning Commission in 1981. The revised Scheme envisaged certain additional facilities such as the setting up of an assessment room, a resource room, enhanced salary of the staff and other incentives for the teachers and disabled children and provides 100% assistance.

As the training of teachers in special education is special ingredient for the proper implementation of the Scheme, the NCERT has also started such a training course for the key personnel. Besides, the four National Institutes of the Handicapped are also cxpected to play a pioneering role in the training of teachers in special education and also in the preparation of equipment required by the disabled for education in integrated schools.

In India the cultural milleu is diverse as far as language, art, religion, caste, communities, etc. are concerned. There are also large scale disparities between different sections of the population, among regions etc.

There is consequently an urgent need for bringing about social and national integration. ID education, therefore, various policies are being pursued to, achieve the goal of social and national cohesion. The National Service Scheme, social service and community education and community service scheme, labour and social service corps, NCC and Nehru Yuvak Kendra Camps are given priority in the: curricular and co-curricular activity in school curriculum.

Educational policies also stress the promotion of national consciousness, an understanding of cultural heritage and the creation of strong sense of nationalism. Hence, teaching of language and literature, philosophy, religion, history, painting, art, music, dance and drama have been included in the school curriculum. The ten-year curriculum frame work lays down stage-wise objectives of general education. Among the objectives listed are those that have a direct bearing on developing linkages between education and culture of the country.

## Higher Education System

Coordination and determination of standards in higher education is a special responsibility of the Central Government. This responsibility is discharged mainly through the University Grants Commission. Besides, the Government has established agencies for promotion and coordination of research efforts in specialised fields. There are three such national agencies at present, namely the Indian Council of Social Science Research, the Indian Council of Historical Research and the Indian Council of Philosophical Research. The Gov- ernment has also been implementing a number of schemes in the field of higher education and research, including those relating to academic collaboration between India and other countries.

In the field of higher education, the growing facilities have attracted a larger number of people to universities and colleges. However, our economic development has not kept pace with this expansion. Consequently, unemployment among the educated, in particular, has been showing a rising trend. Although the ultimate solution to the problem of unemployment lies in the rapid industrial and economic development of the country, efforts arc afoot to make higher education more relevant to the needs of the people and to increase the employability of graduates.

## Technical Education System

The Technical Education System of the country is designed to meet the technological needs of economy both on short-term and long-term basis. The development of technical education is, therefore, regarded as an area of high priority in economic planning. In order to meet the urgent requirements of the nation, major emphasis has been on (a) optimum utilisation of existing facilities, (b) consolidation, (c) expansion of facilities in areas where weakness exists, (d) creation of infrastructure in areas of emerging technologies vital for the development of the country, (e) improvement of quality and standards of education, and (f) furtherance of national efforts to develop and apply science and technology as an instrument of country's socio- economic progress.

Besides the schemes instituted in the earlier years the following new plan schemes have been instituted :

— *National Manpower Information System* : The main objective of the National Manpower Information System is to provide uptodate and meaningful manpower information on a continuing basis to enable the concerned authorities to anticipate areas of growth in the field of science and technology and consequently plan for technical manpower development on the proper lines. The system will help in many ways including collection, storage, updating, retrieval and analysis of manpower information to formulate necessary development plans on scientific lines to meet the national requirements.

— *Quality Improvement Programme* : The programme of quality improvement was initiated with a view to improving the quality and standards of technical education system in India. The scheme continued to play its important role in the faculty development and curriculum development in the technical institutions. Quality improvement programme consists of (i) faculty development, and (ii) curriculum development which includes preparation of instructional material, textboks and laboratory development.

— *Community Polytechnics* : The scheme was instituted in the year 1978-79 under which 36 Polytechnics were selected to be developed as community polytechnics. in addition to offering diploma courses in different. branches of engineering and technology, these polytechnics are also required to interact with the environment and serve as focal points to promote transfer of technology to the rural sector.

— *Advanced Technician Course*: The scheme of Advanced Technician Course has been started from 1981-82. The main objective of this Scheme is to provide avenues of advancement to diploma holders and also to provide higher courses at advanced level to enable the technicians to advance professionally in their own lines.

— *Institutional Network Scheme* : The Institutional Network Scheme, which was introduced in 1981-82, continued with vigour during 1983-84. Collaboration between the Indian Institutes of Technology and Regional Engineering Colleges continued in the areas of laboratory development and faculty exchange programme.

— *Expansion of Faculties in Areas where Weakness exists.* The Scheme was instituted in 1981-82 to strengthen and expand facilities in the areas where weakness existed. The primary object of the scheme was to improve areas of Computer Science, Electronics, Maintenance Engineering, Instrumentation, Product Development and Bio-Sciences and Management Sciences etc.

— *Creation of Infrastructure in Areas of Emerging Technology.* The Scheme, which was introduced in 1981-82, envisages to create and develop facilities for research and education, and training in the areas of new emerging technology so important for the development and advancement of the country in this respect. These include Microprocessor application, Remote Sensing, User Technology Atmospheric Sciences, Environmental Engineering, Energy Sciences, and Water Resources Management. The strengthening and creation of facilities in these areas would be of immense help in accelerating the pace of development in the country.

— *Modernisation of Engineering Laboratories and Workshops*: The Scheme envisages to meet the changing situations in the industry and curricular changes. The laboratories are being modernised with more relevant and useful equipment. The scheme is expected to help improve the situation in this respect.

In the field of Agricultural Education, most of the universities have introduced agricultural courses at under-graduatelevel. The Scheme of Agricultural Polytechnics (Krishi Vigyan Kendras) at the post- matric level has been developed.Polytechnics have also been set up in tribal areas.

### Non-Formal Education

In 1979-80, the Government of India, Department of Education launched a program of Non-Formal Education (NFE) for children of 6-14 years age group, who cannot join regular schools. These children include school drop-outs, working children, children from areas without easy access to schools etc. The initial focus of the scheme was on ten educationally backward states. Later, it was extended to urban slums as well as hilly, tribal and desert areas in other states. The program is now functional in 25 states/UTs. 100% assistance is given to voluntary organizations for running NFE centers.

Bal Bhavans centers, which are operational all over India, aim to enhance creative and sports skills of children in the age group 5-16 years. There are various State and District Bal Bhavans, which conduct programs in fine-arts, aeromodeling, computer-education, sports, martial arts, performing arts etc. They are also equipped with libraries with books for children. New Delhi alone has 52 Bal Bhavan centers. The National Bal Bhavan is an autonomous institution under the Department of Education. It provides general guidance, training facility and transfer of information to State and District Bal Bhavans situated all over India.

### Distance education

India has a large number of Distance education programmes in Undergraduate and Post-Graduate levels. The trend was started originally by private institutions that offered distance education at certificate and diploma level. By 1985 many of the larger Universities recognized the need and potential of distance education in a poor and populous country like India and launched degree level programs through distance education. The trend caught up, and today many prestigious Indian Universities offer distance programs. Indira Gandhi National University, one of the largest in student enrollment, has only distance programs with numerous local centers that offer supplementary contact classes.

# 2

# System of Educational Administration

India is a Union of States with a written Constitution. It enjoys a Parliamentary form of Government at the Union and State levels. According to the Constitution, Central Government is solely responsible for the subjects mentioned in the Union list of the Constitution. Similarly, the State Governments are responsible for the subjects mentioned in the State there is also a Concurrent List which is the joint List. responsibility of Central and State Governments.

By a Constitutional Amendment in 1976, education was placed in the Concurrent List. Prior to this Constitutional Amendment, the Central Government was directly responsible by virtue of entries in the Union List for several educational sectors including (a) co-ordination and determination of standards in institutions for higher education and research and scientific and technical institutions; (b) union agencies and institutions for professional, vocational or technical training; (c) promotion of special studies or research; and (d) Central universities and any other institutions declared by Parliament as institutions of national importance.

In discharging this constitutional responsibility, the Govern- ments at the Centre and the States have enacted legislation to govern the educational institutions and administer the programmes at various levels and in different fields. The statute books of the States, for example, cover legislations relating to: school education, State Universities, Boards of Secondary Education, Compulsory primary education, etc., while those of the Centre include University Grants Commission Act, Acts governing the Central Universities and the five Indian Institutes of Technology, Apprentices Act etc.

The Ministry of Education and Culture plays a major role in ensuring a coordinated development of education all over the country and in developing national programmes in some essential areas like elementary, adult and secondary education and research. State Education Departments share the major responsibility in administering education particularly at the school level.

The Union Ministry of Education and Culture is guided in the main by the Central Advisory Board of Education the members of which include the Ministers of Education in the States and educationists. There are a few advisory and expert consultative bodies like the All India Council of Sports and the All India Council for Technical Education, the National Council for Teacher Education, the National Council for Women's Education and the National Book Development Board. To carry out its responsibilities, the Ministry during the years has built up a number of offices and organisations. The important amongst them are: The University Grants Commission, the National Council of Educational Research and Training, the National Institute of Educational Planning and Administration, Indian Institute of Advanced Study, Central Schools Organisation, Central Board of Secondary Education, Central Hindi Institute, Central Institute of Indian Languages, National Sanskrit Institute, Lakshmibai National College of Physical Education and Netaji Subhas National Institute of Sports. In the field of technical education there are five Indian Institutes of Technology, the Indian Institute of Science, fifteen Regional Engineering Colleges, three Institutes of Management, four Technical Teachers' Training Institutes, Indian School of Mines, School of Planning and Architecture, National Institute for Training in Industrial Engineering, and National Institute of Foundary and Forge Technology. While scientific research is promoted in a chain of specialised research laboratories under the Council of Scientific and Industrial Research set up by the Central Government and in the Universities, three significant organisations viz. Indian Council of Social Science Research, Indian Council of Historical Research and Indian Council of Philosophical Research have also been set up to promote research in the social sciences, history and philosophy.

In every State there is an Education Minister, who is, in some States, assisted by Minister of State/Deputy Minister. The Secretary is the Head of the Education Department which has a Secretariat for Policy and Coordination and Directorate of Education that perform the functions of direction, regulation and inspection in various sectors of education. There are State Institutes of Education and State Councils of Educational Research and Training in the States to look after the academic aspects, which are replicas of the National Council of Educational Research and Training. Functional Inspectorates or Bureaux like Inspectorates for Physical education, Audiovisual education, Vocational guidance bureau, Evaluation units also function in the States.

Both at the Centre and in the States, educational programmes are looked after by a number of Ministries/ Departments, besides the Ministry/Department of Education. Medical education is looked after by the Ministry/Department of Health and Agricultural education by the Ministry/Department of Agriculture. In some States technical education remains with a department other than Education viz. Department of Industries.

Educational Planning is the joint endeavour of the Central and State Governments. The Planning Commission in the Centre and the State Planning Departments decide the policy and approach in the field of national development. A Planning and Monitoring Division in the Central Ministry works in close liaison with the Education Division of the Planning Commission, on the basis of the broad guidelines issued by the Planning Commission, draft Five-Year and Annual Plans are prepared by the Central Ministries and the State Governments. These plan programmes are discussed and examined at various levels before they are finally approved for implementation. Joint consultation on educational planning between the Centre, the States and the Planning Commission is promoted in all India forums like the Central Advisory Board of Education or State Education Ministers' Conference, Official meets and Annual Plan discussions.

## EDUCATIONAL FINANCING

Educational financing in India has developed to be a multisource system although the State has been taking an increasingly commanding position in this behalf since Independence. Education is now financed by the Central Government, State Governments, local authorities and through fees and other sources that include endowments, donations and voluntary contributions.

Educational financing by the Central Government and the State Governments is of two categories, viz., Plan and NonPlan. Plan allocations cover development expenditure while Non-Plan allocation provide for maintenance. The Central Government, however, is directly responsible for the development programmes in the fields within its purview. It also takes up schemes known as Centrally Sponsored Schemes and Central Schemes administered by the States which are of common interest and utility to the State Governments and represent nationally identified objectives. The Central Government has in the post-independence period, been extending increasing financial assistance to the State Governments besides incurring considerable direct expenditure on the Central and Centrally Sponsored Schemes.

## Educational Structure

Educational structure has become comprehensive and differential. The educational system is being reorganised to the changing needs and realities. Educational system has undergone several assessments in order to improve and to become responsive to the challenges of modernisation and goals of national developments. Demographical changes have been made. Alternate strategies of education have resulted in restructuring of education and emergence of alternate structures. Alternate nonformal structures as complementary to formal structures have been developed parallel as complement or supplement to formal education structure.

Educational content/curricula/teaching-learning materials are becoming more functional and less academic, more diversified and less omnibus, and more operational and less disciplinary. The approach for developing the learning materials has become an integrated approach to knowledge with focus on reallife problems. Divergent learning materials are being developed. Local specific learning sequences are being experimented. Content is being based on relevance, flexibility, needs, and local specifics. Curricula are being revised to contain new areas of population education, health and nutrition education, community education, and value-oriented education.

Educational methodologies are undergoing substantial changes due to correspondence education, computer-assisted instruction, educational technologies, micro-teaching, distance learning, non- formal education, programmed instruction, personalised instruction, radio-vision, systems approach, ungraded schools/ units, video- education, work-experience, instructional television and open school education. Open education has been instituted for depressed areas and under-served sections of the population. Part-time eductation is in progress. Electronic media is evolving its own pedagogical methodologies and strategies. Multiple approaches are being evolved to cater to the needs of dis-interested learners, slow learners and defiant learners. Language laboratories and children's media labs are revolutionising educational methodologies.

Educational Broadcasting in India is now available from forty- four stations which originate the programmes and 27 Auxiliary Stations which relay them. This indicates the importance given to educational broadcasts in our country.

All India Radio's Educational Broadcasts for schools are mainly designed as a support to the curricular Organisation of various States and Union Territories of the country. The scope of the programme is both enrichment and direct teaching type. The objective is to re- enforce and consolidate the learning/teaching situation in the class rooms by means of new techniques, help of specialists and approaches which are normally beyond the capacity of an average school. Besides giving support, the programme also gives a lead by up-dating and filling curricular gaps and bridging contemporary developments in the scope of the programmes, thereby closing the gaps between the class room and the outside world.

Planning is done State-wise or Territory-wise with the help of experts from the respective education departments on an yearly basis.

Programmes for primary schools are planned on the basis of the environment of the children and are of enrichment type, trying to bring some life and outside world in the class rooms, whereas the secondary school broadcasts are more syllabus-oriented and textbooks based.

The format of programmes is of various types, such as talks discussion, feature, drama, interview, debate, quiz, music etc. A programme service for teachers is also available to familiarise the teachers with the new challenges in the curricula, the latest educational methodology, and practices and also to up-date the teachers content-wise on the subject they teach. Broadcasts for post secondary school listeners are put out either as a separate university service or as part of the programmes for youth.

All India Radio is giving more and more importance to the planning and production of Science Programmes with a view to acquainting the listeners with up-to-date scientific knowledge, build in scientific temperament.

All India Radio is committed to support the National Adult Education Programme with appropriate programme in terms of motivation, training and publicity.

Ministry of Education has set up a Centre for Educational Technology, which has helped to bring the educators and broadcasters closer with a view to solving the educational problems of a vast and diverse country like India more effectively and meaningfully.

Educational evaluation is rapidly changing towards testing and measurement of higher abilities instead of memorisation, knowledge and understanding. Emphasis is being shifted from summative evaluation to formative evaluation with good deal of guidance, counselling and remedial instruction. From the evaluation, of the cognitive areas, there is a move towards assessment of non-scholastic areas as well. At places, criterionreferenced evaluation uses specific criteria for evaluating learning tasks.

Curriculum development movement dates back to the 1960s. The main thrust in the, early phase was in sciences and mathematics. This was followed by the work-oriented curriculum of the 1970s which aimed at equipping the students with efficient work habits, skills and healthy attitudes towards work, manual work in particular. Present thinking in the 1980s veers down to the fact that curriculum is to be value-oriented to bring about the desired changes in values and attitudes in the learners. The school curricula are becoming need- based, life-related, childcentred and environment-oriented.

The science education development has been under implementation since 1967 for upgrading of science kits, promotion of science clubs, Organisation of science exhibitions and summer institutes in science. These activities are supplemented by inservice training programmes for teachers, supply of laboratory equipment, improvisation of teaching aids, electronic kits, and science films and radio broadcasts.

Population education project since 1969 has been attempting to introduce population education concepts in all stages of school education. Innovative structures and approaches to population education are advocated. India is probably the first country to have formulated a population policy as early as 1962 to ensure that the younger generation does not grow up without adequate awareness of the population problem and a realisation of, its national responsibility in this regard. Efforts are being made to develop textual materials in population education for various school classes, preceded by base-line population education surveys in the country.

Use of satellite television for instructional purposes was start- ed in 1975. Indian Space Research Organisation and/or Space Application Centre worked partially for production and fully for transmission of educational programmes in several parts of rural areas in India during 1975-76, on an experimental basis. With the launching of INSAT-IA/IB in 1982-83, NCERT continues training programmes in telecommunication, electronic systems, space applications, video-tape recording, film technology, and satellite communications. Courses are undertaken in ETV programmes, script-writing, portable video, multi-media packages, school broadcasting etc.

## Educational Innovations

The National Council of Educational Research and Training brings out school level textbooks, teacher guides and supplementary readers. These publications are models of their own kind and emerge from the research and development work conducted by its more than 25 departments, 4 Regional Colleges of Education and 17 Field Units. The Council has developed about 400 textbooks and over 100 supplementary readers during 1962-83 pertaining to class I to XII in sciences (physics, chemistry, mathematics, life-sciences); and social sciences and humanities ('economics, political science, civics, history, geo- graphy, commerce, social studies, Hindi, Urdu, English, etc.). In addition, about 30 teachers' guides and about 20 workbooks have also been developed during this period.

The Council has been working in audio-visual teaching aids with special reference to graphics and low-cost materials. It has developed textbooks illustrations, charts, models, flashcards, flannel graphs, film stencils, etc. It promotes the use of dioramas and study-kits to enrich teaching-learning processes. Integrated science kits and electronic kits have been designed. Learning cards have been evolved. During 1981-83, it has produced 40 educational films, 30 filmstrips, 200 audio-tapes, and 30,000 kits. On an average, about 10,000 educational films are lent to 0.2 million schools every year by the Central Film Library maintained by NCERT.

Examination Reform Project seeks improvements through research, studies, training and extension programmes and production of sample education materials. National Test Development Library is being developed in the Council to serve, as a good reference library for use in educational measurement. National Talent Search Examination of the Council aims at identifying talented students in various subjects at school stage so that they could be provided with scholarships for enabling them to complete their education up to Ph.D in sciences, mathematics, and social sciences or take up professional courses in areas like engineering and medicine.

Twelve national integration camps and community singing for students and teachers are organised every year at different places to foster, in the participants, spirit of national integration as they become familiar with each other's life and culture. During this period, thirteen songs of different languages with national integration theme have been recorded on cassettes to be made available to the 22 States and 9 Union Territories for duplication and distribution amongst schools.

The University Grants Commission is implementing the following innovative programmes for improvement of quality :

(i) Assistance to selected Centres of Advanced Study and Departments of Special Assistance in Science, Engineering, Technology, Humanities and Social Sciences.

(ii) Support for Departmental Research Projects in Science, Humanities and Social Sciences.

(iii) Assistance for (a) College Improvement Programme, (b) College Humanities and Social Improvement Programme, and (c) University Leadership Programme.

(iv) Setting up of special committees and working groups to prepare detailed curricula including modernisation of laboratories, and development of innovative courses in Electronics, Physics, Chemistry, Mathematics and Biology.

(v) Assistance to support research activities of) University scientists for undertaking an integrated Indian Scientific Programme called the "Indian Middle Atmosphere Programme", as a multi-department/agency activity.

(vi) Special Programme relating to development, research and extension work, in Enviromnental Engineering and Pollution.

(vii) A minimum Programme of examination reforms in universities, and introduction of Mini-computers in selected colleges.

(viii) Setting up of educational media and audio- visual Research Centres to improve the quality of education. Production of balanced and effective programmes of higher education for broadcast through INSAT-I-B.

## Educational Research

The National Council of Educational Research and Training Supports educational research by providing financial assistance to individuals and outside organisations. It also awards fellowships so that educational problems are investigated and a band of competent research workers is created. Besides supporting the research efforts of others, the Council itself conducts significant research in different areas of. education. The priority areas of research are quality of school life, characteristics of school environment, academic difficulties of students, alternative strategies of education, learning outcomes, value changes, equality of educational opportunity, qualitative improvement of education, etc.

The Council conducts all India educational surveys, provides data processing service, analyses sample data, compiles selected information, collects educational statistics, provides training in survey methods and orientation in sample surveys. It has completed so far four all-India Educational Surveys. During this period, 4th Survey was supplemented by secondary analysis of the data, environmental studies for demography, educational facilities planning studies, district development plans, and the school mapping exercises.

The Council has been concentrating its efforts in identifying the various limiting factors particularly those which relate to the status of women in society and curricular irrelevance which prevent women from taking full benefits of education and facilities. This helps promote education of girls and women. A survey of educational backwardness of girls was taken in the States identified as educationally backward. This project is being funded by UNICEF.

Tools for monitoring and evaluation of universalisation of elementary education programme have been developed during 1981-83 and a pilot try-out conducted. The tools ·cover enrolment, retention, attendance, transferability from non-format schools, etc. The tools envisage monitoring, physical, academic, teacher, financial and administrative aspects. Monitoring is undertaken at school, block, district, state and national levels. It is done on monthly, quarterly, half-yearly and annual basis.

During these years, the Council undertook evaluation of textbooks at school level from the standpoint of national integration. For this, tools and techniques have been developed, guidelines have been drafted, state agencies have been identified, and textbooks evaluation was taken up in 23 States and Union Territories.

## UNICEF Projects

The specific objective of the UNICEF assisted project on Primary Education Curriculum Renewal (since 1975) is to develop innovative need-based curricula, instructional materials and strategies which can satisfy the educational requirements of the underprivileged children of the disadvantaged sections of the society. The project is implemented through 2,465 primary schools and 183 teacher training institutions covering 11,000 teachers and 0.4 million students.

The main objective of the UNICEF-assisted project on Com- prehensive Access to Primary Education is to develop for out of-school children of age-group 6-14, a large number of learning materials (episodes) based on local specific problems on modular approach to learning/ instruction. The project is being implemented, since 1979, through 974 teacher training institutions and 19 in-service teacher training centres. About 13,000 draft modules have been developed so far.

The specific objective of UNICEF assisted project on Development Activities in Community Education and Participation, since 1975-76, is to develop programmes and instructional materials to provide opportunities of formal and non-formal education to cater to the needs of the age-group 0-3, 3-6, 6-14, 15-35 and others. The project is implemented through 102 community education centres all over India.

UNICEF assisted project on Nutrition, Health, Education and Environmental Sanitation attempts to integrate concepts and practices of nutrition and health education in. the curricular programmes of rural schools in 15 centres. It aims at development of environment-based instruction package on nutrition, health education and sanitation for primary school pupils, teacher-educators and supervisor's for more than 2,500 schools.

In children's Media·Laboratory, set up with UNICEF assistance in 1975, the Council endeavours to develop and discover inexpensive, non- formal and effective media of educational value for children in age- group 3-8.

During the years 1982 and 1983, the University Grants Commission approved 488 major research projects in science subjects and 54 in humanities and social sciences involving a total grant of Rs. 444.88 lakhs. Besides, the Commission approved 1,880 minor research projects in science and 655 in humanities and social sciences involving an assistance of Rs. 147.32 lakhs.,

In the field of Technical Education, five Indian Institutes of Technology, which are apex institutions for engineering education and research, intensified their activities in the areas of continuing education and by starting new inter-disciplinary academic programmes and pursuing research and consultancy services.

The Government of India is directly assisting 12 State Governments and 20 Non-Government institutions for the development of their post-graduate courses as a part of the continuing scheme under the scheme of Development of Post-Graduate Courses and Research Work in Engineering and Technology.

The Review Committee on Post-graduate Education and Research in Engineering and Technology, inter-alia, recommended restructuring and Organisation of Post-graduate courses, identification of emerging areas, revision in the norms of assistance, faculty improvement etc.

The School of Planning and Architecture, with a view to further broadening its academic programmes relating to human settlements and the environment and also to promote research and extension, carried on effectively all its activities/programmes during this period.

The National Institute of Educational Planning and Admi- nistration, inter-alia, conducts research and studies and acts as a clearing house of information in the field of educational planning and administration. During the years 1981-83, the Institute took up a number of research studies, besides completing those already in hand.

The Indian Council of Social Science Research promotes and coordinates social science research in the country. The programmes and activities of the council continued during this period. The Council approved a large number of research projects and received completed reports in respect of the projects sanctioned earlier. Besides, the Council continued its support. to two sponsored research programmes, and assistance to 17 research institutes in the field of social sciences.

The Indian Council of Historical Research, inter-alia, sponsors historical research programmes. During the period under report, the Council continued to promote and facilitate historical research, which included grant-in-aid programme, sources programme, execution of special projects, holding of seminars, publication of journals/books and collaboration in the field of research. The Council sanctioned several research projects, fellowships and Study-cum-Travel/Contingent grants.

### International Relations

For its efforts at improving the quality of education, National Council of Eucational Research and Training receives assistance from international agencies like UNESCO, UNICEF, UNDP and UNFPA. During this period, Council's officers were deputed abroad for Science Equipment; Technical Education; Documentation Service; Educational Research; Instructional Materials; Educational Technology; Examplar Modules; Special Education; etc. Foreign visitors to the Council visited in connection with textbook preparation; audiovisual aids; science teaching; educational television; textbook production; science kits; environmental education; population education; etc.

The Council functions as the secretariat of the National Development Group for the Asian Centre for Educational Innovations and Development (ACEID). The Council as an associated centre of the APEID, hosted the programmes on upgrading basic sciences; in-service teacher education; integrated curriculum; productive work in teacher education etc . During this period, the Council signed contracts with UNESCO for undertaking studies on technology in education; drop-out problem; inservice training modules; problems of urban, marginal areas; graphic communications; alternative structures in education and contemporary world problems.

The Council acts as a major agency for implementing the provision of the Bilateral Cultural Exchange

Programmes that are signed by the Government of India with different countries as far as school education is concerned. Council's officers were deputed abroad for vocational education, and educational information system. Visitors to the Council included those who came in connection with pedagogical personnel training; examination techniques; curriculum development; and school television.

The Indian Council of Historical Research sent 9 historians to attend the International Congress of Human Sciences held in Tokyo. Besides, 5 scholars were sanctioned grants for visiting foreign countries in connection with their research pursuits/International Seminars. The Indian Council of Social Science Research maintained and developed contacts, exchanges, co-operation and collaboration outside India. Under the Indo-French Cultural Exchange Programme,6 French scholars visited India and 5 scholars from India visited France during the years 1982 and 1983. A scholar visited Czechoslovakia under Indo-Czech programme. Fifty Indian scholars visited different countries to collect data and to attend international conferences The Council hosted the Unesco meeting on Women Studies and Social Science at New Delhi in, October, 1982. A seminar on New International Economic Order was held at New Delhi in December, 1982.

The Shastri Indo-Canadian Institute, New Delhi, awarded fellowships to 20 Canadian scholars during 1982 and 1983 for undertaking research in humanities, learning Indian languages and in the field of performing arts. The Institute awarded travel grants to 16 Canadian scholars to participate in seminars/workshops held in India. Two Indian scholars were also selected by the Institute to visit Canada under the Social Sciences and Humanities Programmes.

Under the Indo-USSR Cultural Exchange Programme, 49 and 39 Russian teachers were assigned to various Indian Universities/Institutions for teaching Russian Language and literature during 1982 and 1993, respectively.

Under the Berkeley Professional Studies Programme in India, 6 scholars during 1982 and 7 scholars during 1983 came for study/internship in the fields of medicine, law, engineering, textiles, architecture, agriculture and health.

The American Institute of Indian Studies, New Delhi awarded fellowships to 226 scholars during the years 1982 and 1983 for doing research in social sciences, humanities etc.

Eighty seven American scholars/students came to India during the period 1982-1983 for doctoral and post-doctoral research under the United States Educational Foundation's programme and also for assignment as visiting professors in Indian Universities. Similarly, 92 Indian scholars were awarded Lecturers/Research/student Fellowships to the USA.

India is one of the contributing countries to Colombo Plan Staff College for Technician Education in Singapore. Besides providing annual contribution of its share that is provided by the Department of Economic Affairs, she has also provided two Indian Faculties.

This college conducts programmes, seminars, workshops etc. for the benefit of Senior Administrators, Heads of Polytechnics. Directors of Technical Education and the Faculty of Technicians Institutions. The Ministry makes nominations for the various programmes being conducted at this college after inviting proposals from the State Government and Institutions.

# 3

# Administration of School Education

The system of Education which we inherited while attaining our independence, had hardly any relevance to the needs of the life situation then prevailing in the country. With the passage of time, the educational system continued to drift away from the realities of life. At the same time there was a growing all round realisation of the deficiencies of the system. No society, particularly one like ours, which is passing through an extremely crucial but equally important phase of economic development, can allow such a system to continue. Luckily, the country has designed and accepted a replacement for the out-moded system and is currently engaged in the implementation of the new system commonly known as the 10 + 2 + 3 pattern. This pattern has been on the anvil for almost 60 years and carries on it the imprint of the deliberations of numerous high level academic and non-academic forums. The Central Board of Secondary Education has introduced this system, which has an extremely sound academic base, with effect from the current session in its thousand and odd member schools spread all over the country and outside its borders.

It is of utmost importance that the three principal partners in the successful implementation of this scheme viz., the student, the teacher and the parent, are fully posted about its content and the benefits expected to flow there from. In the following pages various aspects of this revolutionary reform in education have been discussed by eminent educationists. I am therefore particularly happy to place this brochure in the hands of the reader.

## Pattern of School Education

The adoption of the common pattern of 10+2+3 for school and college classes has been an important reform whose implementation has long been overdue. The reform was first recommended, about 55 years ago, by the Calcutta University Commission (1917-19). At that time, the Matriculation Examination, which marked the end of the school course and also constituted an entrance examination to the universities, was held in different provinces at the end of 10-12 years of schooling. But in spite of this large variation of the duration of the school stage, these examinations, though conducted by different agencies, were regarded as equivalent to each other in all parts of the country. The Matriculation Examination was followed by a two-year intermediate course at the end of which another public examination, the Intermediate Examination was held. Then came a two-year period of undergraduate education after which the First Degree Examination was held. All these three examinations-Matriculation, Intermediate and First Degree-were held by the universities. The Commission examined in depth the content of education at the intermediate and the undergraduate stages and came to the following conclusions:

(1) That the intermediate stage was really a part of the school course and that the students at this stage could be more effectively taught by school methods than by those which were appropriate at the university stage; and

(2) That the standard of undergraduate education was so poor that the first degree in India was not really

comparable to the first degree in the advanced countries.

The Commission, therefore, recommended that:

(1) The dividing line between the university and the secondary courses is more appropriately drawn at the Intermediate Examination than at the Matriculation;

(2) That the duration of undergraduate course for the First Degree should be increased to three years. and that

(3) A Board of Secondary and intermediate Education should be established for the purpose of reorganising high school and intermediate education on the lines recommended by it and for holding the matriculation and Intermediate Examinations. The universities would thus be left to their proper sphere, namely, the provision of under-graduate and post-graduate education and the holding of examinations for the first, second or research degrees.

This recommendation made a great impression on Indian educational thought and, for a time, it appeared to be on the verge of universal acceptance. But ultimately it was implemented only in one province, namely, the U.P. and that too, in a mutilated form. No steps were taken to increase the duration of the first degree course to three years; not were any effective steps taken to vocationalize the intermediate stage.

The University Education Commission (1948-49) under the Chairmanship of Radhakrishnan had, therefore, to take up the discussion of the problem once again. After examining the problem from all points of view, this Commission also came to the conclusion that it was necessary to adopt the uniform pattern of 10+2+3 for school and college classes. The Commission felt that this pattern would make it possible to vocationalize the secondary stage of education so as to divert students into different walks of life at the end of secondary school and thus reduce pressures on university admissions. It also felt that the lengthening of the undergraduate course to three years, preceded by an intensive preparation at the earlier stage of two years, would result in a considerable improvement of standards in higher education. Unfortunately, steps were not taken to implement these recommendations.

The problem came up for consideration once again when the Secondary Education Commission under the chairmanship of Dr. A. L. Mudaliar submitted its report (1952). The stage was now ripe to re- organise school and university education together, on the lines recommended by the University Education Commission and the Secondary Education Commission and to adopt a common pattern for school and college classes. At this time, throughout India, the duration of the post-Matriculation course leading to the first degree was uniformly four years and it was uniformly divided into two stages - two years of Intermediate and two years of undergraduate education.

The simplest reform would, therefore, have been to add one year to the degree course and to transfer the two years of the Intermediate course to the school stage. But for various reasons, and mainly for financial considerations, this was not done. Instead the recommendation of the Sargent Report of an eleven-year higher secondary school followed by a three-year course for first degree was revived and the pattern of 8+3+3 was adopted. The Intermediate course was therefore broken up into two parts and the first year was either added to the school stage or converted into a pre-university course of one year and the second year was added to the two-year undergraduate course for the first degree to create the three-year degree course. This was an unfortunate decision dictated by the compulsion of economy rather than the logic of academic reform.

The entire position was reviewed once again by the Education Commission (1964-66). It found that, as a result of the decisions taken after the Report of the Secondary Education Commission, there were at least four different patterns of schools and colleges in the country which may be stated as follows:

(1) Kerala was the only State where the pattern of 10+2+3 had been adopted, with the two-year stage being located in junior colleges;

(2) The pattern of 10+2+2 prevailed only in Uttar Pradesh where a ten-year school was followed by a two- year intermediate course and a two-year course for first degree;

(3) The pattern of 11+3 prevailed in the Delhi Union Territory and the State of Madhya Pradesh where an eleven year higher secondary school was followed by a three year course for the first degree; and

(4) The pattern of 10 (or 11 or even 12 in some cases) + 1+ 3 was followed in the other States where a school stage of 10 to 12 years was followed by a year of pre-university course and a three-year course for the first degree.

The Commission examined this situation from all points of view and came to the conclusion that, on sound academic considerations detailed in its report, it would be highly desirable to adopt the uniform pattern of 10+2+3 for school and college classes in all parts of the country. The Commission was also definitely of the view that the school stage should consist of 12 years (10+2) and that every effort should be made to vocationalize the higher secondary stage so that, ultimately, 50% of the enrolments at this stage would be in the vocational courses. The Commission also recommended a detailed programme for bringing about these important changes.

These proposals of the Education Commission have found general support in the country. Even before the Report of the Commission was submitted, the National Integration Committee appointed by the Ministry of Education under the chairmanship of the late Dr. Sampurnanand recommended that, from the point of view of national integration, the uniform pattern of 10+2+3 should be adopted for school and college classes in all parts of the country. This recommendation was also supported by the Committee of Educationists and student leaders appointed under the directive of the National Integration Committee and also by several conferences of students organizations. The Central Advisory Board of Education has also unanimously supported the proposal and expressed the view that it should be implemented on a priority basis and that, at any rate, the programme should be completed in all parts of the country by the end of the Fifth Five Year Plan. The Resolution of the Government of India on the National Policy of Education also supports the uniform adoption of this pattern.

The pattern has since been introduced in the States of Andhra Pradesh and Karnataka. Steps have been initiated to introduce the pattern in the States of Maharashtra, Gujarat and West Bengal. Several other States have set up committees to examine the issue and it is hoped that they will also follow suit in the near future.

### Basic Academic Considerations

While due weight must be attached to this series of weighty recommendations of important Commissions and Committees and the steps already taken to implement them, it is also necessary to examine these proposals on academic grounds and to satisfy ourselves that they are in the best interests of the country.

The first point to be decided, on academic grounds, is the stage or age at which a student should be deemed to be fit to enter the university system. In all the advanced countries of the world, a student entering the universities is expected to be 18 years of age or more. It is only then that he can be adequately prepared for entering upon a course of higher education and also be mature enough to study on his own and to profit by, the methods of teaching which are appropriate to the university stage. This necessarily implies a total duration of at least 12 years for the school stage (including elementary and secondary education), because the age of admission to the school system is generally six years. At present, when the total duration of the school stage is sometimes only 10 or 11 years, and the age of admission to the school system is five years or even less, very young students aged 14-17, often enter the university system. They are really children who deserve to remain at school and continue to be taught by methods appropriate to the school stage rather than young persons who are mature enough to profit by a course of higher education. This is bad for the schools that lose in their stature by a cut in their total duration. It is bad for the universities because it adversely affects their standards. What is even more important, it is not good for the students themselves. If this situation is to be improved, it follows that the total duration of the school stage (including elementary and secondary education) should be not less than twelve years.

The next question to be discussed refers to the duration of the secondary education course. The duration of elementary education is eight years in some States such as Uttar Pradesh, and seven years in others such as Maharashtra. If the total duration of school stage is to be twelve years, it follows that the duration of the secondary course would be four years in some States and five years in others. The Education Commission had an open mind on this issue and did not insist on a uniform pattern of seven or eight years for elementary education. It was, however, very emphatic on one point: secondary education should not form an integrated continuous course, but should preferably be broken up into two sub-stages: the lower secondary and the higher secondary. It further recommended that the elementary and lower secondary stage should cover the first ten years of school and that the higher secondary stage should cover the last two years. It is necessary to understand the reasons which led the Education Commission to make these recommendations.

The Education Commission found that whenever the course of secondary education is made continuous and unbroken, as in the higher secondary schools of Delhi or Madhya Pradesh, two undesirable consequences follow. The first is that the expansion of secondary education is much larger than necessary or desirable. This is because the principle of selective admissions cannot be introduced at the beginning of the stage (Class IX) when the students are too young and because every student who enters the stage has to continue till the very end because of the continuous character of the course. Such a system therefore prevents the students from leaving the school at the end of Class X, although they would be eligible for admission to many vocational courses at this point. Secondly, the continuous character of the course compels the student to decide upon his future career at a very premature stage when he is entering Class IX and is about 13 or 14 years old. This is academically undesirable and in fact, Dr. D. S. Kothari has condemned it as a system of "child marriage". The Education Commission was therefore strongly of the view that the secondary stage should be broken into two parts at the end of Class

X, that the students should continue to receive general education till the end of this stage, and that in the next higher secondary stage of two years, two distinct streams should be introduced, one stream preparing the students for admission to universities and the other preparing them for different vocational courses which would be terminal in character. The Commission also felt that the enrolment in courses of a vocational or terminal character should be as high as 50 per cent of the total.

It must also be pointed out that the Education Commission was not happy with the existing higher secondary pattern of 8+3 which provides seven different streams-Humanities, Science, Technical, Commercial, Agriculture, Fine Arts and Home Science and requires every student to join one stream of his choice. The vocational courses provided in this pattern have one major weakness their vocational content necessarily remains weak because the total time available is limited. These courses, therefore, do not become terminal and do not prepare the students for the pursuit of a vocation at the end of the secondary stage. In fact, they do not even prepare them for admission to the corresponding vocational courses at the university stage. The vocational courses in this stream have therefore never become either popular or terminal. Since the programme of vocationalization of se- condary education is extremely important and since it is obviously urgent to divert a fair proportion of students into different walks of life at the end of the secondary stage and thus reduce the pressures on university admissions, the Education Commission rightly came to the conclusion that the existing higher secondary pattern of 8+3 should be replaced by the proposed higher secondary pattern of 10+2.

Two important points must be mentioned in regard to the proposed reorganisation of school education:

(1) In the old days, and even in the multipurpose system introduced by the Secondary Education Commission, science and mathematics tended to be neglected. They were studied only till the end of Class VIII, and thereafter the student had the option to omit them if he so desired. In many secondary schools, even the provision for the teaching of these subjects did not exist. The net result was that more than 50 per cent of the students at the secondary stage were deprived of basic education in science and mathematics. Adequate teaching of science and mathematics is essential in the modern world based on science and technology. It is equally necessary to improve the quality of education and to avoid the dangers resulting from a dichotomy of the "two cultures" of science and of humanities. Above all, a society like ours, which is committed to the ideals of socialism, has to ensure vertical mobility to the manual workers, whether engaged in industry or agriculture. For this purpose, it must provide the necessary grounding in science and mathematics to every person as a part of his school education because, without this, vertical mobility is not attainable. The Education Commission, therefore, rightly recommended that the teaching of science and mathematics should be obligatory till the end of Class X.

(2) While a student should ordinarily be expected to decide whether he will go in for a vocational course or into the university stream at the end of Class X (when he is about 16 years of age), it goes without saying that such decisions would be tentative and that some young persons may like to change from one stream to the other at a later stage. The Central Advisory Board of Education, therefore, specifically recommended that such later transfers from one

stream to the other should not only be permitted but also facilitated by due provision for transfer of credits on this account. The importance of this recommendation is obvious.

Even as early as 1919, the Calcutta University Commission had recommended that the course leading to the first degree should have a duration of three years. With the passage of time, the opinion on the subject has now become even stronger for three main reasons.

Firstly, there is now a much greater demand for specialization on account of the explosion of knowledge and, at the same time, there is also a demand for greater general education to enable the young persons to face successfully the complex societies of the modern period.

Secondly, there is now a much greater demand for inter-disciplinary courses and for the provision of greater elasticity to the students to choose subjects of study to match their individual capacities and interests.

Thirdly, there is also a greater emphasis on providing practical experience, op- portunities for field work and project-oriented studies at the under- graduate stage to improve the standards of education and to bring the system of higher education in close contact with the community around, through programmes of social and national service. If these important purposes are to be satisfactorily achieved, it goes without saying that a two-year duration is extremely inadequate for the undergraduate stage and that the new courses for the first degree will need a minimum duration of three years.

The foregoing discussion will show that the new pattern of 10+2+3 for school and college classes is an educational reform of great significance, that it is based on several important academic considerations, and is vastly superior to the alternative patterns that now prevail and that its universal adoption in all parts of the country will bring in several advantages among which the following may be mentioned:

(1) The school stage will be strengthened and its standards will improve because of its lengthening to twelve years and because of the inclusion, within it, of the intermediate stage which will bring in better teachers and better facilities.

(2) The two-year higher secondary stage will have several advantages. It will enable us to control expansion to some extent because an element of selective admission can be introduced at this point. The students will also be mature enough, when they enter Class XI to make a tentative decision about their future career and to embark upon some programmes of prespecializations. It will enable the schools to prepare their gifted students intensively for the University and also to provide remedial action for any shortcomings arising from weaknesses in earlier education. Above all, it will be possible to vocationalise this stage intensively so that a fair proportion of students (ultimately as large as 50 per cent) can be diverted into different walks of life, thus reducing the pressures on university admissions. An important and necessary innovation at this stage would be to provide for transfer of credits to a student who may desire to change from one stream to another.

(3) The standards in higher education will also improve as the students going into the university stream will now be better prepared and more mature.

(4) The three-year degree course would be a definite improvement on the existing two-year course for the first degree. With this longer duration, it will be possible to meet the demands of specialization as well as of a broad based general and

interdisciplinary education and to make adequate provision for practical experience, field work and project-oriented studies. The introduction of problem-oriented interdisciplinary courses at the Master's degree level would also be greatly facilitated with the adoption of 10+2+3 formula.

## Misconceptions

In spite of all these academic considerations in favour of the uniform adoption of the common pattern of 10+2+3 for school and college classes, it is really unfortunate that there are several misconceptions on the subject which interfere with a proper implementation of the programme. It is necessary to clear these misconceptions if the programme is to succeed.

There is an unfortunate tendency, in certain quarters, to regard the arithmetic of the pattern (whether it is 11+ 2 + 2 or 11 + 1+ 3 or any other combination) as far more important than the substance of the reform which consists of the vocationalization of the higher secondary stage and improvement of standards, both in school and university education. I would like to state it categorically that the arithmetic of the structure is of no consequence whatsoever and that even the structure of the educational system is of little importance. We should not, therefore, look at this proposal of adopting a new pattern of school and college classes on a uniform basis throughout the country either as an arithmetical problem or even as a purely structural problem. We must regard it as a fundamental educational reform for strengthening both the school and university stages of education and of making the secondary stage terminal through a programme of vocationalization. If these basic objectives are not emphasised and achieved, a mere adoption of some other arithmetic or a different structure will not serve any useful purpose.

Another common misconception is that, in adopting a common pattern of school and college classes, we must look elsewhere for precedent,%. and support our argument with illustrations from other countries. This is hardly necessary and in fact would be an incorrect procedure. I have had the opportunity to study the pattern of education in many friendly countries. I have found that there is no uniform pattern of school and college classes in the different countries of the world, and not even in the socialist countries whose educational systems tend to be uniform. Each country has evolved its own pattern in accordance with its own peculiar circumstances. It is therefore, not desirable to change our pattern of school and college classes on the basis of the patterns prevailing in other countries. The Education Commission rightly emphasised that we must outgrow this imitative attitude and should introduce changes in our pattern slowly "on the basis of our own indigenous thinking after taking into account what is happening outside, but without being dominated by it".

Yet another misunderstanding, which is often propagated by certain vested interests is that the adoption of the new pattern will adversely affect the interests of school and college teachers. Nothing can be farther from truth. The school teachers have everything to gain by the adoption of the pattern because more posts will be created at the school stage at higher levels. Even the college teachers have nothing to lose because we have insisted that in spite of a temporary setback in enrolments, there should be no retrenchment. The setback in enrolments also will be more than made up in three or four years by the natural increase in enrolments that will necessarily take place from year to year. What is even more important, the teachers in higher education will have much better job satisfaction because of the qualitatively better students that will now be entering the university system.

There is also a misunderstanding that the new pattern can be implemented quickly in a year or two. This can only be disastrous. The Education Commission pointed out that a good deal of careful preparation is needed for the adoption of the new pattern and that the programme will have to be phased over a few years. That is why, in the Delhi Union Territory, it is proposed to introduce the new syllabus in Class IX in the first instance and then to revise the syllabus for subsequent standards year after year. A good deal of preparatory work is also needed to identify vocational openings appropriate to this stage, to prepare fairly reliable estimates of manpower needs or employment opportunities, to prepare the curricula and to set up the essential institutional structure for vocationalization. The preparation of teachers for the higher secondary stage is also important and will consume considerable time and resources. Due attention will have to be paid to all this preparation if the programme is to succeed and result in improvement of standards.

### New Pattern of Education

The Central Board of Secondary Education has introduced the new pattern of education, commonly known as 10+2 in all its schools beginning with IX class, with effect from May 1975. The first course leading to the examination at the end of X class (corresponding to the present Matriculation examination) will include three languages, Mathematics, Physical Sciences, Life Sciences and Social Sciences, also work experience and Health and Physical Education-a general undiversified education for all.

The second stage to end with the 12th year is an improved Higher Secondary course with more accent on vocationalization, involving diversification and specialization in subjects best suited to the genius of the pupil. For Most Students, this will be the terminal stage of education and stepping-stone to careers in life. After that the academically disposed scholars Could go in for the three-year degree course.

A radical feature of this scheme is that it makes work experience or community service compulsory. The pupil can choose from a long list of subjects like electric gadgets-their servicing and repairs, electronics, agriculture, photography, leather work, typing and tailoring. This part will consist of practicals only, no theory or written paper, and the assessment will be internal and cumulative at school. The traditional system of evaluation will also be reformed. There will be no pass or failure as such. There will be Grades for each subject-5 Grades in all: G-1, Outstanding; G-2, Very Good, G-3, Good; G-4, Fair and G-5, Poor; and this will be a surer guide for employers who look for special proficiency in their one special trade and also for admissions to higher professional or technical courses.

Forty years ago, Mahatma Gandhi advocated Basic education or work-centred education or learning through doing. He said that in a poor country like India, where 80 per cent of the population is agricultural and another 10 per cent industrial, it is a sin to give a purely literary or liberal education. The traditional education has a negative role, it makes pupils more unemploy- able: a farmer's son who passes B.A. and M.A. becomes unfit for unsophisticated farming; the housewife's daughter who passes M.A. looks down on housewifery and is all for a white collar job, which is in such short supply. It is anti-national to continue such a system.

The work-centred education will develop self-reliance and self- confidence through earning capacity instead of a feeling of helplessness without a routine job. It will instil dignity of labour found in all advanced countries but absent in India; it will produce the spirit of initiative and enterprise that will create openings and opportunities where there are seemingly none. Of course, mere education will not end unemployment; that depends on economic development and many other factors. But it will make our young men and young women fit to face new challenges in life and to transform both our society and its economy through innovations and unsuspected adventures.

**New System of Evaluation**

The new system of evaluation reflects also the new needs of a fast changing society. To declare a pupil as a failure in any class at so early an age will give him an inferiority complex for life and stunt his growth. Gandhi, Tagore, Edison, Einstein and Ramanujam all did poorly at school examinations but later became world figures. Why dub a child as a failure if he does badly in one or two subjects that he is compelled to study with or without his will? His interests may lie elsewhere. Give him a poor Grade in that and a good Grade in subjects in which he shines. That is simple justice to the young.

The new system is the first step towards revolutionary changes in the educational scene. And there is the rub. Everyone clamours for a wholesale change in the system of education and examination. There are no two opinions that the present system ha. outlived whatever limited utility it once had. It produces neither employment nor character nor discipline. Laymen look on schools and colleges as time-filling institutions. The experts express their dissatisfaction with it. Yet as soon as there is a real prospect of a radical change some members of the intelligentsia fiercely rally to the Support of the system of which they themselves have been critics. Our main problem seems to be that our radical thinking is not matched by radical action.

**Soundness of New System**

The new system has got overwhelming support from expert educational opinion. It was recommended by the Kothari Commission, it conforms to the National Policy Resolution on Education (1968), it has been approved by the Central Advisory Board of Education and by various all-India forums and seminars. If such massive commendation is not enough to launch it into practice, nothing can be. Let the dissenters not wince before the challenge of change which they have been advocating so frequently. The new system seems to be the best under the circumstances and deserves an honest and sincere trial.

The no-changers warn us that the new system will encounter many difficulties. Nothing great was ever achieved without surmounting huge difficulties. If men remained confined within the safe familiar limits, there would have been no aeroplane, no space travel, no adventurous inventions. A verse in the Panchtantra says, "Low men do not start any venture for fear of meeting obstacles; the middling ones do make a start but leave off when there are obstacles but the high-minded persist in the right course, though again and again beset with difficulties".

The prophets of doom warn us that the new scheme will founder on the rock of finance. Where from will come the huge funds and local expertise to teach many odd items of work experience in a thousand schools? Where there is a will, there is a way. Money is never any bar to real progress.

India has over-abundance of human resources and acute scarcity of finance. Our policies should be man-power centred and not money- centred. Human effort and human ingenuity work wonders, while mere money power proves a non-starter. Indian education would have been in a far happier position today, if Gandhiji's ideas of developing education around work experience had been adopted 2 to 4 decades ago. But then the no-changers had their day and Gandhiji was too busy with more urgent programmes to secure independence for India, to devote his whole time and attention to educational reform.

## New Approach to Work Experience

Of all the changes contemplated under the new 10+2+3 pattern of education recently adopted by the Central Board of Secondary Education in its member-schools, the introduction of work experience as a compulsory part of the school curriculum is the most vital.

This however, has raised doubts and misgivings in the minds of some people, which is not unnatural, considering that this change envisages a drastic departure from the age-old conception of education which kept learning and earning strictly apart. In all societies, when education was first started in an organised manner, it was confined to a selected few. We have travelled far from those days and we are in an era when education is not for the selected few but is sought to be made universal. It is now universally agreed that education should be relevant to life and should not only train the mind, refine the intellect, and culture the emotions, but it should also improve the productive capacities of the individuals.

The change has been received very enthusiastically by most people who have hailed it as a reform long overdue. There are however, some isolated voices of resistance which mainly arise because of lack of proper awareness about the nature and scope of work experience at the school level.

The first obvious question is, what is work experience? This seems to be a very simple question but if not handled pragmatically it can result in a lot of academic discussion and hair-splitting which can only result in thwarting the starting of this programme.

A new concept like work experience would offer obvious difficulties if it is sought to be reduced to a one sentence defini- tion. It is essential that this new discipline is taught on the basis of certain commonly accepted concepts which will get refined as we go along on the road of implementation.

Work experience has been introduced to provide a corrective to some of the Deficiencies of the present system of education, and to make it more relevant to life. In fact, it provides one of the most essential dimensions to education which has been missing so far and which has been acutely felt by all right thinking persons.

The present system of education, except for a few good excep- tions, has been producing young people who are not found easily employable and what is worse, who themselves are lacking in self confidence because they have not been trained in any skill or creative activity which could enable them to face the challenges of life. The introduction of work experience is a step to remove this handicap, not because it will create jobs for everybody (that depends upon economic factors) but because it will make the products of education relatively more employable and it will imbue them with greater self-confidence because of their experience of having produced something.

It has, therefore been decided to adopt a very simple concept of work experience meaning thereby inculcation of skills and knowledge through creative and productive activities which may result in the students acquiring ability to produce goods and services which are marketable. A creative activity and its productivity in terms of its market value are the two essential characteristics of the concept of work experience. It is hoped that some important values will be inculcated as automatic by-products. The courses have been so designed as to accelerate the realization of educational values, like inculcation of dignity of labour, capacity to work hard, love of aesthetics, innovation and experimentation and greater confidence to face challenges.

**Inflexibility**

The concept of work experience will in future be more and more sharply defined and the curriculum and courses will be redesigned to realize the educational values in a much more direct and explicit manner.

Long years of teaching-learning process have more or less fixed the contours at various levels of most traditional subjects and the instructional ritual has almost got fixed with little incentive or encouragement to explore unchartered areas. This has generated a rigidity and inflexibility about the whole process which makes routine practices safer and more acceptable to all concerned because of their familiarity. There is left not much scope for innovation on the part of the teachers although some imaginative persons have tried experiments and innovated ideas even in these areas with very fruitful results.

Routinism in any sphere is harmful to real progress, but in education it is more so because it leads to sterility of thinking and offers no way out of the dreary desert sands of dead-habit. Fortunately work experience at least does not suffer from this handicap and offers to teachers full scope for their imaginative experimentation and innovation.

It is hoped that the teachers, while actually implementing the programme, will enrich this simple concept of work experience through their dynamic thinking and practical efforts. They will bear in mind that they are pioneers in this field and can legitimately feel proud that it has fallen to their lot to work out this revolution in educational thinking which seeks to liberate us from centuries of inertia which has kept earning and learning delinked from each other.

This does not, however, mean that the teacher is left entirely on his own without any directions or guidelines. After a good deal of deliberations, a list of about 40 work experiences has been suggested by way of illustration and a student is free to choose any one out of these in accordance with his own aptitude and facilities provided by the school. For most of these suggested work experiences, broad syllabi have also been prepared to make the level of proficiency in each work experience as unambiguous as possible.

The teacher has also been given a four-week training in various areas of work experience during the summer recess. About 1,000 teachers, at the rate of one teacher for each affiliated school, have been put through this practical training. For this purpose the facilities and expertise available in our Engineering Colleges, Technical Teachers Training Institutes, Polytechnics and Regional Colleges of Education have been utilized.

Work experience will be no blind alley for the students because it will be followed by vocational stream in the XI and XII classes. The students doing very well in work experience will have the choice of joining the vocational stream, which will be all integrated programme of academics and vocations. Even at the University level, some Universities are already thinking of starting some vocational courses.

There are obviously two ways of implementing the programme of work experience, either by taking the workshop to the school or by talking the school to the workshop. To begin with, we start with the alternative where most of the factors are under the control of the educational institutions, i.e. work experience

Teachers acquiring workshop skill will be mostly done in the school itself and that obviously would restrict to some extent the choice of work experience on the part of the schools. The use of community facilities in the neighbourhood or making arrangements with a factory or workshop or productive centre in the neighbourhood is not precluded. In fact the latter has to be encouraged and large scale co-ordination will have to be developed with other agencies concerned with productive activities. This will be a real breakthrough and we shall then be able to take up more sophisticated and more refined work experiences. This may take a little time but this arrangement will have to be worked out because it will not be possible to set up all the necessary workshops in the schools themselves.

As the programme develops, it is certain that such co-ordination will be forthcoming. The success of all educational enterprises depends upon the joint efforts of parents and teachers and work experience needs this joint effort Much more than any other project.

## Renewing Science Education

In an age when education is sought to be made universal it would be incongruous to continue with the legacies of the elitist traditions of education evolved mostly in the context of the requirements of leisured classes. Education cannot continue with its ivory tower approach and cannot go on merrily oblivious of the changes in the social and economic scene. Education has to assume a dynamic role and has to become meaningful, purposeful, useful and relevant to life. This necessarily involves appropriate changes in the curricula and content of courses as also methods of teaching, apart from the overall change in the general approach which has to permeate throughout under the new pattern of education. It is a pity that in the popular mind the structural aspect of change as reflected in the years to be spent for various stages of education under the new pattern, has received great attention to the almost exclusion or the very great changes in contents and methods of instruction. In the new approach, the gap between the world of work and the world of learning is Sought to be bridged. Education is not only to stimulate thought but also to inculcate skills for improved action. This coordination between thought and action is sure to generate a two-way process resulting in improvement in both. Whereas work will be improved with the application of knowledge itself will benefit and become more purposeful and realistic when put to use in refining and improving action.

Teaching of science in this country has been becoming more and more theoretical and getting away from the realities of ordinary life resulting in loss of popularity. It is essential to evolve a new methodology of teaching science which will make the subject more interesting, more readily assimilable by the students and also restore to various science disciplines their fading vitality and popularity. Any subject which is not constantly reviewed in the matter of its contents as well as methodology of instruction in order to retain its relevance to the changing life situation, is likely to get fossilised and suffer the fate of the classics. Science can be a discipline for specialised and sophisticated action, or its applicability to life situations can be underlined for the benefit of the citizens. Science, if it is to help any country in ushering in an era of science and technology, cannot ignore the needs of the citizens and has to be reoriented to help in solving problems of daily life.

The new change sought to be introduced in the method of teaching science through the scheme of project technology seeks to give a more practical bias to science teaching, pointing out at every step the relevance of science to various life situations and the way it can help to solve various problems. The whole idea is to develop science teaching around some chosen projects allied to technology. This will stimulate innovative thinking among students and will inculcate among them the scientific temper, originality, creative and improvisational abilities, which are so necessary in a society, which is trying to become increasingly technological. It also involves doing things with the hands by the student and this naturally develops greater interest and elimi- nates some of the passivity and boredom which are associated with the class-room situation.

Science education which is really meant to train students to observe, to analyse, to infer and to generalise, has not been having its full impact. Following the new method of project technology, it is hoped that proper scientific attitudes and creative abilities will be stimulated and quite a few young students will be launched on voyages of discovery on their own.

### Inter-disciplinary Approach

Another advantage of the project technology is that it very often encourages the interdisciplinary approach which develops a wider understanding of the unity underlying all knowledge and also brings people from various disciplines together fostering a team spirit which in these days is most essential for any significant achievement in any field. This method also eliminates the isolation of science from the community by creating an awareness of the social, economic and moral problems.

Recently the method of project technology was tried by the Central Board of Secondary Education in a

Workshop at Lawrence School, Sanawar, which was attended by 21 teachers from schools in different parts of the country and was guided by experts from India and abroad. This quiet workshop away from the maddening crowds, generated tremendous interest among the participants. As a matter of fact their absorption in their work all the day long was to be seen to be believed. Their complete concentration through long hours indicated the strong motivating effect of project technology. If the introduction of this programme in schools results in the same motivation and the development of the same interest among students, it will be a breakthrough in solving many of the ills of the present-day education. This small workshop has thrown up very fruitful ideas and has shown the great potentialities of the project technology for more purposeful teaching of science.

It has been decided that suitable follow-up action will be initiated with the help of these 21 teachers and it would be possible to generate a snow-ball movement in order to cover all the thousand schools affiliated to the Central Board of Secondary Education in about a couple of years. Some of the projects designed and completed at Sanawar were very interesting and useful. The chief characteristic of these projects was that very cheap and improvised material had been used. It is hoped that the habit of improvisation, experimentation and innovation when properly developed and emphasized would become a life-long asset and for our socio-economic development this type of asset is most urgently needed.

### Challenges of Modern Education System

It was with the appointment of Calcutta University Commission in 1917, popularly known as Sadler Commission, that for the first time the idea of an educational structure formed an important part of discussion. This commission recommended that the dividing line between the University and secondary courses should more properly be drawn at the Intermediate Examination rather than at the Matriculation. The Commission desired the Government to establish Intermediate Colleges which would provide instructions in Arts, Science, Medicine, Engineering etc. A faint re-echo of this 58 years old idea may be discerned in the proposed New Pattern. The 30 years between the Sadler Commission and the independence, chronicled several recommendations emanating from various academic forums and were mainly intended to answer the then existing needs and for welfare of the masses. The Hartog Committee in 1929 recommended the branching off of more students into industrial and commercial channels at the end of the middle stage. The Sapru Committee in 1934 recommended diversified courses at the secondary stage-one for entering the University and the other for getting into the Vocational stream.

The University Education Commission (1948-49), the first Education Commission in independent India, thought it unfortunate that the importance of Intermediate College in educational system of India had not been realised and recommended that the admission to the university should be preceded by 12 years of schooling. The objective was to raise the standard of University Education.

The Conference of Vice-Chancellors (1962), the All India Council for Secondary Education (1963), the Conference of State Education Ministers (1964)—all recommended a 12-year course of schooling before admission to a 3-year degree course. as the goal towards which the country must move.

The Education Commission of India (1966) emphasised that there is a direct link between education, national development and prosperity and stated that this can be vitalised only when the National system of education is properly organised, both qualitatively and quantitatively. This Commission also pointed out that the existing system of education was largely unrelated to the life, needs and aspirations of the people and there was a wide gulf between its contents and purposes as well as interests of National development. One of the major weaknesses of the present educational system is that secondary education fits students for college and almost unfits them for everything else.

In any well designed National system of education, secondary education must have two specific objectives:

(1) to prepare a student for the University, or

(2) to become terminal and prepare a student for some vocation in life.

Realising that the total period of education and the duration of its different stages have a direct bearing on the quality of education imparted for achieving the goal, the Education Commission recommended:-

(1) Broadly uniform pattern of education;

(2) Extension in the total period of schooling to bring about a general rise in the standards of attainment; and

(3) Vocationalisation of education.

### National Policy Statement

Bearing in mind the recommendations of the Commission, the Government of India issued in 1968 a National Policy statement on education for the country. In this statement, the Government of India stated that it was convinced that a "radical reconstruction of education on the broad lines recommended by the Education Commission, is essential for economic and cultural development of the country, for national integration and for realising the ideal of a socialistic pattern of society. This will involve a transformation of the system to relate it more closely to the life of the people, a continuous effort to expand educational opportunity, a sustained and intensive endeavour to raise the quality of education at all stages, and emphasis on the development of Science and technology and cultivation of moral and social values".

The policy statement also stated that it would be advantageous to have a broadly uniform educational structure in all parts of the country. The ultimate objective should be to adopt the 10+2+3 pattern.

The conference of Education Secretaries and Directors of Public Instruction held on 15th & 16th September, 1972 passed the following resolution:

"Adoption of a uniform pattern of school and College classes (10+2+3).

(1) A uniform pattern of education of 15 years, duration, leading to the first degree, should be adopted by all the States.

(2) There should be very close co-ordination between the vocational courses attached to the higher secondary stage, the Industrial Training Institutes and the Poly- technics. Courses selected should have close affinity to the skills and services in demand in the locality. This will involve man-power studies and production centres as well as financing of the skilled personnel on cooperative or institutional pattern for self-employment or employment in production centres.

(3) The scheme of Vocationalisation of Education as well as work experience deserves the highest priority in the Plan and should be assisted fully.

(4) Vocational courses prescribed in the Institutions would need constant review and replacement as technology, materials and demands change. They would have to keep pace with development of local industries also, particularly the small scale, cottage and consumer industries".

The recommendations of the Conference of the Education Secretaries and Directors of Public Instruction were endorsed by the Central Advisory Board of Education in its 36th session held on 18th and 19th September, 1972, in New Delhi.

Almost simultaneously the Government of India, Ministry of Education and Social Welfare appointed a National Committee under the chairmanship of Dr. P. D. Shukla, with the following terms of reference;

(1) To suggest practical steps to be taken for-the implementation of the uniform pattern of 10+2+3 for the school and college classes in all States and Union Territories of the country.

(2) To estimate the cost of implementing the programme.

**New Pattern in CBSE Schools**

In view of the overwhelming national importance of this matter the Central Board of Secondary Education set up a special committee to suggest ways and means to implement the new pattern in the member- schools of the Board and advise it on the educational innovations which should be introduced. With this Committee were associated eminent educationists and the experts from sister agencies like Directorate of Education, Delhi, Kendriya Vidyalaya Sangathan, National Council of Educational Research & Training and other such bodies. This committee favoured the introduction of the change for the following reasons:-

(1) It will provide an opportunity and a means to re-vitalize and rationalize school curricula and to structure them on more scientific lines so as to serve the social and economic needs of the adolescent in a better manner.

(2) It will help initiate other educational reforms such as modernization of teaching methods and evaluation techniques, essential to raise the general standard and quality of education, particularly at the school stage.

(3) A broadly uniform pattern in all States and Union Territories will facilitate the Board to share its resources and experience with other such bodies, in the areas of production of books and reading materials, teaching aids, training of teachers and their movement, reconstruction of syllabi and improvement in examination practices.

(4) It will do away with the present practice wherein a student is required to take a decision at too early an age about the particular stream of education to be taken up by him for future studies. At the same time it will help reduce pressure for admission on Universities and other centres of higher education.

(5) The improved academic and intellectual equipment of the student will provide him with an edge to face the challenges of modern life.

(6) A broadly uniform pattern of education all over the country will strengthen national integration.

(7) It will remove difficulties in the matter of education of children of the mobile population, to which this Board specially caters.

(8) It will serve as a vehicle of social transformation.

From what has been detailed heretofore it is apparent that this change has been long overdue to give a new direction to education.

**Syllabi & Courses**

In keeping with the objectives set by the National Policy on Education, The Central Board drafted syllabi and courses for classes IX & X, the first stage of the new structure, on modern lines incorporating latest pedagogical techniques. A large number of seminars of teachers & educationists were held in which the draft syllabi & courses with particular reference to their coverage and feasibility, were discussed. The new courses aim at the promotion of higher intellectual capacities as also the harmonious development of the physical, emotional and other aspects of the pupil's personality. They seek to provide a wide range of knowledge to develop students into well-informed citizens and train them for democratic living and community service; at the same time to imbibe a scientific outlook for modern living.

A few of the salient features of the new courses are mentioned below:-

(1) They provide a comprehensive general education with work experience as an integral component.

(2) Science and Mathematics. formerly denied to almost 50% of the students, are now available to every student, which are so essential for the day-to-day life in the existing context.

(3) These envisage compulsory Health & Physical Education.

(4) They aim at Optimum relevance to the current life situation.

(5) Through community service, a sense of involvement in national reconstruction is planned to be generated in the student.

(6) Work experience makes learning possible by the use of hand and pave the way for vocational education at the subsequent stage.

(7) These aim at the development of the student upto the stage when he can successfully branch off into the academic stream or the vocational channel in accordance with his aptitude.

### Modernising Evaluation Procedures

Educationists all over the world are unanimous on the inherent drawbacks in the prevailing system of assessment through examination. In actual practice, the entire system of education tends to focus on the score in the examination. The new scheme of assessment, therefore, aims at rationalisation and imbibes the following features:-

(1) Internal Assessment along with external examination.

(2) System of Grading instead of marks.

(3) Standardisation of raw scores.

(4) Question Banks.

(5) Improving quality of question papers.

(6) Improving evaluation procedures.

The new pattern of school education has come into force in 1000' and odd member-schools of the Board scattered all over the country and abroad, from the academic session 1975-76.

(1) The syllabi, soon after finalization. along with the lists of equipment for science subjects and work experiences, were circulated well in advance among the member-schools so that they could do the required spade work in time.

(2) To further strengthen the syllabuses and explicate them in more operational terms the Board undertook to prepare quality textbooks for the subjects of English, Hindi, Sanskrit, Punjabi, Economics and

Civics, while National Council of Educational Research & Training prepared those for Mathematics, Physics. Chemistry, Life Sciences, History & Geography; thus covering all the compulsory subjects laid down in the scheme. In this venture help of other expert agencies like Central Institute of English, Hyderabad and Directorate of Education, Delhi was also secured to have books on improved lines.

(3) Besides ensuring quality, a set of new textbooks for classes IX and X now costs only about Rs. 60/- as against Rs. 150/- to Rs. 190/- earlier for the higher Secondary classes.

(4) Science equipment and work experience materials worth Rs. 20 lakhs have been made available to the schools during 1974-75. Funds to the tune of Rs. 30 lakhs are planned to be invested in various inputs during 1975-76.

(5) The successful introduction of the new pattern primarily depends on the timely orientation of teachers in the philosophy and contents of new courses. This summer vacation, about 5000 teachers of the member- schools of the Board were provided in-service training through Summer Institutes of 2 weeks to one month duration. These institutes were organised not only in Delhi but in different parts of India also.

4

# Management of Elementary Education

At the time of Independence, India inherited a system of education which was not only quantitatively small but also char- acterised by structural imbalances. Only fourteen per cent of the population was literate and only one child out of three had been en- rolled in primary school. The low levels of participation and literacy were aggravated by acute regional and gender disparities. As education is vitally linked with the totality of the development process - education being "the basic tool for the development of consciousness and reconstitution of society," in the words of Mahatma Gandhi - the reform and restructuring of the educational system was recognised as an important area of state intervention.

The need for a literate population and universal education for all children in the age group of 6-14 was recognised as a crucial input for nation building and was given due consideration in the Constitution as well as in successive Five Year Plans. This has resulted in a manifold increase of spatial spread, infrastructural facilities, increased coverage of various social groups; but the goal of providing basic education to all could not be achieved. There has been a spectacular increase in elementary education during the post-Independence period. The elementary education system of India has expanded into one of the largest in the world. The number of primary schools increased from 209,671 in 1950-51 to 572,541 in 1992-93; the corresponding increase in upper primary schools was from 13,596 to 153,921. These 726,462 schools together with 2.7 lakhs non-formal education centres enrolled 150 million children as compared to 22.3 million in 1951. Universal provision of education has been substantially achieved at the primary stage (classes IN). According to the Fifth AR India Education Survey (1986), 94.5 per cent of the rural population had schools within a walking distance of 1 km. and 83.98% of the rural population have an upper primary school within a walking distance of 3 km. The survey estimated that there were 31,815 habitations in the country which had a population of 300 or more but did not have a primary school within the walking distance of one kilometre. Most of these habitations are situated in educationally backward states such as Uttar Pradesh, Rajasthan, Madhya Pradesh, Bihar, Jammu and Kashmir, Assam and Arunachal Pradesh.

## Enrolment

Since Independence, there has been a substantial increase in enrolment at all levels of education. Enrolment at the primary stage increased about five fold from 19.2 million to 105.37 million in 1992- 93; the increase in the upper primary stage is far higher from 3.1 million to 38.7 million.

The gross enrolment ratios of children in the age group 6-11 increased from 42.6 per cent in 1950-51 to 105.7 per cent in 1992-93. Likewise, the gross enrolment of 11-14 age group increased from 12.7 per cent in 1950-51 to 67.5 per cent in 1992-93. An analysis of the enrolment data reveals that the population of children moving up from the primary to upper primary stage has been increasing steadily, from 16.3 per cent in 1950-51 to 36.72 per cent in 1992-93. While the gross enrolment ratios (GER) at the primary stage in the country as a whole and in most of its states exceed 100 per cent there are quite a few states where the ratio is considerably lower. These include Uttar Pradesh, Bihar, Rajasthan, Haryana, Jammu and Kashmir, and Meghalaya. At the upper primary stage these states and in addition, Andhra Pradesh, Orissa and Sikkim have GERs lower than the national average. Most of these states have literacy rates lower than the national average. There is thus a strong regional dimension of UEE. The problem gets more complicated as the drop-out rates, though declining, continue to be high. Nearly half the children who entered Class I drop out before reaching Class V, and two-thirds of the children dropout before reaching Class VIII. Regional disparities also abound in rates of the dropouts.

## Gender Disparities

As with any educational indicator, gender disparities are conspicuous in regard to enrolment and retention. Girls' enrolment has grown at the primary stage from 5.4 million in 1950-51 to 42.4 million in 1991-92 and at the upper primary stage from 0.5 million to 13 million. The rate of growth of enrolment of girls has been higher than that of boys but disparities still persist - girls still account for only 45.7 per cent of the enrolment at the primary stage and 37.73 per cent at the upper primary stage. The drop-out rates of girls at the primary as well as the upper primary stage are higher than those of boys.

Regional disparities are also conspicuous. High female literacy states (above 50 per cent) have by and large universalised primary enrolments among girls. Even in regard to upper primary enrolments Kerala, Goa, Pondicherry and Lakshadweep fare very well. In states with medium female literacy status (40-50 per cent) enrolment of girls appears to be satisfactory at the primary level. The situation in low female literacy states (20-40 per cent) causes concern. These states have more than half of the country's population, with just four of them (Uttar Pradesh, Bihar, Madhya Pradesh and Rajasthan) accounting for 40 per cent of the country's population.

## Dropping Out

The 42nd round of the National Sample Survey (July 1986-June 1987) provides valuable information on the reasons for non-enrolment and dropout. Nonavailability of schooling facilities seems to account for only about 10 percent of the "never enroled" in rural India and about 8 percent in urban India; the difference between the sexes is very small in rural areas but somewhat larger in the urban sector

However, nearly 30 percent of the persons surveyed, both in rural and urban India, gave the reason for "never enroled" as being "not interested". The difference between the sexes here is large: a larger proportion of "never enroled" females gave this reason in comparison with the males. The reason for being "not interested" could be considered as a demand side constraint to access: some authorities however, consider it as a supply side constraint rooted in poor facilities and quality of education.

About 52 percent of urban males and 29 percent of urban females could not avail of the educational services because of participation in household economic activity and other economic reasons. Attending to domestic chores restrained around one percent of the males, both in rural as well as urban India, from ever enroling as students. Nevertheless, this reason was one of the major demand side constraints on access to education for the females: for 9.9 percent of them in the rural and 10.7 percent. of them in the urban sector Most of the young females are denied access to education because they look after their siblings besides performing a variety of domestic, housekeeping chores. Significantly, the proportion of currently "not enroled" decreases with the increase in per capita household income.

A little over one-fourth of all "drop-outs " in rural as well as urban India gave "not interested in education/ further study" as the reason for discontinuance of education - with the proportion among females being somewhat higher - 33.3 percent as against 26.5 percent for males in areas and 28.5 percent as against 23.6 percent for males in urban areas. Another 16.3 percent of rural and 20.3 percent of urban "dropouts" cited 'failure' to pass examinations as the reason for discontinuance. Again, it is a Moot point whether this is a supply side constraint due to the poor quality of eduction services or a demand constraint, or a combination of both.

## Scheduled Castes and Scheduled Tribes

According to the 1991 census, the population of Scheduled Castes (SCs) was 138.2 million (16.33 per cent) and that of Scheduled Tribes (STs) 67.8 million (8.01 per cent) of the country's population.

Both SC and ST populations are not homogeneous target groups in all respects. There are wide variations between different SC and ST groups regionally. Thus SC girls in Kerala are likely to be better placed than non-SC boys in some of the more backward states and districts.

Because of the affirmative policies of the government, the enrolment of SCs and STs has increased considerably at the primary stage. The participation of SCs and STs is now more or less in proportion to their share in population at the primary level. Drop- outs, though declining over the years, are significantly large. Gender disparities are very conspicuous among SCs and STs also.

## Handicapped Children

Handicapped children are a distinct target group where basic learning needs have to be catered to by special programmes. Handicapped children would include those who are orthopaedically handicapped, those with hearing impairments, visual impairments, the mentally handicapped and others. NPE, 1986 called for integration of "the physically and mentally handicapped with the general community as equal partners to prepare them for normal growth and to enable them to face life with courage and confidence."

The POA, 1992 estimates that about10.39 million children with disabilities are to be provided education in the school system. Out of these, about half a million require vocational training.

The statistics on participation of these children are not firm. At the end of 1991-92 about 30,000 disabled children were availing of special benefits under the scheme of Integrated Education for Disabled Children (IEDC). In addition, about 60,000 children with mild disabilities received resource support without special benefits. A large number of children with disability are also receiving education in 1,035 special schools.

## Learning Achievement

If the fact that half the children drop out before reaching Class V is shocking, far more shocking is the level of learning achievement of those remaining in school. A sample study of learning achievements of students was conducted in 48 districts as part of the DPEP. In the final year of primary schooling, in none of these districts the maximum average score for reading skills was higher than fifty two per cent; the achievements in arithmetic were worse.

### Challenges of Elementary Education

Inspite of the substantial accomplishments since Independence, India has the dubious distinction of having the largest number of illiterates and out-of-school children in the world - 30 per cent of the world's adult illiterates and 21.87 per cent of out-of-school children. About 19 to 24 million children in the age group 6-14 are out of school of whom about 60 per cent are girls; about 121.3 million are adult illiterates in the age group 15-35 of whom 62 per cent are women. Given the demographic pressure the numbers are likely to increase further.

The benefits of investing in basic education, both for its intrinsic value in enhancing human capabilities, as well for its instrumental worth in contributing to social development and economic growth, greater efficiency and better functioning of democratic institutions are well established. Of equal significance is the ability of education to empower women and men to acquire greater control over the circumstances that dominate their lives. It is now recognised that fertility regulation cannot be a matter of mere promotion of contraception but has to strongly promote the socio- economic factors which strongly influence fertility behaviour such as female literacy and education. The low level of social indicators such as fertility rates, Infant Mortality Rate (IMR), sex ratio are related to the failure to achieve Universalisation of Elementary Education (UEE). If the East Asian experience has any relevance the criticality of UEE for the economic reform process cannot be over emphasised.

It is evident from the above that UEE has strong regional and gender dimensions. The Indian experience encompasses the entire Third World experience. At one end we have states such as Kerala which has achieved universal literacy as well as UEE in terms of school participation - though not in terms of learning achievement - with social indicators as good as the best among the Third World, if not the Scandinavian countries. On the other extreme we have states like UP, Bihar, Orissa and MP with indicators as worse as Sub Saharan Africa. To the extent that gender disparity is pronounced UEE is the problem of the girl child.

Teacher competence, motivation and performance are areas which require greater attention. These are crucial inputs in UEE. Whatever policies may be laid down, in the ultimate analysis, these have to be interpreted and implemented by teachers, as much through their personal example as through teaching-learning process.

Except in a few places where the ethos of Panchayati Raj system has been internalised the school remains rather isolated from the local community.

Experience in India and elsewhere has established that universal participation cannot be delinked from the operations of quality and relevance of education and from learning achievement. The challenge before the nation is to enhance universal participation and universal achievement of certain minimum levels of learning. In terms of numbers alone this is the greatest challenge that human society had ever faced - more so if one were to adhere to the goal set up in the National Policy on Education, 1986 of universalising elementary education before the commencement of the twenty-first century.

### Legal Framework for Elementary Education

Several articles in the Constitution of India bring into focus the general principles governing educational development in the country. These articles are rooted in India's struggle for independence. Basic education was one of the important goals of the freedom struggle and Mahatma Gandhi, even while leading the epic struggle against colonial power, evolved an alternative education system. The Directive Principle contained in Article 45 of the Constitution enjoins that "the State shall endeavour to provide, within a period of ten years from the commencement of this Constitution, for free and compulsory education for all children until they complete the age of fourteen years." The expression "the State" which occurs in this Article is defined in Article 12 to include the Government and Parliament of India, the government and the legislature of each of the states and all local or other authorities within the territory of India or under the control of the government of India.

Article 29(1) of the Constitution provides that any section of the citizens, residing in the. territory of India or any part thereof having a distinct language, script or culture of its own shall have the right to conserve the same." Article 29(2) lays down that "no citizen shall be denied admission into any educational institution maintained by the State or receiving aid out of State funds on grounds only of religion, race, caste, language or any of them." Article 30(1) enjoins that "all minorities, whether based on religion or language, shall have the right to establish and administer educational institutions of their choice," while Article 30(2) lays down that "the State shall not, in granting aid to educational institutions, discriminate against any educational institution on the ground that it is under the managment of a minority, whether based on religion or language." Article 350-A lays down that "it shall be the endeavour of every State and of every local authority within the State to provide adequate facilities for instruction in the mother-tongue at the primary stage of education to children belonging to linguistic minor- ity groups."

Special care of the economic and educational interests of the under-privileged sections of the population is laid down as an ob- ligation for the State under Article 46. As per this Article, "the State shall promote with special care the educational and economic interests of the weaker sections of the people, and in particular, of the Scheduled Castes and the Scheduled Tribes and shall protect them from social injustice and all forms of exploitation."

Till the 42nd amendment of the Constitution when it was brought into the Concurrent List, education was in the State List except for certain specified items in the Union List like determination of standards in institutions for higher education or research, establish- ment and maintenance of central universities as well as specified institutions for scientific or technical education and research.

The objective of incorporating education in the Concurrent List was to facilitate evolution of all-India policies in the field of education. Though the parliament was thereby empowered with the authority to legislate on education, the Centre has been relying on a consensual process to promote educational development. The concept of concurrency was given an operational meaning by the National Policy on Education (NPE) 1986. This policy envisages concurrency as a "meaningful partnership between the Centre and the States" and placed on the Union Government a larger responsibility in regard to the national and integrative character of education, quality and standards, manpower planning, research and advanced study, and international aspects of education, culture and human resource development.

## Policy Priorities

The late Prime Minister Rajiv Gandhi called for a comprehensive review of the existing educational system and the National Policy of Education (NPE) came into effect in 1986. Within the comprehensive framework enunciated by the NPE (1986), the developments and experiences since then were incorporated into the NPE in 1992 and a revised Programme of Action POA (1992) was formulated. Along with its Programme of Action (POA), the NPE provides a comprehensive framework to guide the development of education. Overall, the NPE is committed to:

— address all aspects of education: equity, efficiency, relevance, quality, content and process, linkages with culture, values, society, polity and economy, resources and management.

— emphasize the organic unit of early childhood education, primary education, non-formal education, adult education and post literacy and life long continuing education.

— tilt the balance away from quantitative expansion of institutions towards quality and equity.

— give unqualified priority to UEE, adult literacy and education for women's equality; this priority is reflected in the budget allocations during the current Five Year Plan (1992-97).

Shift the emphasis from enrolment per se to enrolment as well as retention and achievement.

NPE, 1986 also broke away from stereotyped confines of thinking and promoted thoughtful introspection and key strategies such as:

i) the shift from the States to the district as the unit of planning for implementation of elementary education and adult literacy;

ii) social mobilisation to promote basic eduction; and

iii) integration of adult literacy and non-formal programmes with socially relevant themes such as small population norms, health care, environment and nutrition.

## GOALS OF EDUCATION FOR ALL

Against the background of the demographic implications and the complex ground realities of the Indian scene, the goals of Education for All (EFA) in India constitute :

1. Expansion of Early Childhood Care and Development Activities especially for poor, disadvantaged and disabled children, through a multi-pronged effort involving families, communities and appropriate institutions.
2. Universalisation of Elementary Education (UEE) viewed as a composite programme of :
   — access to elementary education for all children upto 14 years of age;
   — universal participation till they complete the elementary stage through formal or equivalent non-formal education programmes;
   — universal achievement of atleast minimum levels of learning.
3. Drastic Reduction in Illiteracy, particularly in the 15-35 age- group, bringing the literacy level in this age group to atleast 80 per cent in each gender and for every identified disadvantaged group, besides ensuring that the levels of the three R's are relevant to the living and working conditions of the people.
4. Provision of opportunities to maintain, use and upgrade education and provision of facilities for development of skills to a persons who are functionally literate and those who have received primary education through formal and non-formal channels.

5. Creation of necessary structures, and the setting in motion of processes which could empower women and make education an instrument of women's equality.
6. Improving the content and process of education to relate it better to the environment, people's culture and with their living and working conditions, thereby enhancing their ability to learn and cope with the problems of livelihood and environment.

## Role of NGOs

The NPE recognises that Voluntary Agencies or groups of public spirited individuals could provide a useful supportive framework for promoting universalisation of elementary education. After 1986, schemes are in place for enlisting NGOs in elementary education.

Voluntary agencies can contribute significantly to universalise elementary education through a number of measures such as:

— implementing non-formal education programmes and alternative school programmes in more people friendly and innovative ways in terms of pedagogy,instructional materials, training, organisation and management.

— providing resource support to teachers, schools and continuing education.

— training of teachers, local functionaries, Village Education Committee members and others.

— establishing linkages between education and other social services such as health, nutrition etc.

## Interventions in Elementary Education

Major interventions in the years since 1986 include :

**Operation Blackboard**

This programme is designed for improvement of primary schools and provision of support services. it envisages conversion of all single teacher schools into double teacher schools ensuring that at least one of the teachers is a woman and provide all such schools at least two reasonably large rooms.

Under this scheme 1,10,000 teachers (of them 57 per cent were women) have been recruited and 1,36,000 classrooms were constructed. This scheme has been expanded to cover upper primary schools and also provide a third teacher to primary schools with enrolment more than 100.

**Non-formal Education (NFE)**

This has become an important alternative channel for children who cannot attend full time schools. Although the focus of the centrally sponsored scheme of NFE is still on the ten educationally backward states, namely, Andhra Pradesh, Arunachal Pradesh, Assam, Bihar, Jammu & Kashmir, Madhya Pradesh, Orissa, Rajasthan, Uttar Pradesh and West Bengal, it covers urban slums, hilly, tribal and desert areas and areas with concentration of working children in the other states as well.

Financial responsibility is shared by the Central and state Governments in the ratio of 50:50 for co-educational centres and 90:10 for girls'NFE centres. Assistance to the extent of 100 per cent is provided to voluntary agencies for running NFE centres for experimen- tal and innovative projects.

The number of NFE centres increased from 126,000 in 1986 to 255,000 by March, 1994 and the enrolment from 3.65 million to 6.4 million. During this period the number of girls centres has incresed from 20,500 to 96,766. Over 425 voluntary agencies are participating in this programme. Alongside, around 50 experimental and innovative projects and 22 district resource units are in operation for in-depth work. Though the coverage has expanded a major challenge is the development and scaling up of effective NFE models that can help the learners to learn at their own pace.

**Minimum Levels of Learning**

The NCERT has developed the National Curricular Framework and within this framework the minimum levels of learning have been laid down for primary level and concerted steps are being taken to achieve these levels.

The strategy to improve learning acquisition in school focuses attention on what is happening in the class room, and seeks to bring the principles of equity, quality and relevance to bear upon it. The strategy aims to lay down learning outcomes expected from basic education at a realistic, relevant and functional level, prescribes the adoption of measures that would ensure that all children who com- plete a stage of schooling achieve these outcomes. These outcomes define the Minimum Levels of Learning common to both school and equivalent NFE programme.

The main steps by which MLLs are being introduced in schools are:

i) an assessment of the existing level of learning achievement;

ii) a definition of the MLLs for the area and the time-frame within which it will be achieved;

iii) reorientation of teaching practices to competency based teaching;

iv) an introduction of continuous comprehensive evaluation of student learning;

v) review the textbooks and revision, if required;

vi) the provision of inputs as necessary including provision of physical facilities, teacher training, supervision and evaluation, etc., to improve learning acquisition to the MLLs.

The endeavour is to monitor learning achievement, to direct greater resources where levels of learning are lower, and to consciously accelerate the pace of development in the needy areas, thereby to reduce disparities, equalise standards and govern inputs for quality improvement in the performance of the system.

## TEACHER TRAINING

The NPE perceives teacher education as a continuous process and its pre-service and in-service components being inseparable have been incorporated in the new restructured programme of teacher education initated in 1987. Setting up of District Institutes of Education and Training (DIETs) is a significant institutional mechanism in this direction. Eventually DIETs are expected to provide academic and resource support to basic education and also to engage in action research and innovation. As of now, DIETs are being set up in 380 districts out of the 462 districts in the country; in 190 districts DIETs are already conducting training programmes. It is proposed to set up 425 DIETs by the end of the eighth plan (1997-98). Efforts are afoot to strengthen the SCERTs so that they can provide the resource back up.

The National Council of Teacher Education (NCTE) has been setup as a statutory body for determination and maintenance of standards of teacher education. This is expected to improve the quality of pre-service training, and upgrade the syllabi and curricula of teacher training programmes.

# 5

# Resource Requirement of Education System

The National Policy on Education 1986 has reiterated the nation's resolve, as recommended by the Education Commission (1966) and promised in the National Policy on Education 1968 by the Government of India, to invest six per cent of national income in education from the eighth Five Year Plan onwards. The Policy modified in 1992 also reiterated the same. The goal has now been postponed to the next Five Year Plan, i.e. , the ninth Five Year Plan. Realization of the goal, compared to about four per cent of gross national product (GNP) that is being invested in education Presently, requires scaling up of the allocation of resources substantially to education in the next few years.

Secondly, the new economic policies, particularly structural adjustment policies and globalization require increasingly more and more educated manpower. It is increasingly realized both by the Government and the international agencies that promote the structural adjustment policies that the success of the structural adjustment programme critically depends upon human resource development, particularly education. In other words, the new economic policies necessitate higher levels of investment in education.

Thirdly, the sustenance of the several programmes launched during the post 1986-Policy period requires significant increase in the allocation of resources to education. Some of the notable programmes in this context include the operation blackboard, and the District Primary Education Programme (DPEP) it case of elementary education, vocationalization of secondary education, and improvement of quality in higher education and development of open learning systems. All these programmes require increased allocation of plan as well as non-plan resources for education.

As education was brought into the concurrent list, and as the National Policy on Education 1986 promised "meaningful and challenging partnership" between the centre and the states in education, both the central government and the states have a responsibility to make special efforts to finance education and to realize the several goals, including the target of investing six per cent of national income in education.

## Role of Finance Commission

The centre-state shares in financing education (and other sectors) depend upon their respective fiscal capacities. The level of spending on education in a state depends upon the amount of resources transferred from the centre to the states, besides upon its own budgetary resources. Such transfers from the central government take place through the Planning Commission, and the Finance Commission, besides other grants. The Planning Commission is normally concerned with plan allocations only, and the Finance Commission with the non-plan expenditures only. Non-plan expenditure on education increases over the years, and presently forms more than 80 per cent of the total (plan plus non-plan) expenditure on education, and hence the role of the Finance Commission becomes increasingly important.

The Finance Commission has to recommend the allocation of resources to the states based on requirements of the states, as forecasted by the states themselves for already existing educational institutions. The states submit to the Finance Commission their requirements on the non-plan account for a five year period, keeping in view their own budgetary positions and the requirements of various sectors, including education sector. The Finance Commission receives these detailed estimates from the states, in general "distrusts the state estimates which are based on solid experience", scrutinizes them, and "provides their own estimates based on unspecified criteria differentially applied to different states".

It has been found that the Finance Commission has an important but restricted role to play in improving the mechanism of allocation of resources to the states. This does not mean that Finance Commission cannot consider equity, even though non- plan expenditure on educationally advanced states should be higher. Strengthening of the existing infrastructure and facilities, better maintenance of the existing schools and colleges, which are treated as non-plan activities, also contribute significantly to improvement in the educational levels of the states.

The Sixth Finance Commission for instance, gave some weightage to the backward states. taking into account the unfinished tasks in elementary- education. The Seventh Finance Commission considered poverty and the inverse of state domestic product. (SDP) per capita while making its reassessments.

The Eighth Finance Commission included the requirements for up- gradation of the standards of administration in education in its awards and allocated additional resources for clearing the backlog in the construction of school buildings and for providing teachers for single teacher schools. The Ninth Finance Commission (1988) also provided for construction of school buildings in ten educationally backward states, according to the norms of the Operation Blackboard.' Thus' the Finance Commission could play a significant role in pursuing equity in education.

The actual method adopted by the Finance Commission in recommending their awards is not generally known. But the general presumption is that the Finance Commission has had to work based on a very limited data base. The present paper attempts at filling up this gap to a significant extent, by providing a very detailed data set for about a decade beginning 1980-81 and ending with the most recent period for which reliable statistics are available, which is mostly 1991-92.

Generally, the Finance Commissions have been recommending their awards to fill the gap between the projected receipts of the states and the expenditures in revenue accounts of the states. In many cases these projections were mere extrapolations of the past trends. The Finance Commissions also seem to have followed no explicit criteria other than scrutinising these state forecasts, based on

(a) the requirements of the state governments under the revenue account to meet expenditure on administration and non-plan commitments or liabilities,

(b) provision for wages and salaries for government employees,

(c) commitments on interest charges on debts,

(d) transfer of resources to local organizations,

(e) maintenance of capital assets,

(f) maintenance of plan schemes completed in the earlier plan, and

(g) requirement of the backward stages for upgrading standards in general education.

However, the Ninth Finance Commission was required for the first time to adopt a "normative approach" on the requirements of various states and in the awards of the Finance Commission. Accordingly, the Ninth Finance Commission has made its recommendations in several sectors based on cost functions. The Tenth Finance Commission is also hoped to follow a normative approach. The exercise here is also in the same direction.

## Sources of Data

The main source of data on plan and non-plan expenditure on education in the states has been Analysis of Budget Expenditure on Education, published by the Ministry of Human Resource Development. In the present context, this is supplemented by published and unpublished data collected from the Department of Education, Ministry of Human Resource Development. The data on enrollments are collected from Education in India and Selected Educational Statistics. State domestic product (SDP) deflators are derived from data on SDP available in current and constant prices in National Accounts Statistics (Central Statistical Organization). Population projections are drawn from the Report of the Standing Committee of Experts on Population Projections (October 1989) , and other Census reports.

The annual rates of growth are generally high both in current and constant prices in several states. As expected, rates of growth in constant prices are obviously less than rates of growth in current prices. But for this, there are no uniform patterns emerging. The growth in plan expenditure is not smooth; in fact rates of growth in plan expenditure in a few states are negative (e.g., higher education in Gujarat, Karnataka, Tamil Nadu, Uttar

Pradesh, secondary and technical education in Kerala, and technical education in West Bengal) , while in a few other states rates of growth in the same (plan expenditure) are very high (e.g., 27 per cent in elementary education in Uttar Pradesh, and 39 per cent in Jammu and Kashmir).

The rates of growth in non-plan expenditure in constant prices are reasonably smooth and positive. In case of, elementary education, the rate of growth ranges between 2.46 per cent per annum in Kerala and 12.90 per cent in Tripura, and in case of all levels of education together, it ranges between 3.69 per cent in Kerala and 10.93 per cent in Tripura.

Based on the available data given in Table 1 on plan, non- plan and total expenditure on various levels of education in the 18 states, two alternative types of projections of expenditure on education are attempted here:

First, assuming that the rate of growth realized during the 1980s continues during the 1990s, mere projections of likely trends in plan, non-plan and total expenditure on education are made until the end of the century. These projections are also presented in current and constant prices, and both by levels of education. These projections, that can be treated as just extrapolations projecting the past into future, are obviously oblivious of the recent policy changes and their effects on education. Neither the unit costs of education, nor the enrollments do explicitly figure in these calculations. Hence these estimates may be viewed as the minimum levels the expenditure on education should grow to during the 1990S.

Alternatively, taking the unit costs of education explicitly, and the enrolment targets into account, the total requirements of expenditure on education can be estimated. For instance, the Ninth Finance Commission adopted a "normative approach" and estimated cost functions in making their awards. Following the same approach, the requirements of resources in each state are forecasted here, by estimating the following simple equation:'

In Andhra Pradesh, Assam, Gujarat, Karnataka, Madhya Pradesh, Tamil Nadu and Rajasthan the projections based on recent rates of growth are higher than the requirements estimated through cost function, suggesting that these states performed well in the recent past, and if the same trends continue, the resource position of the elementary education system would be very good.

According to the estimates of the Standing Committee on Population Projections, the population, particularly the 6-13 age group population, in Tamil Nadu is likely to decline. The declining trend is to continue even after the turn of the century. So with the target of universalization of elementary education, the projected trends in enrollments show a negative rate of growth. This has produced a declining trend in plan, non-plan and total expenditure on elementary education.

Secondly, the enrollments in elementary education in Kerala already exhibited a declining trend during the 1980s. One might have expected a similar trend to continue. But the target enrollments (based on the estimates of population of 613 age-group, as estimated by the Standing Committee) by 2000 AD require a reversal of the trends in enrollments. The results of the cost function based on the declining enrollments in the past, produces awkward results regarding requirements of resources in the future. Hence in stead of using the cost function, we have considered the 1989-90 level of per student expenditure (in 1980-81 prices), and the projected enrollments in making the estimates regarding requirements of resources in the future.

It may be noted that though these projections of requirements of resources are based on a simple and crude methodology, without considering the specific programmes, and items of expenditure, they are based on a sound logic of unit costs, enrollments and past trends in the same. From these long and detailed array of estimates, it is hoped that necessary implications can be drawn by the Finance Commission.

At the end, a few issues may be underscored, as a proposal to the Finance Commission:

Though education is regarded as "a unique investment in the present and the future". and that it presents "a crucial area of investment for national development and survival" (Government of India, 1986, p. 3 and p. 29) , rarely education sector in India received any special treatment as far as allocation of resources is concerned. As a result, many educational goals remained unfulfilled. Educational levels of the population, and/or simply literacy levels are being rightly viewed as an important indicator of measuring levels of development in general, and human development in particular. The Finance Commission may like to consider this variable in measuring the overall backwardness of the states, along with, inter alia, state domestic product per capita and poverty ratio in making its awards.

In view of the recognition of the need to lay special thrust on elementary education,' universalization of which is repeatedly postponed and is still elusive, it is necessary that the Tenth Finance Commission accords a high priority and a special treatment to elementary education. The need and scope for significant increase in the levels of investment in primary education are abundant both for improvement in quality and quantitative expansion. The District Primary Education Programme makes it clear.

Second, as long as the backlog exists in the construction of school buildings, and provision of basic inputs like the Operation Blackboard material, it is necessary that the Finance Commission makes, in addition to actual unit cost based recommendations of resources, grants for construction of school buildings, and provision of teachers in single and two teacher schools.

Thirdly, appropriate norms on cost per school (with a desirable level of infrastructure and facilities) should be considered while making provision for opening of schools.

Recognizing the need, for example, the Government of India hosted the Education for All Summit of Nine High Population Countries in December 1993.

Tenth Finance Commission suggest that the requirements of the states for modernization of administration, e.g., computerization of records, should be taken into account, while making the awards by the Finance Commission. Modernization of administration and computerization of statistical information is important not only in case of land records etc., as noted in the 'Terms of Reference' but also in sectors like education — both at institutional level, and also at macro (state and national) level. This does require additional resources.

The terms of reference for the Tenth Finance Commission also clearly suggest that the Finance Commission should provide for the maintenance and upkeep of capital assets and maintenance expenditure on plan schemes to be completed by the end of the eighth Five Year Plan.

Since our estimates based on actual trends in unit costs of education do not take into account these considerations separately, it is necessary that the actual awards by the Finance Commission for the education sector in various states need to be much higher than estimated here.

# 6

# Staff Appraisal

Substantial gains have been made in providing access to education to Indian children over the past four decades; however, much remains to be done. Forty-eight percent of India's population is still illiterate and the number of illiterates increased from 302 to 324 million between 1981 and 1991. While nearly all children have physical access to a school, the holding and teaching power of most rural primary schools is very weak.

About seventy-five percent of the 102 million children reported to be enrolled in primary school attend one of 565,000 schools that offer the lower primary cycle of education. States differ in administration and definition of the steps on the educational ladder, but most have adopted the national model of five years of lower primary plus three years of upper primary schooling; some states have adopted a four plus three structure for lower and upper primary schooling. Together, lower and upper primary cycles are referred to as elementary education. Lower secondary school, also called high school, comprises two or three years and higher secondary consists of two additional years of secondary education which is the Plus 2 stage.

While the stated gross enrolment ratio (GER) at the primary level is high, 102.7 percent in 1992, a proportion of the children reported as enrolled in grade 1 are listed on school ledgers but do not attend beyond a few days. In addition, the reported GER includes repeaters, who are not identified as such. The Government of India (GOI) thus discounts the reported GER by 20 percent for planning purposes. Internal efficiency is extremely low. Nearly one-fourth of children who are reported to be enrolled drop out before reaching the second grade and about half drop out before grade five. Although gaps in access and completion have been closing in recent years, nationwide a disproportionate number of non-enrolled and dropouts are from the poorest households, girls, members of Scheduled Castes (SCs) and Scheduled Tribes (STs).

Approximately 250,000 non-formal education (NFE) education centers provide equivalent primary education for an estimated seven million children in the 9-14 age group who do not enter or who drop out of school, and literacy programs are provided for adults in selected districts.

Primary education in India is the joint responsibility of the central and state governments, although most financing is provided by the States. In the Seventh Five Year Plan (1985-1990) the states provided 63 percent of the plan resources invested in primary education and 96 percent of non-plan recurrent costs.

After the National Policy on Education was issued in 1986, central government assistance for primary education expanded in the form of grants to states for specific programs. During the Seventh Plan, 70 percent of central government assistance was delivered through Operation Blackboard (OBB), through which grants are provided for an additional teacher and educational materials in single-teacher rural schools. An important provision is that one of the two teachers in OBB schools should be female. In addition, the GOI provides grants for non-formal primary education for girls and working children and for improved primary teacher education through the establishment of District Institutes of Education and Training (DIETs) in the states. DIETs are intended to provide training, curriculum and planning and management support for elementary education at the district level. A centrally financed National Literacy Mission (NLM) has been established to implement total literacy campaigns (TLC) in selected districts.

Two autonomous national resource institutions are financed by the GOI to provide professional and academic leadership in education. These are the National Council for Educational Research and Training (NCERT), and the National Institute of Educational Planning and Administration (NIEPA). Both are located in New Delhi. These institutions work closely with counterpart organizations in the states, providing training, research and planning support.

### Sub-sector Efficiency and Effectiveness

The effectiveness and efficiency of primary education in India need to be improved. Weak outcomes signal low returns to investment or, from another point of view, failure to capture the significant benefits in poverty reduction, economic development and social returns that primary education has been shown to generate, internationally and in India. Addressing the principal constraints on sub-sector efficiency and effectiveness through expanded and better investment is a significant challenge to Indian education.

Despite substantial improvements since 1986, the outcomes of primary education, as measured by literacy statistics, dropout and learning achievement are unsatisfactory. Available data also suggest that there is considerable variation on these indicators both between and within states, indicating a substantial degree of regional inequity.

Ten large northern states have overall literacy rates ranging from 38 to 55 percent, and female literacy rates from 20 to 40 percent, all well below national averages. By contrast, Kerala has achieved universal enrollment and comparatively high levels of completion of the lower primary cycle. Near universal literacy has been attained. Among other major states, dropout rates in grades 1-5 range from 21 percent in Tamil Nadu to 66 percent in Bihar. Female dropout rates are five or more percentage points higher than male rates in six large northern states and in Karnataka; they are lower than male dropout rates in a number of smaller states.

Within state disparities on basic indicators are also marked. For example, of Maharashtra's 29 districts, 20 have female literacy rates above the national average of 39 percent, but the rates in 9 fall below the average. For Assam, the comparable figures are 13 and 10 districts, respectively. In Haryana, 9 districts are above the national average and 7 are below. Three of Tamil Nadu's 20 districts have female literacy rates below the national average.

Many of the students who do complete primary school learn relatively little. Project studies of student learning achievement in the second and final year of lower primary school in seven states show that, on average, students have mastered fewer than a quarter of the curriculum objectives. Learning achievement is very low even in states that have achieved full enrollment and comparatively low dropout, such as Kerala and Tamil Nadu.

The effects of these disparities are readily seen in social indicators. The sex ratio is an indicator of gender discrimination. In a high literacy state such as Kerala, there are 1016 females for every 1000 males, and the infant mortality rate is 28 per thousand births. By contrast, in the low literacy state of Bihar there are 930 females for every 1000 males, and the infant mortality rate is 117 per thousand births. Nationally, household sample survey data show that completing primary education is associated with significant improvements in contraceptive use, pre-natal care and child immunization among rural women. On the basis of dropout rates alone, more than half of rural girls are leaving school ill-equipped to take advantage of these important development services.

## SUB-SECTOR CONSTRAINTS

With the issuance of the Revised National Policy on Education and a National Programme of Action in 1992, the GOI has accelerated central leadership and support for primary education development. The challenges are substantial. Historically, the ability of states to invest in primary education has varied widely, but limited federal resources have not been well targeted to offset these variations. The institutional mechanisms needed to manage expanded investment and to provide technical leadership have received little past attention.

Reforms will now need to be carried out in a changing institutional environment caused by th implementation by states of the Seventy-third and Seventy-fourth amendments to the Constitution of India (1992) that provide for increased responsibility on the part of elected local governments (Panchayat Raj institutions) for social programs, including primary education. Having achieved the comparatively easy objective of putting schools in reach of most children, reforms will need to address the much less tractable problems of improving the quality of education in order to reduce dropout and improve learning achievement, and to improve the equity of access to and completion of primary education for girls, scheduled caste (SC) and scheduled tribe (ST) students.

Historically Inadequate Financing. With the introduction of new economic policies in 1991, and the launching of the Eighth Plan in 1992, India has substantially increased financing for elementary education.2/ Projected Eighth Plan investments in elementary education by the Government of India and the states would be on the order of US$3 billion; in the Seventh Plan (1985-90), combined investment totalled less than US$1 billion. This sharp increase in planned investment comes after decades of gradual increases in both Plan (investment) and Non-plan (recurrent) expenditures on education and, within education, on elementary education. Average annual state expenditures on elementary education have risen from 5.2 percent of total budgets in 1985/86 to 10.2 percent in 1990/91.

Recent trends are thus encouraging. However, the present primary education system shows the effects of past under-financing. In real terms, the rate of growth in expenditure per student at the elementary level was only 0.4 percent from 1980/81 to 1987/88, reflecting both the priority given to expanding enrollments and the continuing growth of population at 2 percent annually. More than 90 percent of expenditures continues to go to salaries.

In consequence, expenditures on the quality of education — in-service training, learning materials, maintenance of facilities, educational research and development, system planning and management — have been severely constrained. Household survey data show that about 40 percent of dropout is explained by lack of interest in education and by failure in school; both factors can be attributed at least in part to the low quality of education. Very poor absolute levels of learning achievement across the states provide a further indicator of poor quality.

The challenge for the balance of the century is thus to target substantially increased resources on improving educational quality. This will require an enhanced leadership and management role for the GOI in a complex federal system of education in order to ensure equitable allocation of enhanced resources and to assist states in developing institutional planning and management capacity at state and district levels.

## System Management

Prior to the National Education Policy of 1986, the central government's role in primary education was marginal. States provided the largest share of investment and recurrent cost financing, but, with few exceptions, states gave low priority to primary education. State planning and management mechanisms were poorly developed, and primary education systems were characterized by routine administration of inadequate finances to districts, which in turn built and supervised schools. Change and improvement in primary education was limited to small scale pilot efforts in a few states.

Beginning in 1986, the central government has sought to expand its leadership and financing role in basic education through national grants schemes and mobilization of external assistance. The centrally sponsored grant schemes (OBB, Nonformal Education, DIETS) focus on one element of the education delivery system. They provide standard packages of inputs, regardless of the varying conditions of states and districts and targeting is imprecise. Other than DIETS, there has been little investment in the development of district, state or national institutional capacity for the planning and management of large scale education reform programs or for educational evaluation and research. Implementation difficulties have reduced the effectiveness of the OBB and NFE schemes.

External assistance has been mobilized for integrated state basic education development programs in Bihar, Rajasthan and Uttar Pradesh, and to expand the earlier ODA-assisted project in Andhra Pradesh. In these projects, most of which have been launched since 1990, the development of state institutional capacity has begun to receive attention. Registered "societies"3/ have been established to manage the flow of resources and to provide a nucleus for the planning and management of reforms. In Uttar Pradesh, a State Institute of Education Management and Training is being established to provide technical planning, management and research services. In most states, however, institutional development has yet to begin.

At the national level, capacity to finance and manage a sustained, large scale program of financial and technical assistance to states for educational reform and improvement has yet to be developed. The bulk of technical, professional training and research resources of NCERT and NIEPA have been directed at secondary and higher education.

A 1993 national survey of more than 130 universities and social science research institutions identified only four with any ongoing work on primary or elementary education. Less than one percent of the publications of NCERT and NIEPA have addressed issues in primary education. In the GOI Department of Education (DOE), supervision of existing state primary-level projects and planning for initiatives is being handled by a team of four persons, with assistance from a team of ten NIEPA and NCERT faculty.

The size of the country, the diversity and complexity of the federal system, and the scope of the task to be accomplished mandate the creation of a strong planning, monitoring and management function within the GOI to assist in the development of state institutional capacity and to support and supervise programs and projects aimed at improving the quality of primary education.

### Decentralization and Role of Local Governments

The 73rd and 74th Amendments to the Constitution of India (1992) mandate the creation of locally elected governments in all states. States have latitude in determining the structure and functions of these governments through enabling legislation. It is anticipated that such legislation will be passed and elections for local bodies held in all states by 1995.

Primary education is to be one of the major areas of responsibility for elected local governments. A committee of the Central Advisory Board for Education (CABE) has recommended the functions to be performed at district, block and community levels with respect to primary education. Long-standing national policy for the creation of effective school/community organizations has been strengthened. The CABE report has been endorsed by state ministers of education."

In a nation of the size and diversity of India, moving responsibility for primary education to lower levels of administration holds considerable promise, as does expanded community involvement. However, patterns of authority and financing are likely to vary across states and are at present undecided. District-level tax-based financing is unlikely in most states in the near future. District- level planning and management capacities are largely undeveloped. There are risks that state education agencies would be unable to provide the technical support needed at lower levels of government, and that changing patterns of fund administration may result in inefficient administration of investment programs, including those for primary education.

Gaining the potential benefits of decentralization poses an additional challenge to state and national education agencies. International experience shows that effective decentralization requires not only real transfer of authority, but also training and technical support to enable officials to carry out new responsibilities.

## Education Quality

While universal access to basic education remains elusive, high primary gross enrollment rates suggest that the system has at least largely caught up with the backlog of unenrolled children. However, expansion of facilities to meet population growth, to improve equity of access for girls, SC and ST students, and to reduce overcrowding in classrooms will continue to be needed. The major challenge at this point is to improve internal efficiency and learning achievement in schools that serve the 100 million children who appear on the enrollment ledgers at the beginning of the school year.

The large scale, sample-based learning achievement studies conducted in 33 districts in seven states in the past three years support the conclusions of extensive observations of rural primary schools. The basic inputs for learning are found in most schools across India: students, textbooks, a blackboard, and teachers. This is, by itself, a notable achievement. However, as results demonstrate, it is not sufficient.

Students are poorly prepared for school. In low-literacy districts, two-thirds or more of students are first-time learners from illiterate homes. Early childhood education (ECE) reaches about 40 percent of such children through the Integrated Child Development Services (ICDS) and other state-run pre-primary education programs. Research in India and elsewhere has demonstrated that high quality ECE improves primary school attendance and learning achievement. But project learning achievement studies failed to find a positive relationship between attendance in ECE as offered in these districts and learning in school. Observations indicate that the potential of ECE is constrained by inappropriate curricula and learning materials, untrained teachers, and inadequate supervision.

The quality of school inputs is low. Textbooks are overly difficult, with many students unable to read them; their publication quality is low, and state textbook publication systems suffer, in varying ways and to varying extent, from inefficient practices. While there are blackboards, consumable supplies and educational aids are conspicuous by their absence and, when present, by low utilization. Although most teachers are highly educated and have formal pre-service training, they have not been trained for multi-grade teaching in rural schools. Less than 6 percent of teachers had received any in-service training in 1986/87.

In some states, weak supervision leads to high rates of teacher absenteeism; in small schools, this results in high effective student- teacher ratios and, too often, children without teachers. Buildings are poorly designed, inadequately maintained, and largely unfurnished. According to a 1986/87 national survey, 44 percent of lower primary schools did not have proper buildings; 66 percent had no furniture for students; 74 percent lacked libraries; and 95 percent lacked toilets. While the situation has improved in intervening years, conditions are still poor in many places. Project baseline studies in three districts in Tamil Nadu, for example, revealed that more than 90 percent of schools lacked toilets, a quarter lacked furniture for students; in four districts of Assam, 80 percent of schools lack safe drinking water and fewer than 10 percent have toilets. In such circumstances, it is not surprising that many students lose interest in education, or leave school because of academic failure.

The challenge to national, state and district education authorities is thus to improve the quality of basic services: pre-primary education, textbooks, learning materials, teacher competencies, and facilities. Nationally-sponsored research and development work aimed at improved curricula and textbooks began in response to the 1986 Policy.

Known as Minimum Levels of Learning (MLL), this program has identified basic competencies in language, mathematics, and social/environmental studies. With trials largely completed, the challenge is to implement MLL standards through improved textbooks and in-service training of teachers. This will be a massive task, requiring substantial investment and greatly strengthened institutional capacity for implementation, for supervision and monitoring, and for evaluation and research to determine the cost-effectiveness of alternative intervention strategies for achieving MLL.

## EQUITY

Priority given in the 1986 National Policy on Education to increasing the enrollment of girls in lower primary school has begun to pay off. Female enrollment grew at 3.7 percent annually from 1981 to 1991; male enrollment grew at 2.5 percent annually during the same period. However, the national Gross Enrollment Rate for girls and boys in 1991 still stood at 88 percent and 116 percent respectively. Nationally, average female dropout rates are roughly equivalent to boys. But despite relative overall progress for girls, considerable variation across states on both enrollment and dropout indices remains. In 1991, female GERs in lower primary school ranged from 56 percent in Bihar to 128 percent in Tamil Nadu. Female dropout rates ranged from zero percent in Kerala to 60 percent in Rajasthan and 70 percent in Bihar. Studies of learning achievement, however, show relatively equal average levels of learning for boy and girls. On three tests administered in 21 districts to students in the final year of primary school, boys outscored girls 40 to 23, but the differences are small. In three districts in Haryana and one in Karnataka girls outscored boys on all tests. Consistent with national policy, states have sought to reduce gender disparities by reviewing curricula and textbooks to eliminate gender bias and by increasing the proportion of female teachers.

Gross enrollment rates for SC boys are comparable to national averages, though GERs for SC girls lag substantially. SC students also tend to score lower than average on achievement tests, although again differences are small and SC girls outscored the average for all girls on two or more tests in two districts in Maharashtra and one each in Kerala, Karnataka and Tamil Nadu. For the most part, SC students are enrolled in integrated schools and speak the regional language. With the exception of Assam, project states have sought to increase enrollment and retention through a variety of incentive programs, including scholarships for SC girls and attendance allowances. Less attention has been given to educational strategies such as teacher sensitization.

Enrollment rates for ST boys approach national averages, but those for girls lag substantially. Dropout rates are higher than average for both boys and girls. ST children outscored district averages about 45 percent of the time on learning achievement tests, suggesting that they do not lag behind others on this indicator 5/ Tribal children are found both in integrated schools and in coherent tribal communities, the latter often found in isolated locations with little access to social services.

As established by the Seventh Amendment to the Constitution, states and local authorities are to provide instruction in the mother tongue at the primary stage for all linguistic minorities, including tribal children. Policies seek both to preserve minority languages and to facilitate participation in the dominant society and economy. However, tribal languages are not widely used as the medium of instruction. In Assam, for example, the instruction at primary level is offered in Assamese, Bengali, and Hindi; in areas inhabited by the Bodo tribe, instruction is provided in the Bodo language.

Implementation of the policy also has been constrained by the presence of over 400 tribal languages and dialects, 60 of which are written, inadequate financing, and the lack of a coherent approach to policy implementation at national and state levels. Project studies of ST education indicate that ST parents generally would prefer the use of regional languages as the medium of instruction, but the baseline learning achievement studies indicate that language difficulties are a major constraint on classroom processes not only for ST children, but also in areas with multiple regional languages. Textbooks and learning materials have been developed in relatively few tribal languages. Historic lack of access to and completion of primary and secondary school severely limits the potential number of teachers able to provide instruction in tribal languages, and the remote nature of many tribal communities reduces the willingness of teachers to accept or persist in posts. The dominant role of Tribal Welfare Departments in providing schools in tribal areas, with teachers and materials provided by state education departments, has led to division of authority and responsibility in states. Tribal Welfare Departments also provide scholarships and other incentives for ST students.

Improving equity of access to and completion of primary education for girls, SC and ST students thus remains a significant challenge. The data on learning achievement indicates smaller disparities than have commonly been thought to exist. While the comparisons suggest that a degree of equality in learning has been achieved, it is equality at a very low level of achievement. Rural primary students tend to learn equally little, regardless of gender or caste.

For girls, the potential of intensified training for teachers, enhanced roles for women in school/ community organizations, and a greater role for women's development groups in encouraging enrollment and attendance needs to be realized. Similar strategies for SC students, especially SC girls, need to be developed and tested. For ST students, a substantially increased state commitment to policy implementation, backed by adequate resources and appropriately involving state Tribal Welfare Departments, is needed. National technical and managerial leadership and support for this effort will be important.

## Policy Framework for Educational Development

The Revised National Policy on Education (1992) and the 1992 Programme of Action provide the basic policy framework for central and state investment in primary education development. The objectives for primary education, in order of priority, are to (a) reduce dropout, (b) improve learning achievement, and (c) expand access for unserved students. Girls, SC and ST students are to be given priority attention. Decentralization of responsibility for planning and management of primary education development programs to the district level, and strengthening of school/community organizations, are advocated as means of developing locality specific strategies and implementation plans and of increasing ownership of schooling by communities. The policy framework is thus well-aligned with principal sub-sectoral constraints.

To achieve these policy objectives, the GOI has established the District Primary Education Program (DPEP) as a cabinet-approved, centrally sponsored program of financial and technical assistance to states and districts for primary education reform."' Developed through extensive consultations with states, DPEP would finance primary education development programs in selected districts and the strengthening of both state and national institutional capacity for planning, management and technical support. It is the intention of the GOI to channel the bulk of external assistance to primary education through the DPEP to ensure consistency with policy and equitable allocation of resources.

DPEP Guidelines were issued in April, 1993. In a major departure from previous vertical schemes focused on specific inputs, such as OBB, DPEP would provide grant financing for integrated sub-projects developed at district and state levels aimed at improving the quality of basic education services.

DPEP would thus emphasize improved and expanded non-salary inputs for primary education; institutional development; more and better textbooks and educational materials; improved classroom teaching and facilities; strengthened community/school organizations; and expanded technical and managerial support. Incentives and scholarship programs already in place would continue to be financed by state governments outside of DPEP.

Key managerial features of the program include:

(a) targeting of resources;

(b) decentralized planning at the district level with substantial popular participation;

(c) appraisal of district and state proposals against DPEP criteria and categories of assistance;

(d) flexible implementation arrangements at the state level;

(e) incremental implementation and expansion based on performance;

(f) intensive technical support and supervision from strengthened national agencies and resource institutions; and

(g) substantially increased financing through the budget of the GOI DOE.

DPEP financing would be targeted to districts with female literacy rates below the national average of 39 percent, as well as to districts where Total Literacy Campaigns have generated substantial enrollment increases in primary education.

Proposals for DPEP financing would be developed first by district planning teams, following DPEP criteria and guidelines, with technical support from state and national agencies. Proposals for institutional development at the state level to provide enhanced support to district projects would then be developed. Parents, teachers, NGOs and education officials would be consulted and involved in the preparation of district and state proposals.

DPEP program staff would appraise both district and state proposals against program criteria and guidelines. Appraisal would focus on conformance with program objectives and priorities, and technical and managerial feasibility. During appraisal, DPEP would assess the capacity of the states to finance their share of the investment program and to sustain the recurrent costs of program investments on non-plan budgets when sub-projects are completed.

States would establish registered societies to receive, disburse and account for funds, and to manage the implementation of sub-programs. These state implementation societies would be closely modeled on precursors established to manage externally-assisted state projects in Bihar, Rajasthan and Uttar Pradesh. Societies are governed by Councils representing key state and national agencies, NGOs, and educationists, and are directly managed by Executive Committees.

Participation in DPEP is voluntary on the part of states. Initially, a limited number of districts (3-5) and investments in state institutional capacity would be considered. Assessment studies would be conducted in each program district to establish baseline indicators for enrollment, dropout and learning achievement. 7/ These studies would be replicated every third year to gauge progress against program objectives. Funds would be released through an annual review of district and state progress reports and proposals for the subsequent year. Depending on progress, states would be eligible to propose additional districts for financing over time. Major reviews of performance would be conducted following the completion of the periodic assessment studies. DPEP could drop non-performing districts from the program and, with appropriate appraisal, shift resources to other districts. It is intended to launch the project in approximately 8 states that do not currently have externally assisted basic education projects. These latter states, as well as additional states, could apply for DPEP financing as the program expands.

Initially, DPEP would focus on building national, state and district institutional capacity, and on reform of lower primary education. Once satisfactory progress is being made at the lower primary level in low-literacy districts, states could apply for financing of sub-projects aimed at upper primary education.

Supervision and Technical Support. The program would be managed by the DPEP Bureau in the GOI Department of Education, which would be responsible to an empowered committee representing key GOI Departments, including Finance and the Planning Commission (DPEP Project Board). The DPEP Bureau would be fully staffed and equipped to provide appraisal for and regular supervision of state and district sub-projects, to manage flow of funds and disbursements, to oversee procurement, and to provide liaison with international donors. It would be supported by substantial technical and professional consultant services. The DPEP Bureau would develop national technical assistance, training and research and evaluation capacity through contracts with national and state resource institutions.

The Finance Ministry and the Planning Commission have approved an increased allocation for primary education of US$650 million to the DOE for implementation of DPEP over the balance of the Eighth Plan period. These funds would finance 85 percent of district and state projects through grants, with the balance being provided as additional allocations in state elementary education budgets and, for national components and activities, the budget of the DOE.

## IDA Strategy

Promoting economic reform for broad-based, efficient economic growth, accelerating poverty alleviation and developing human resources are the focus of IDA's country assistance strategy. Education development is central to strengthening human resources, and primary education is a necessary foundation. Low educational achievement, especially among the poor, Scheduled Tribes, Scheduled Castes and women is a major constraint to their social and economic improvement.

IDA's strategy for education is to focus medium-term assistance exclusively on primary education, given its underdeveloped status in India, its high returns, and its importance to the poor. IDA assistance for this project would provide the financing and technical experience needed to establish DPEP program management and technical support capacities, as well as to initiate sub-projects in a substantial number of districts and states. Previous support for basic education in India, consistent with the objectives of this program, has been provided by IDA through the Social Safety Net Adjustment Program (Credit 2448-IN), and through the Uttar Pradesh Basic Education Project (Credit 2509-IN).

Without continued IDA involvement, the proposed DPEP mechanisms for management, super-vision and evaluation would be less well developed, and the quality of sub-project implementation reduced. IDA has advanced the analytical underpinnings of is work through studies of student learning achievement and primary school effectiveness in Uttar Pradesh and Tamil Nadu and a public expenditure review for education. The analytical basis for the project is further strengthened by studies of education for girls, scheduled caste and tribal students completed by Indian scholars, as well as the 1986/87 national survey of education.

Additional project studies have been carried out in collaboration with UNICEF, NCERT and NIEPA during project preparation, including: baseline beneficiary assessments in the six IDA DPEP states; textbook production, distribution, and costs; girls' education; tribal education; teacher training, education and motivation; and state education finance.

The first substantial external assistance for primary education was provided by ODA for a project in Andhra Pradesh; approximately US$35 million was provided through 1992. UNICEF has disbursed around US$5 million from agency funds for the Bihar Education Project, and has pledged to raise up to US$92 million more from other donors. In Rajasthan, the Swedish International Development Authority has provided or pledged approximately US$100 million for basic education projects.

The Netherlands have provided and pledged approximately US$30 million for Mahila Samakhya, the women's empowerment program managed by the GOI DOE. IDA approved a credit of US$165 million for the Uttar Pradesh Basic Education Project in 1993 (Credit 2509-IN). Under the agreements of the Program to Strengthen the Social Safety Net (Credit 2448- IN), the European Community (EC) has agreed to provide ECU 150 million as program support to DPEP; this is the first program of external financing for DPEP. EC funds would be released through two mechanisms.

First, an annual fixed grant would be made contingent on adequate budget provision for elementary education by the GOI; tranche releases would be tied to issuance of annual budget documents.

Second, grants of approximately US$1.7 million would be made on the initiation of DPEP assisted district sub-projects. 8/ In addition, the EC program earmarks US$5 million for external technical assistance and training. ODA and UNICEF have agreed to place future financial assistance through the DPEP program. GOI would keep separate all donor funds by earmarking them to different districts.

While India has long employed central grant programs as a mechanism for GOI investment in state-managed development activities, the DPEP would incorporate a number of structural innovations. The DOE has gained four years of satisfactory experience with the use of registered societies for project implementation (Bihar, Rajasthan, and Uttar Pradesh), and lessons learned have been incorporated into the model Memorandum of Association and By-Laws that are to be used by each participating DPEP state.

For other innovations, including decentralized planning, formal appraisal and supervision mechanisms, and performance management, there are few lessons of experience, other than implementation difficulties associated with their absence. The presence of these structural innovations underlines the need for phased start of the program and effective monitoring and management.

From experience with previous vertical schemes such as OBB, the GOI has learned the importance of integrated education development programs that address inter- related constraints through coordinated efforts to improve basic services. Experience with state projects in Bihar, Rajasthan and Uttar Pradesh has demonstrated the importance of formal annual reviews and work program proposals, and the importance of focusing on improving the quality of ECE, textbooks and learning materials, and strengthening teacher in-service training.

Experience with IDA-assisted Population and Human Resources Projects in India has demonstrated the importance of strong project management arrangements, annual budget financing sufficient to cover anticipated project expenditures, clear mechanisms for the advance of funds and for timely completion of disbursement requests, and supportive supervision from IDA, especially in start-up phases of projects. The development of effective supervision activities by project agencies also emerges as significant given the geographic scope of highly decentralized social service delivery programs.

The program would also draw on wider international experience in primary education development." This experience substantially validates the DPEP emphasis on ECE, improved textbooks and learning materials, intensified in-service teacher training, and enhanced community participation in the operation of schools.

The proposed IDA credit is for a specific investment project that would finance the development and operation of the DPEP Bureau in the GOI DOE to serve as a financial and technical program intermediary organization, as well as an initial set of state capacity building and district sub-projects in 23 districts (3-5 per state) in the states of Assam, Haryana, Karnataka, Kerala, Maharashtra and Tamil Nadu." The number of initial districts exceeds the minimum number agreed to by the World Bank and the GOI in the Program to Strengthen the Social Safety Net (Credit 2448-IN). The proposed credit would support the first of three phases of GOI DPEP, which focuses on establishing DPEP as the principal financing and technical support mechanism for the development of primary education in India, and testing intervention strategies in a limited number of districts.

As a newly developed and complex program" that would develop key Institutions while initiating district action programs, GOI DPEP would need to be implemented in a carefully phased manner. In the first year of operation, GOI DPEP would focus on the development of key national and state institutions and technical support programs, and on initial start-up activities in district sub-projects based on seven year investment plans and detailed first year implementation programs. District sub-projects would emphasize the development of district management capacity, initial in-service training designs and materials, and limited civil works. Detailed plans for expanded implementation of the GOI DPEP would be prepared for review at the beginning of the second and each subsequent year of program implementation. Annual reviews would be conducted by the DPEP Bureau, with full participation of program donors.

The GOI DPEP would extend support lo participating states in phases. In Phase I, the proposed district sub-projects would be financed in Assam, Haryana, Karnataka, Kerala, Maharashtra, and Tamil Nadu. These states have a combined population of 243 million and contain 38 of the 242 districts, nation-wide, with below average female literacy rates. ODA assistance to Andhra Pradesh, currently partially present in all districts, would expand to full coverage, resulting in coverage of 50-52 low female literacy districts. In Phase II, GOI DPEP would be expanded to include additional states and additional districts in the initial set of states. In later phases, present state projects could be considered eligible for expansion. At full expansion, the program would cover an estimated 373 districts, including all falling below the average female literacy rate, in 14 of India's largest states, with a combined population of 770 million.

The proposed IDA credit (the proposed DPEP project) would finance implementation of Phase I of the GOI DPEP. It would also finance preparation and initial activities in states and districts proposed for Phase II of the GOI DPEP. It is also anticipated that, depending on implementation progress, the proposed IDA credit would be followed by a second operation to support Phase II of the GOI DPEP.

### Goals of National Policy

The goals of national policy for lower primary education are to (a) build institutional capacity, (b) reduce dropout, (c) improve learning achievement and (d) increase access for unserved groups. Reducing the disparities in dropout, learning and access for girls, SC and ST students has high policy priority. To address these goals, the proposed credit would assist the GOI DPEP in achieving achieve key objectives at national, state and district levels by the end of the project period. Specific objectives and monitorable indicators have been established for the development of national program management and technical assistance capacity and operations, for state capacity building and for district sub-projects.

The DPEP Bureau in the DOE would be fully established and functioning. National technical assistance and research and development programs for development of improved textbooks and learning materials, in-service teacher training, educational planning and management, program evaluation and research, and ST education development would have been established and provided substantial support for the development of counterpart agencies in project states. A computerized school statistics MIS would have been developed, tested and installed in all DPEP assisted states.

State Implementation Societies would be fully functioning, providing sub- project preparation and supervision support to districts and reporting quarterly on progress and expenditures. A new generation of textbooks based on MLL would have been tested and put in use. Publication quality and distribution efficiency would be improved. Textbooks and learning materials would be available in major tribal languages.

State Councils for Educational Research and Training (SCERTs), or equivalent organizations, would be providing enhanced support for improved classroom practices and teacher in-service training. State Institutes of Education Management and Training (SIEMTs), or equivalent agencies, would be providing technical assistance and training support for education staff at state and district levels. SCERTs, other state research agencies, and NGOs would have completed evaluations of DPEP activities in each state.

### Capacity Building

District sub-project teams would be fully functional, implementing sub-project activities and reporting quarterly on progress. DIETs would be functioning, with augmented staff and equipment, providing support for planning and management, teacher in-service training, development of learning materials, and program evaluation.

#### Reducing Dropout and Improving Learning Achievement

School/community organizations would be fully functional for at least 50 percent of schools, and dropout rates would be reduced to less than ten percent. Learning achievement in language and mathematics in the final year of primary school would be increased by 25 percent over baseline estimates.

#### Improving Equitable Access

Enrollment disparities by gender and by caste would be reduced to less than 5 percent.

Achieving these objectives equally for girls, SC and ST students would reduce present disparities for those groups currently ranked lowest on key indicators. For the 23 proposed district sub-projects, it is estimated that the program would enable 1,500,000 students to complete primary education who would otherwise have dropped out, of whom 785,000 would be girls. An additional 1,400,000 places would be created in primary schools or NFE classes. Learning achievement would be increased for an estimated 14 million students.

The GOI DPEP is a centrally sponsored program of financial assistance to states for primary education development investments that are planned and implemented by state and district planning and management teams. The program would be managed by the DPEP Bureau in the DOE, which functions as an intermediary organization to identify, appraise and finance sub-projects proposed and implemented by state governments. Sub-projects are appraised against a set of program eligibility and financial criteria. Continuing eligibility of and financial allocations to sub-projects would be based on annual reviews of implementation performance and work program and budget proposals. In the third and sixth year of the project, impact on development objectives would be measured. Baseline levels of dropout rates, learning achievement and enrollment have been established for each district sub-project, and monitorable indicators of national and state capacity development have been established for state and national sub-projects.

The GOI DPEP was officially established with approval by the Cabinet in November, 1993. In the start-up stages of development the program has been managed by a team in the DOE. Over the past year the DPEP project development team has completed a project cycle of identification, pre-appraisal and appraisal for 42 districts and 7 states.

The proposed IDA credit would assist in further development of the GOI DPEP appraisal, financing, supervision and management capacity. On-going technical assistance, research and development programs would be intensified and expanded. Funds would be provided to sponsor DPEP innovations and for the preparation of additional sub-projects. The credit would finance international fellowships and technical cooperation as designed and managed by the DPEP Bureau.

The credit would support a first phase of state sub-projects in Assam, Haryana, Karnataka, Kerala, Maharashtra and Tamil Nadu aimed at strengthening capacities in education management, planning and research, textbook and learning materials development and publication, and teacher in-service training. The credit would also assist in the financing of 23 district sub-projects intended to reduce dropouts, increase learning achievement and increase access to primary education for unserved students in the same states. The proposed DPEP project would finance educational materials, training, staff salaries on a declining basis, consultant services, international fellowships and technical cooperation programs, research studies, pilot projects, civil works and equipment. The proposed DPEP project would have three components:

(a) building national institutional capacity,

(b) building state institutional capacity, and

(c) improving quality and access in primary education.

## Building Institutional Capacity

The innovative nature of DPEP would require a management structure with good policy access, substantial authority, a high degree of flexibility in appointing staff and consultants, strong professional competence, and access to good information on program activities, accomplishments and problems. To meet these requirements, the GOI would establish the DPEP Bureau in the DOE and related governing and support bodies.

The credit would finance the formalization, expansion and strengthening of the DPEP Bureau in the GOI DOE and associated national technical assistance and research and development programs. The credit would finance salaries of additional staff on a declining basis, consultant services, equipment, vehicles, and the costs of sub-contracts.

The DPEP Bureau would serve as an intermediary organization to appraise, finance and supervise state and district sub-projects according to established criteria and procedures. The DPEP Bureau would in turn be assisted by an implementation support group employed under contractual arrangements to the DOE (program technical services). Through this contract, the DPEP Bureau would acquire substantial flexibility with respect to appointment of temporary staff and consultants, including levels of remuneration. The DPEP Bureau would be governed by a General Council, which would review policies and progress annually, and a DPEP Project Board, which would be fully empowered for program, financial and staffing approvals. The new units would have significant staff continuity with project preparation teams.

### Staff Continuity

To finance technical assistance to states and districts for the preparation of sub-projects, and to appraise sub-project proposals, in 1993 the DOE established a DPEP Project Development Team comprising a joint secretary and three deputy secretaries, with support staff. A National Core Team made up of faculty from NCERT and NIEPA, and consultants, was established to conduct project studies and to provide technical training and support to national, state and district planning teams. Over the course of 15 months these teams have led the development of proposals from 7 states and 42 districts and completed an ambitious program of project studies. This work has provided an extensive program of action training, through which the GOI and partner institutions have gained experience with the conduct of large scale field research in primary education and with project preparation and appraisal. Experience gained has been the basis for the design of the GOI DPEP management structure and of the proposed technical assistance and research and development programs.

This experience would be incorporated into the proposed national management and technical assistance programs through continuity of staff. The experienced project development team would be appointed as the initial key staff of the DPEP Bureau that would be established to manage the program. Proposals for national technical assistance programs have been prepared by the NCERT and NIEPA faculty who have provided these services during the project development process.

### General Council

The General Council would provide policy direction to the DPEP and facilitate center-state coordination; it would meet annually and be chaired by the Minister of Human Resources Development. Members would include DPEP state Ministers of Education, secretaries of affected central departments, and the Joint Secretary of the DPEP Bureau.

### DPEP Project Board

The General Council would be assisted by a DPEP Project Board (PB), an empowered body assigned full financial and administrative powers to implement the program.

The broad functions of the PB would be to recommend policies, consider annual work plans and budgets (AWPBs) of state and national sub- projects, approve changes in norms for new program components and activities, promote convergence of services, review DPEP progress, and provide guidance to the DPEP Bureau.

**DPEP Bureau**

The DPEP Bureau, headed by a Joint Secretary, would be responsible to the Project Board and General Council for the implementation of the program within DPEP Guidelines and in agreement with donors. The DPEP Bureau would have the responsibility and authority to appraise, supervise and evaluate district, state and national sub-projects and to approve staff appointments to the program technical services. It would comprise two units, with program and policy functions, staffed by deputy secretaries.

The Policy Division would be responsible for servicing and implementing the decisions of the PB, release and reimbursement of funds, maintenance of accounts and compliance with procurement norms of donors. The Program Division would supervise the work of the program technical services, be responsible for overall coordination with states on implementation of DPEP, and represent the GOI on the state implementation societies. The GOI has appointed the joint secretary, 3 deputy secretaries and key support staff for the DPEP Bureau in the DOE. To ensure that implementation procedures are well understood at national, state and district level, an implementation manual has been prepared and reviewed by the Association.

**DPEP Technical Services**

The DPEP Bureau, assisted by full time senior technical and professional experts on contract, supplemented as needed by short-term consultants, would provide the key technical services needed for program management:

(a) Appraisal: technical assistance and appraisal for state and district sub- projects.

(b) Supervision: organizing DPEP supervision missions, coordination of biannual joint supervision missions with program donors, assisting DPEP Bureau state coordinators review procurement and disbursement activity, and preparing reports.

**Benefits and Risks**

The proposed credit would provide substantial financial and technical support at a critically important point in the development of primary education in India. Through the DPEP, the GOI has made an unprecedented commitment to a sustained effort to reach the large majority of the population who exist at the fringes of the modem economy. Improving the human capital of the poor is the best way to help them move out of poverty, enabling them to improve their benefits from social services, to raise their productivity in agriculture and traditional occupations and, in the medium term, to share in the benefits of a liberalizing economy. The proposed credit would establish the institutional framework through which targeted assistance would reach the schools of the poor over a phased and sustained effort over 15-20 years. The potential magnitude of the impact of DPEP at full implementation is suggested by the number of beneficiaries in the initial 23 IDA-assisted districts out of the total of 373 districts to be reached by DPEP: 1,500,000 students who would complete primary schooling rather than dropping out; 14 million students with a better chance of mastering the curriculum; and an additional 1,400,000 primary education places.

While confident that the activities that would be financed by the proposed credit are feasible and sustainable, IDA staff and project authorities also recognize the significant financial and implementation risks associated with the program.

The DPEP is aimed squarely at historically low levels of investment in primary education, by providing investment assistance to states to, in effect, drive up both investment and recurrent expenditures on primary education. IDA's financial analysis indicates that the states participating in the proposed IDA credit can meet the investment costs and sustain the recurrent expenditures of the initial set of district and state activities. However, full implementation of DPEP across all targeted districts would require unprecedented levels of investment and recurrent cost financing for all states. For some, the revenue situation suggests that some of the growth in outlay can be met through enhanced revenues. For most, however, sustaining the investment program would require substantial reallocations within state budgets toward primary education. Past experience is an uncertain guide to the willingness of the states to do so. The GOI would partly offset state financial risks by phasing the program over two or three Plan periods in order to provide an opportunity for the effects of economic adjustment and stabilization to improve state revenues and to support reform of state budget priorities. However, the possibility of rapid deterioration in state financial circumstances can not be ruled out, only monitored.

At the national level, political commitment to enhanced financing for primary education has led to substantial additional financial allocations by the Planning Commission for DPEP. The Prime Minister has announced that outlays for education would be increased to six percent of GDP in the Ninth Plan. However, the GOI is experiencing difficulty in reducing the budget deficit, and this could affect allocations to the proposed program.

Thus, for IDA and other donors, the financial risks resolve to one: the sustainability of political commitment at the national and state levels. Initial signs are encouraging. The enhanced Eighth Plan allocation to DPEP by the GOI is a clear sign of increased national priority. State participation is voluntary, and those states choosing to participate have, through their own financing studies, become aware of the medium term investment and recurrent cost implications. In the present political climate, the benefits of primary education of acceptable quality for the poor, and for the economy as a whole, are increasingly well understood. In the medium term, a strong and effective DPEP could reinforce political commitment.

Close monitoring of the indicators of political commitment, notably annual budget allocations, would be a priority for IDA and other donors. In this respect, it is worth noting that the EC would release approximately US$90 million to the program in four equal tranches tied to maintenance of FY91/92 budgets for elementary education in real terms in annual GOI budgets for the DOE. Subsequent credits from IDA would be dependent on satisfactory financing and implementation progress in the first credit. These macro-incentives could provide continuing support for existing high levels of political commitment to primary education and to the DPEP.

IDA staff conclude, on balance, that the present high level of financial and political commitment, supported by close monitoring and macro-incentives, justify the financial risks associated with the proposed credit.

Managing a program of the scope and complexity of DPEP will not be easy. The risk is further raised by the necessary move away from relatively easily-administered central programs based on norms to a program that seeks, in principle, to provide integrated development assistance tied to local conditions. To achieve the necessary level of management capacity, the DPEP would need to create new management structures at national, state and district levels.

There is a thus a risk that implementation would be uneven across the states in the initial stages of activity. This could lead to slow disbursements in early years.

There is also risk attached to the proposed efforts to mobilize national and state expertise to support and, over time, improve the quality of implementation and interventions at the district level.

These risks are balanced in part by the way the proposed project has been developed, in part by elements of program design and in part by actions taken by the GOI and states. However, residual uncertainties regarding implementation arrangements would remain, as is the case for most innovative projects in constrained financial circumstances.

The project preparation process gives some assurances that these management structures can function as intended. The pace of preparation for the proposed project has been swift. The accomplishments of the GOI, states and districts in project preparation have been substantial, indicating significant political commitment and ownership. A high degree of popular participation has been achieved.

A number of elements of the program design combine to strengthen risk management. First, in designing the DPEP the GOI has drawn explicitly on lessons of experience from externally-assisted state primary education projects. This experience has demonstrated the importance of strong institutional capacity, a key objective of DPEP. Second, the proposed DPEP Bureau would be well staffed for supervision and appraisal and would operate through an annual management control mechanism, with full participation of donors. Third, there is an explicit provision for a start-up year focused on a limited set of key activities, including institutional development.

Substantial actions designed to facilitate effective startup would be taken by the time the proposed credit would be presented to the Bank's Board. At the national level, the entire project development team would be appointed to key program management positions in the DPEP Bureau. All key officials and state and district levels would be appointed, with substantial continuity with project preparation teams. Program rules and regulations and finance and accounting systems would be in place, supported by an implementation manual. Contracts for key services would have been pre-approved by IDA and ready to sign. Detailed first year work programs and budgets would have been approved by program authorities. Substantial funds would have been released by the GOT to state implementation societies and the program would have been launched.

The program would create incentives for good performance. In combination with performance measurement, the management mechanism would create incentives for quality implementation by states and districts. Program guidelines would permit non-performing districts of states to be dropped from the program. By putting financial incentives in place to support key national and state technical support programs, the DPEP would introduce a new approach to mobilizing expertise in the social sectors. Extensive popular participation has generated substantial interest in the benefits of the program in blocks and communities. If these interests are met through effective implementation, growing demand from beneficiaries should provide another incentive for implementation at the lowest levels of the program.

International donors would mobilize considerable technical resources to support DPEP. IDA and the EC would strengthen their technical expertise in resident missions to support implementation. IDA human resources staff based in the New Delhi Mission would provide continuous technical and managerial support; the Procurement and Disbursement Unit in the Mission would provide technical assistance in these key areas. The EC is posting a senior human resources expert to New Delhi to manage a US$5 million technical assistance fund for DPEP. UNESCO has also expanded its New Delhi staff to include an expert in educational statistics and monitoring to support DPEP. UNICEF has committed its extensive local expert staff resources to project preparation and would continue to assist with implementation. Finally, periodic beneficiary assessments and a substantial program of evaluation and research should provide a well-substantiated flow of academic and public information on program performance, strengthening the incentive structure for national and state program management.

**Financial Flows**

DPEP would create a new system of financial advances to state implementation societies. The system has been created to overcome diversion of development assistance by state finance departments and thus to improve implementation and disbursements. New accounting and auditing arrangements would be established. There is a risk that despite careful design and appraisal, new systems would not function as intended. This risk, however, must be balanced by the problems inherent in present systems.

**Relationships between State Governments and Societies**

While previous experience with state implementation

societies is encouraging, the proposed scale of operations through societies is unprecedented. The GOI has designed societies to function as project implementation structures for state governments, with direct state control through the composition of governing councils and executive committees, and through annual control (with the GOI) of funding for society activities. During appraisal, IDA voiced concerns regarding the nature of the legal relationships between societies and state governments.

**Relationships with Local Governments**

The establishment of locally elected governments (Panchayat Raj bodies) in all states draws on long national commitments to local democracy. However, with implementing legislation only recently passed in all states, there is considerable uncertainty regarding the possible impact of local governance on primary education. The extent to which district governments would control financial allocations and teacher appointments, for example, could have major and varying implications for the implementation of DPEP, both positive and negative.

The capacity of the proposed program to monitor and manage these risks would be strengthened through the proposed credit. Both project authorities and IDA recognize these residual risks, and would agree to monitor and discuss developments annually. It has been agreed that an independent management review of the functioning of societies, including financial mechanisms, would be conducted in the third year of the project. DPEP would carry out a continuing program of studies to monitor the impact of the Panchayat Raj legislation, and discuss these studies with IDA.

# 7

# Development of Compulsory Education

Envisages provision for free and compulsory education for children. The State shall endeavour to provide, within a period of ten years from the commencement of this Constitution, for free and compulsory education for all children until they complete the age of fourteen years.

The National Policy on Education (1986), gives the highest priority to the programme of Universalisation of Elementary Education and recommends that it shall be ensured that free and compulsory education of satisfactory quality is provided to all children upto the age of fourteen years before we enter the 21st century. The Programme of Action 1992 outlines relevant strategies to be acted upon.

14 States and 4 Union Territories (UTs) have passed acts making education compulsory.

— *States*: Assam, Andhra Pradesh, Bihar, Gujarat, Haryana, Jammu & Kashmir, Karnataka, Madhya Pradesh, Maharashtra, Punjab, Rajasthan, Tamilnadu, Kerala and West Bengal.

— *UTs*: Chandigarh, Delhi, Pondicherry and Andaman & Nicobar Islands.

These legislations have three parts :

(i) Power vested in the state government to notify the area in which the Act can be implemented;

(ii) Penalties for not sending children to school.

(iii) Power in a vested authority to grant exemption from the legislation.

Tamil Nadu recently replaced the earlier Act. While the earlier Act had envisaged certain areas to be notified, the present Act extends to the whole state. All State Governments have abolished tuition fees in Government schools upto upper primary level. Education in schools run by local bodies and private aided institutions is also mostly free. However, unaided Institutions (3.7%) do charge fees. Other costs of education such as textbooks, uniforms, school bags, transport fee etc. are not borne by States except in few cases by way of incentives to children of poor families and those belonging to SC/ST categories. The reason being 96% of expenditure on Elementary Education goes in meeting the salaries of teaching and non-teaching staff.

The Compulsory Education Acts enacted in 14 States amd 4 UTs have remained unenforced due to socioeconomic compulsions that keep the children away from schools. There is no central legislation making education compulsory. The consistent position has been that compulsion contemplated in Article 45 of the Constitution is a compulsion on the State rather than on the parents.

The thrust in elementary education is on three aspects:

(i) Universal access and enrolment;

(ii) Universal retention of children upto fourteen years of age; and

(iii) To bring about substantial improvement in the quality of education to enable all children to achieve essential levels of learning.

The Government policy is to motivate children to attend the school regularly and to improve upon the facilities in the school system, provide training to teachers and upgrade learning acquisition of children; to enforce compulsory education with punitive measures.

In spite of our consistent efforts, a quarter of the total school going age population is outside the formal educational system. As of now, the gross enrolment ratio in the country as a whole is 104.5 for classes IN and 91.2 for classes I-VIII. After adjustment is made for average and underage children, the corresponding ratio is 86.7% for classes I-V and 75.7% for classes I-VIII. In terms of numbers it is estimated that around 28 million children are out of school, constituting one of the largest groups of out of school children in the world.

Supreme Court Judgement:

i) In Unnikrishnan Vs. State of Andhra Pradesh (Writ Petition No.607 of 1992), Supreme Court held that citizens of this country have the fundamental right to education and the said right flows from Article 21 of the Constitution. This right is, however, not an absolute right. Every child/citizen of this country has the right to free education until he completes the age of fourteen years. Thereafter, his right to education is subject to limits of the economic capacity and development of the State.

ii) In the case of Common cause Vs. Union of India (Writ Petition No.697 to 1993) wherein the petitioner requested the Court to direct Government to provide all facilities for attaining the goal of universal, free and compulsory education for children upto the age of fourteen years, latest by end of 1999, Hon'ble judges after hearing the, arguments declined to grant any relief to the petitioner and advised him to withdraw the petition.

The question is, how do we move towards UEE at a faster pace? Can a legislation for compulsory education help? If so, how should it be framed? Who should enact it - central government or state government? Should it contain penal provision? If not, would the law have a deterrent effect? If yes, can its misuse by petty bureaucracy be minimised? These are some of the issues which need to be addressed, deliberated upon and a national consensus evolved.

The desirability of enacting a law for compulsory elementary education and its impact on enrolment has been discussed and debated extensively in recent years. Prof. Myron Weiner of Massachusetts Institute of Technology, an ardent protagonist of compulsory primary education has presented a very incisive analysis of the positive impact compulsory schooling can have on eradication of child labour in his book "The child and the State in India". He also made a presentation on "Compulsory Education and Child Labour" at the Rajiv Gandhi Centre for contemporary Studies.

He argues that what has been done historically by every developed and, now, by many developing countries is to declare that all children aged six to twelve or fourteen must attend school. That no matter how needy, will not be permitted to remove their children from school, that school attendance will be enforced by local authority and that government will be obliged to locate a primary school within reasonable distance of all school age children. It is, therefore, a legislation in which the child, the parents, local bodies and the government have specific obligations.

Myron Weiner believes that compulsion does not necessarily imply prison sentences or heavy fines. Local officials, teachers, members of local school boards, can visit the houses of parents who have removed their children from school to inform them that school attendance is compulsory. Within a few years of implementation a norm is established in the country that all children must attend school, a norm more enforced by community pressures than by the authorities. In essence what Myron Weiner says is that penal provisions need not be invoked; Law acts as a deterrent and therefore, parents can be better persuaded by VEC's, teachers and others. An argument in favour of legislation is that it is an expression of political will and it would send out a strong signal to International Community that India is serious about eradication of child labour.

As opposed to Myron Weiner's thesis, there is a School of thought which believes that legislation may not be an effective solution in the existing circumstances in our country. Researchers like Christopher Colclough quote the experience of Africa where there is some evidence of an inverse relationship between compulsory schooling legislation and the value of gross enrolment ratio. His argument, primarily, is that regulation like this should not be introduced when large numbers of school children do not attend school because sufficient places are not available. He admits, however, that compulsory schooling regulations do promote continued high levels of enrolment once school places for all children are genuinely available. In states which have near universalized elementary education like Kerala and Tamil nadu, legislation may help 'mopping up' the out of school children. But what about other States where out of school children constitute a significant proportion? J.P. Naik had once observed that with a Compulsory Primary Education Legislation, in some States, there may be more parents in jail than children in school.

This School of thought advances the argument that it is necessary to not only increase public expenditure on education but also introduce measures to mitigate the costs of school attendance. Even this would be a partial solution, they feel, more important being the attitude of parents who may perceive the opportunity costs of schooling to be too high.

It is essentially seen as an attitudinal problem - attitude of the parents towards their children's education, state's attitude towards child labour and towards improving the quality of educational system.

The stand we have been taking in international forums is that child labour would be abolished in a phased manner. By enacting a legislation for compulsory education would we not be detracting from our current stand. Is this not liable to be used by developed nations as a lever for enforcing social clauses of trade by developed countries?

The Legislation focus Hobsons' choice - If the law does not have deterrent penal provisions the law becomes redundant and if such provisions are incorporated they are liable to be misused by petty bureaucracy.

Our experience in other Social sectors indicates that negative incentives or coercive strategies like in family planning programme, can be counter-productive. If this be so, should we embark on a coercive legalistic measure in a realm of attitudinal reorientation and qualitative upgradation of the systems and processes.

A legislation cannot be self enforcing. A strong enforcement machinery may have to be installed. Apart from being an additional burden on the exchequer, it is likely to misuse the power.

## Compulsory Schooling

It seems fairly obvious that a government which genuinely intended to provide sufficient school places for all, and that these should be fully utilized, would introduce legislation to make school attendance compulsory for the relevant age-group. Such legislation is widespread around the world, typically stipulating both the minimum duration of school attendance in years, and the ages during which it should occur. About 85 per cent of developing countries have enacted laws which make schooling compulsory, and that on average they require attendance for about eight years, Both the incidence of legislation and the length of attendance required are less in Africa and Asia than in Latin America. The industrialized countries, on the other hand, have regulations making schooling compulsory, the average duration being slightly more than nine years. The question arises, therefore, as to whether there is any relationship between the non-enactment of legislation and the incidence of low enrolment ratios caused by low demand for schooling. If so, the act of legislating could be expected to be a useful response.

This apparently straightforward question is in fact too complicated to answer accurately, given the available evidence. Observed enrolment ratios are the result of the interaction of supply and demand, and as regards the determinants of supply, the state provision of school places may in any case not be independent of the demand for them. What can be said is that a puzzlingly large number of countries with low GERs have laws making primary-school attendance compulsory. For example, there are seventeen countries with primary GERs of less than seventy having such legislation. Sixteen of these are in SSA, and they include five cases where primary enrolments in the late 1980s were equal to less than one-third of the eligible age- group.

In Africa, there is actually some evidence of an inverse relationship between the incidence of compulsory schooling legislation and the value of the GER: for the group of eleven African countries not having such legislation the mean GER for 1986 was 85, whereas for the continent as a whole it was sharply lower, with a value of 74 for the same year.

We should note that in most cases the legislation exempts children from attending it there is no suitable school within reasonable distance of their homes. The question whether or not such regulations ensure attendance where schools exist thus remains open. However, the cases of Ghana, Liberia, Mozambique, Nigeria, Somalia, Tanzania and Zaire are instructive in the context. In those countries all of which have compulsory schooling legislation, the GER fell by between 10 and 50 per cent over the years 1980-6, partly as a result of economic hardships which caused families to withdraw children from school Here, then, the laws were not sufficient to sustain enrolment in the face of falling demand.

Thus, across developing countries, the existence of compulsory schooling regulations often seems to have had little impact upon the proportion of children actually enrolled. Historically, these laws were introduced in most countries in response to international convention and pressure. Often they date back to the years following the Unesco conferences of the 1960s which, as indicated in Chapter 1, adopted targets for universal compulsory primary enrolment in each region of the developing world.. Sometimes, as in India, Taiwan, North Vietnam, and South Korea, the legislation was on the statute books much earlier, although in India it has never actually been enforced. It is now clear that these regulations were often introduced too early to be of much help: where large numbers of school children do not attend school because sufficient places are not available, it is difficult for the law to insist that attendance should be compulsory for those who do not seek it. The evidence from the industrialized countries suggests that compulsory schooling regulations do promote continued high levels of enrolment once school places for all children are genuinely available. They would thus become important for countries to adopt and enforce as net enrolment ratios move up towards 90. But where the coverage of school systems remains partial, such regulations are probably of little help.

**Mitigating the costs**

One of the causes of the concentration of low enrolment ratios amongst the poorest countries is that state expenditures upon schooling cannot completely remove the costs to poor households of their children's attendance. Even if fees are not charged, there are usually the costs of some books to meet, and often there are school uniforms to buy. Moreover, the opportunity costs of school attendance are, in practice, a negative function of household income. It is the poor who depend upon the income from child labour. For the middle classes, by contrast, household incomes often benefit directly from the child-minding role which full-time schooling provides, and indirectly by allowing more of the time of other members of the household to be spent on income-earning tasks. In order to move gross enrolment ratios up towards 100, it is not only necessary, at given unit cost levels, that public expenditures on education should rise, but it is a requirement that this should also happen within the budgets of private households. By consequence, the poorer are the households concerned, and the higher the direct and indirect costs which they would need to meet, the more likely is it that public measures to increase primary provision would fail to elicit the required enrolment response.

Crucial, therefore, to the success of state policies for UPE and SFA, particularly where (as is usually the case) it is the children of the poorest families who remain out of school, will be the introduction of measures to mitigate the costs of school attendance Methods of community financing at primary level would need to be confined to the wealthier communities and school (with the possible exception, as indicated earlier, of contributions to capital costs via own construction), and all direct costs of attendance, such as tees or charges for books, materials, and other consumables, would need to be reduced and. where possible, removed. In a number of African countries a strong positive enrolment response to the abolition of school fees has already been demonstrated, even in circumstances where such charges were the equivalent of only a few dollars per year. Thus, price and income clasticities of demand for primary schooling are sometimes high. This will need to be both recognized and utilized by strategies for UPE and SFA.

Even so, policies which substantially reduce the direct costs of school attendance may yet prove insufficient to overcome problems of low demand for primary schooling where the opportunity costs of sending a child to school are judged, by its parents, to be high. Unhappily, this happens in a wide variety of countries and circumstances. As household income have fallen in Africa in recent years, the widespread withdrawal of children from school indicated not just an increasing inability by parents to meet the direct costs of schooling, but also an increased dependence by them upon the incomes, however meagre, which their children could earn. More serious, because more long-standing, is the issue of the institutionalisation of child labour which has been tolerated in a significant number of States, particularly those of South Asia and North Africa. In India, as Myron Weiner observes:

Indians of virtually all political persuasions oppose the notion that education should be imposed. The major objection is that poverty forces children to drop out of school to find employment to augment the income of their families. It is an argument widely subscribed to by all political groups ... In the debate over the government's new policy toward child-labour laws, critics were distressed that the government accepted child labour as a 'harsh reality', but virtually no one urged the government to remove children from employment in cottage industries and agriculture by forcing them to go to school, irrespective to their parents' wishes.

These circumstances obtain in India owing to the set of interests served by the system of child labour. Poor parents seek the income it provides. Exploiters, and ultimately consumers, profit from the much lower wages commanded by children in comparison with adult labour. The middle classes find it convenient not to disrupt a system which prevents large numbers of those from poorer backgrounds from entering their own ranks. The conspiracy of silence to which this array of interests leads will not be overcome merely by further reductions in the direct costs of schooling. What is required is a change in attitudes within the State, leading to firmer action against child labour and in support of more universal attendance at school.

If you have been good enough to occasionally cast- a passing glance over this column you would have noticed that it has never before contained an open letter. I avoid writing them, generally, because they tend to have a preachy, pontificatory quality which I dislike. It is my humble opinion that us hacks are really in no position to give lectures to all and sundry despite the fact that it is almost an occupational hazard in our profession.

You are young, Mr. Scindia and, from all accounts, dynamic enough to do something that could make future generations of Indians remember you with eternal gratitude. And, all you need to do to achieve this recognition is to remember that despite your title being Minister for Human Resource Development you are primarily Minister for education. Culture, sports and all the other things that come under you can only begin to happen if we first concentrate on educating our hopelessly illiterate population.

Technically we now have over 50 per cent literacy (52.1 per cent to be exact). In fact, as you and I know, even this shameful figure is fudged because anyone who can scrawl his name legible on a piece of paper is considered literate in our unlettered land. But, even if we accept 52.1 per cent as accurate it is not something we can consider an achievement, not even when we Compare ourselves to other similarly poor countries. To give you only a few figures that your ministry staff, undoubtedly, have full knowledge of. The literacy rate in Sri Lanka is 89.1 per cent, Myanmar 81.5 per cent.

According to Asia Week's latest list of vital signs, there are only seven countries more illiterate than us, Pakistan, Bangladesh, Afghanistan, Bhutan, Nepal, combodia and Egypt. So when we talk of our "achievements" in the field of education since Independence we are quite clearly using the wrong word, We have achieved little so far that we can be proud of.

Then, ask yourself why India has been left so far behind by countries that were as illiterate as us 40 years ago. You may find that the answer to your question is that these other countries made primary education compulsory whereas we decided to reinvent the educational wheel and experiment with our own ideas. The result is that we have pursued a variety of well-meaning schemes but still have only 52.1 per cent literacy.

We have tried coming up with a series of 'new' education policies, we have urged people to reach one, teach one, we even tried, under that governmental all-rounder, Sam Pitroda, to make literacy a mission. But nothing has worked, except in the closed minds of the bureaucrats who run your Ministry. Can we now try compulsory primary education?

You will say, as your predeccessors have, that there is little that you can do because elementary education is a state subject. This is nonsense, and it it isn't, change the Constitution we have often amended it for lesser reasons. It your ministry came up with a model, a plan to make primary education compulsory and helped the state Governments follow it, you know that they can be made to go along with you. In any case, those that didn't would do so at their own risk because in the near future it will become virtually impossible to get a job with-out basic literacy. Whatever your bureaucrats tell you, I urge you to pay attention to the fact that we are running out of time. Even if you did decide to make primary school compulsory it would take the country at least 10 years to achieve this for even the first couple of classes. It is a painfully gradual process which will be even more gradual in a country where inefficiency is the norm rather than the exception.

All over the world adults have often justified what later generations regarded as acts of cruelty toward children. Many revolutionaries, for example, have sent children to wage war, arguing that the martyrdom of children should be regarded by parents as noble. girls have had their sexual organs mutilated to dull their sexual senses so as to prevent promiscuous behaviour after puberty. Girls belonging to higher social classes have had their feet bound to satisfy adult notions of female beauty. Prepuberty children have been bound in marriage to ensure conformity with rules of consanguinity. Girls have been sold into prostitution by their parents. We could go on from one culture to another, from ancient to modern times, to provide example after example of decisions made by parents for their children that most of us would not regard as in the interests of the child.

Of the great ideas that have transformed the world, none is as revolutionary as the idea that children have rights and interests independent of those of their parents. It is an idea that has no single author. It is not written in the French Declaration of Human Rights, nor in the American Declaration of Independence. It is not in the Magna Carta. it is not found in any of the sacred texts, Jewish, Christian, Muslim, Buddhist, Hindu, or sikh. In my research for The Child and the State in India, I found glimmers of the idea in the writings of the early Protestant theologians, in Luther, Knox and Calvin, who insisted that children be taught to read the Bible and thereby have direct access to the word of God, without priests as intermediaries, so they could escape from the sin of birth. To the agnostic an absurd idea, no doubt, but never mind, it was the beginning of the notion that children had rights and parents had obligations.

In time this revolutionary idea spread around the world. different cultures and different ideologies provided a different rationale. Adam Smith argued for compulsory education, not for religious salvation, but for creating a civil society in which men and women were sufficiently well educated to behave rationally and morally so as not to succumb to demagogues. A half century later, John Stuart Mill argued that education was necessary for a child to "perform his part well in life." He wrote that education was necessary for the "members of the community generally who are liable to suffer seriously from the consequences of ignorance and want of education in their fellow citizen." For Mill, education for the poor was essential for self-improvement, social mobility, and citizenship, reflecting his equalitarian and democratic political philosophy.

In time the idea moved from West to East. The Meiji leadership insisted that all Japanese children attend school. "Henceforth, throughout the land," began a famous school regulation of 1872, "without distinctions of class and sex in no village shall there be a house without learning, in no house an ignorant individual. Every guardian, acting in accordance with this, shall bring up his children with tender care, never failing to have them attend school." The Meiji elite believed that compulsory mass education was necessary not only to build a modern country capable of competing with the West but principally as a way of inculcating a national spirit, love and reverence for the emperor, and loyalty to the state. From Japan the idea of state-imposed compulsory education moved to Korea and to Taiwan, both then Japanese colonies. Lenin and his fellow revolutionaries were also proponents of compulsory education. Lenin regarded mass education as essential to create individuals who would not be motivated by the desire for private gain but committed to the collective good. He saw mass education as a means of inculcating loyalty to the party and its socialist ideology. The Soviet Union, and subsequently all the communist states of eastern Europe, china, Nicaragua, Cuba, and Vietnam made education compulsory.

The idea was planted in India in 1882 when several Indian and British officials argued for introducing compulsory education before the Indian Education Commission, but the proposal was never seriously considered. Shortly before World War I, Gopal Krishna Gokhale, then president of the Indian National Congress, took up the issue in the central legislature in New Delhi. He introduced a private bill proposing that local bodies be authorised to introduce compulsory education in their areas. the bill was widely circulated and while it received some support from leaders of the Indian National congress and the Muslim league, a majority of the members of the central legislature, most officials, and respesentatives of the princely states were opposed. The government regarded the proposal as utopian on financial and administrative grounds. In 1918, Vithalbhai Patel introduced a bill in the Bombay legislative council permitting municipal areas of the state to make education compulsory. The bill was passed and thereafter other states under British rule passed similar laws. These laws remain in force today, but It should be noted that all these laws permit but do not require local authorities to make education compulsory. The various state laws are enabling legislation, modelled after an 1871 act of the British parliament which was superseded a decade later by a parliamentary act requiring local authorities to make education compulsory. But because Indian states do have so-called compulsory education acts, and the Indian constitution, in Article 45, makes compulsory education a matter of national policy, many Indians mistakenly believe that India does have compulsory education laws, only that they are not properly enforced. In contrast with the countries of Europe, and many in Asia, the idea of compulsory education was not firmly planted in India.

Where the idea of compulsory education was firmly planted it is clear that no single motivation led governments to make education compulsory. But we can make three generalisations. The first is that education was made compulsory in many countries before the industrial revolution-when per capita incomes were low, poverty was widespread, and parents would have employed their children had they been permitted to do so. Secondly the introduction of compulsory education was not driven by changes in technology which required more skilled educated workers. More to the point, the removal of children from the labour force enabled industries to employ technologies that required higher skills.

And thirdly, it was theologians, with their vision of God- fearing, law-abiding, moral youth: educators with their vision of schools transmitting the Enlightenment Values of Secularism rationalism, cosmopolitanism, and individualism; and revolutionaries, with their romantic vision of social transformation, who provided the driving force behind the idea of compulsory mass education. Theologies and ideologies were the critical determinants. The contemporary view, put forth by the World Bank, UNICEF, UNDP, UNESCO, UNFPA, and by economists and demographers that mass education is needed to increase productivity, reduce fertility, and improve public health-all by now well-proven propositions-did not play a role in the early movement by governments to make education compulsory. Let me note that the 17th century law establishing compulsory education in Massachusetts was not called the Human Resource Development Act, but the Old Deluder Satan Act!

Today, most governments agree that children should be removed from the labour force and required to attend school. They believe that employers should not be permitted to employ child labour and that parents, no matter how poor, should not be allowed to keep their children out of school. Modern states regard education as a legal duty, not merely as a right: parents are required to send their children to school, children are required to attend school, and the state is obliged to enforce compulsory education. It is a view held not only by all developed countries but by the governments of many developing countries as well. In countries of Asia as culturally and politically diverse as Indonesia. Sri Lanka, North and South Korea, China, Taiwan, Singapore, Malaysia and Thailand, virtually all children attend primary school- invariably with an element of state compulsion.

India is a great exception, though others, especially neighbouring countries of South Asia, have also not made education compulsory or banned child labour. Indian policy makers have argued that the Indian government lacks the financial resources for universal compulsory primary school education and that it lacks the administrative resources to enforce child labour laws. They have also argued that poor families need the labour and income of their children and therefore should not be coerced into sending their children to school. Moreover, they say, children and their parents find the schools irrelevant to meet their needs. Finally, it is argued that small scale industries need low wage child labour to survive, and that export-oriented industries needs child labour to be competitive in world markets.

India has a low school attendance rate. The 1981 census-the last one to give us detailed data on school attendance-reported that 52 of India's 6 to 14 age group were not attending school. Only 40 per cent who entered first grade completed four years of schooling, only 23 per cent reached the eighth standard. 82 million children ages 6 to 14 were not in school. the 1993 UNDP World Development Report notes some improvement for 1991 but still 73 million of India's children were not attending primary or secondary school.

There are two major consequences of this low school participation rate. One is that India has a high and increasing number of illiterates. While the literacy rate has improved the absolute number of illiterates has increased-in this past decade alone from 314 million in 1981 to 335 million in 1991, over two million a year. India remains the largest single producer of the world's illiterates, Female literacy is particularly low, reflecting the low female attendance in primary schools. The 1991 census reported the percentage of adult female literates to the total female population is under 40 per cent in

Andhra, Orissa, Madhya Pradesh, Bihar, and Rajasthan. In UP only 26 per cent of women are literate.

Prof. Myron Weiner is pleased and surprised with the impact his book, "The Child and the State in India; Child Labour and Education Policy in Comparative Perspective", has made in India. It is a work fiercely critical of the Indian Government's unwillingness to make education compulsory and its acceptance of child labour. Since the book was published last year in India, he says, "it has been widely and favourably reviewed there. Daily newspapers, magazines and weeklies have written about it. I have been asked to talk on television and I gather it has even stirred up discussion in the education ministries. It is something I feel deeply about, so it's pleasing to realise it has been taken up as an issue by people within the country."

Weiner, an american professor, is a quiet, charming man with a philanthropic conscience that reveals itself quickly. Opening his hands wide, he talks rapidly, with emotion and despair over the face that half of India's children-some 82 million-receive scant, if any, education; that, because of this, their chances of self-improvement or getting further than their parents have in life are minimal; and that the Indian Government apparently has no intention of doing anything about it. In the 20 years up to 1981, the number of illiterates in India increased by one million and the trend continues. Weiner is distressed, "it is vital, if India is to progress in the world and reduce poverty, that it does not have millions of illiterates," he says.

But why should it concern him? Weiner is a U.S. citizen with a secure job as Ford International Professor at Massachusetts Institute of Technology and was recently in Britain, doing a term's lecturing at Oxford University where this interview took place. The answer Weiner said, gazing out over the camp green countryside bathed by a pale winter sun and at the historic grey stone buildings of the town, is simple. He has a passion for India, has been visiting and working there for the past 40 years, intends to do so again, and feels a deep involvement with its fate and fortunes. And, as a father and a humanitarian, watching his own children's development through these years, he was struck over and over again by the contrast between the West's concern with a child's right to a protected childhood and with providing education, and the situation in India where children as young as three can be found in the labour force. One estimate puts the number of children employed at 44 million.

Yet, in India, Weiner explained, "For many people there is not a conception of childhood. The notion that there is a stage of life when children are children does exist in the middle classes, but for the ' lower castes' children are a resource who can contribute to the household income, and sometimes they are seen as the bridge between poverty and absolute poverty. Nor is there the belief I fervently hold that the state has an obligation to give children education, and that children have an obligation to go to school. Only this can ensure they have the opportunities in life which education brings. Half of India's children are denied that opportunity."

Living and travelling in Asia, Weiner saw small, frail children sitting crouched in damp pits in the ground, weaving carpets from dawn to dusk. He saw children, selected for their thin limbs and nimble movements, working in glass factories where they would carry burning loams of glass stuck to the tips of four-foot-long iron rods without handles, or blow the red-hot glass into shapes. Many meet with accidents with burning glass while, others are exposed daily to dangerous chemicals. Many are the risks to children working in the match and fireworks cottage industries; in pottery factories, the airborne silica dust can cause pulmonary fibrosis. A doctor at the local clinic in Khurja, where pots are made, reports that as many as 30 children report with pulmonary complaints each week.

Many of the children work 15 or more hours a day, frequently in poor lighting; they get little or no time to be outdoors or to play and relax. Nor are many given a proper diet. As a result children, who are favoured over adults because they are compiant and work for just a few rupees, are undersized and have pallid complexions and many chronic ailments. Weiner is angered as he considers the life of these children who have no voice to protest and nobody to stand up for them and says Indian scholars have established that child labourers have stunted growth and are in poor health.

The health of children who work with their parents, as many do, may be better, says Weiner, but those working in the fields are usually busy almost all the time. He recalls stopping one morning, during a countryside drive, to talk to a boy in a field with some cattle. Asked why he was not in school, the boy looking surprised said he had never been to school; he had his work. There was no question in his mind. Weiner observes that he should have an option.

But a 10 year old boy who had been to primary school saw things differently when his father said he must leave and work. He begged to be allowed to stay and threatened to commit suicide if he was removed from school. He was allowed to take up secondary education and he even persuaded his father to let his brothers stay. All of them went on to university and got white collar jobs.

Weiner acknowledges that such persuasion may not be possible for all children who wish to stay at school, but he was particularly pleased to come across some teenaged girls, Scheduled Castes (once considered "untouchable") all, who did household work, walked to the village to get water and firewood, tended to a cow or two and cooked for the family. Their days were long but nevertheless they attended evening classes to learn to read and write. He adds: :What was so cheering was to hear these girls say they were determined their daughters should be educated. They spoke articulately about it being the way their children could do better than they have."

Worst off are the bonded labourers such as the small boy who was contracted by his parents to work for their neighbours as a way of paying off the money borrowed for a wedding. Because his work only paid the interest and not the debt, he was unlikely to be free to return to school. Weiner recollects: "He was accepting of this though he said he wanted to go back to school. Often, bonded labourers are exploited children at school... so little resources and have no defence."

"Sympathy and compassion alone, even if it became a national sentiment, would riot get children out of the labour force".

Life is even more cruel to children injured at work. Weiner met a boy who had been scalded by boiling water while working in a silk processing factory, and had been sacked because his arm was too badly injured for him to work any more. He was paid no compensation. For some weeks he wandered the streets, begging, but being bright and inventive he found a way to make money by buying rat poison in bulk, dividing it into samll packages and selling them at a profit. But others in similar circumstances end lip as prostitutes, beggars or thieves. Without education they have no skill to help them better themselves.

The plight of child labourers upsets Weiner but he does not believe that sympathy and compassion alone, even if it became a national sentiment, would get them out of the labour force. The only way to do it, he argues, is for the Government to make schooling compulsory and enfore the decision. He says: I do not think abolishing child labour first is doing it the right way. First you have to make education compulsory. It has to be an obligation of the state to provide education and an obligation for children to attend school. I don't think it is administratively possible to remove children from the labour force and I don't think labour officials can monitor working children. There are too many ways (in which) the labour laws can be evaded. On the other hand, I think compulsory education laws can be implemented. I've looked at this in Taiwan and Mainland China, where they introduced it relatively recently and now the vast majority of children go to school."

It was this recognition which prompted Weiner to write the book and if it (compulsory education) were to happen, he says, laughing suddenly at the simplicity of it, "the problem of child labour would be solved. If the Government enforces attendance at school, the children will be there, not working, and so you get rid of the problem of child labour at the same time that children are being given the benefit of education." But both the, Government and parents argue that it is essential for children to be allowed to work; that it is a necessary evil because families cannot cope without the children's income. That, in turn, means they have a vested interest in producing more children, adding to the country's severe population problem.

The irony, Weiner says, it that the "poverty argument" is wrong. He points to studies by contemporary development theorists which show the connection between mass education and economic growth. Knowledge gives the entire population the capacity to work towards economic growth, and studies show that the returns from primary education are the greatest.

In India, a country which relies greaty on agriculture, this is particularly relevant Weiner suggests. In a survey of devloping countries it was found that the farmers with four or more years of primary education produced 13 per cent more crops than uneducated farmers did and that four years of schooling is a threshold for increasing productivity Each extra year's education raises output by approximately 2 to 3 per cent. Also significant was a research in Hyderabad which showed children from agricultural families who had been to school for five or six years earned higher wages than those agricultural workers who had not. It sounds curious, Weiner agrees, but explains that agricultural wages are paid according to body weight and "children who start work younger are smaller, thinner, and less healthy than those who have been to school." It is information which should be made public, he says with a sudden ferocity.

Another irony, Weiner remarks drily, is that while policymakers shocked him with their lack of apparent concern for mass education, the middle-classes are determined to see their children educated - so much so that the vast majority pay for private education because state education is seen as poor. Their children go on to get the white- collar jobs and so the caste system is perpetuated, Weiner explains. He says: " It would be nice to think that the middle classes, recognising the value of education, would be committed to compulsory education, but the truth is education is largely an instrument for differentiation in India, and there are plenty of people who think education is right for the middle classes but not for the lower classes."

But does it make sense to insist that children spend their time in schools if the quality of education is inadequate? Weiner concedes the problem: "Those responsible for education have put in so little resources they don't feel committed to the notion of it for the lower classes. The schools I visited were often quite unsatisfactory with practically no blackboards, books, chalk and so on. Many have no playgrounds and the curriculum is often unsatisfactory. And teachers frequently do not turn up."

Weiner acknowledges that it is easy for people in affluent, developed countries to talk of the Indian Government's duty to resource its education better; but there is so much poverty and there are so many competing needs. But he points out that a good number of developing countries, including those in Africa with just as serious poverty, have found a way to resource education for all, and he feels sure they will benefit. Weiner observes: There are a number of general benefits for the country as a whole, as well as for individuals who have education. I know of no country that has effectively modernised in this century without a literate population."

One way of at least reducing child labour would be for countries to refuse to import Indian carpets. glassware, pots- or indeed any goods - in the manufacture of which children had been used. The U.S. is currently considering this but Weiner does not see it as ail answer because taking away children's employment does not mean they get to school.

He says:" I am in favour of doing someting to pressure countries not to employ child labour, and I certainly support the efforts the Government makes in India to improve the conditions for working children, but I fear some of the thinking in the U.S. and elsewhere for such legislation is less than pure and I suspect protectionism may have something to do with it."

His book, Weiner admits, has had its share of critics, but far more important, "A number of people seem to have taken up the cause and are carrying on writing and talking about it and that, of course, is the way things can be changed. I am planning now to do research and write an edition for Pakistan because the problem there is very similar," Weiner is confident that if the Central Government were to insist education be made compulsory rather than allow the States to do so, agencies such as the United Nations Children's Fund would provide a great deal of support and would "pay an important role."

But until then, children will go on passing their formative years in dark, airless rooms, crouched and hunched into positions which may distort their bodies for life; they will work hours that make playtime impossible; some will spend their early years inhaling a cocktail of dangerous chemicals, the effects of which may show up years later; others will be maimed in accidents with the red-hot glass or explosive materials used to make matches and fireworks.

That is the side which may attract attention and cause some public anxiety about the fate of children, as happened when a bus carrying load of very young children to a match factory in Sivakasi (Tamil Nadu) overturned, killing all of them. But the daily picture of children toiling is widely accepted and barely noticed. For instance, when Weiner was 'interviewing two researchers from Islamabad University who had collected impressive data on child labour, a small boy walked into the room carrying tea for them. Weiner questioned the child and learnt that he worked as a servant at the University and slept at the back of the building along with other children employed there!

# 8

# Reducing the Academic Load

A curriculum proves heavy for children when (a) it is too lengthy to be completed in time by an average teacher under normal conditions; (b) there is mismatch between the difficulty level of the concepts of course content with the mental level of the pupils; (c) the language used in the textbooks is incomprehensible and the style of presentation is verbose and rhetorical rather than simple and straight forward; (d) the basic assumptions underlying curriculum development are not fulfilled.

A National Advisory Committee was set up by the Government in March 1992 under the chairmanship of Prof. Yash Pal, former Chairman of the UGC to suggest ways and means to reduce academic burden on school students. The Committee popularly known as Yash Pal Committee, submitted its report in July 1993. On receipt of the Committee's report, a Group was set up on 25.8.1993 under the chairmanship of Shri Y.N. Chaturvedi, Additional Secretary, Department of Education to examine the feasibility of implementing the recommendations made in the report of Yash Pal Committee. The Group submitted its report on 5.10.1993.

After studying the problem of curriculum load in detail, Yash Pal Committee identified the following as manifestation of the existence of the problem:

1. *Starting Early.*It has been observed during the last few years that admission age to nursery classes has been progressively lowered down to the age of 2 1/2 years at some places. It appears that the perception has taken a deep root that if a child has to succeed in life, he or she must start education early in life.
2. *Size of school bag.* So far as physical load of the school bag is concerned, the situation has become worse over the past few years. However, the weight of the school bag represents one dimension of the problem, another dimension can be seen in the child's daily routine which includes completion of homework and attendance at tuitions and coaching classes of different kinds.
3. *Examination system.* The major, well understood defect of the examination system is that it focuses on children's ability to reproduce information to the exclusion of the ability to apply concepts and information on unfamiliar, new problems or simply to think. Both the teachers and the parents constantly reinforce the fear of examination and the need to prepare for it by memorising a whole lot of information from the textbook and guide books. This sort of perception about the examination makes things difficult for children.
4. *Joyless learning.* Majority of our school going children view learning at school as a boring, even unpleasant and bitter experience. The limited purpose of preparing for examination is indeed a very important factor for the unpleasantness of learning. The child centred education and activity based teaching learning method are talked about but are seldom practised in our school.
5. *Syllabi and textbook.* The syllabi and textbooks if not prepared properly lead to the problem of curriculum

load. It has been observed that most of the textbooks have high density of concepts and the style of writing is very terse. The language used in the books in some cases is beyond the comprehension of many students.

The Committee concluded that the problem of curriculum load was not an urban phenomenon. In rural areas, where the students have not to carry heavy bags, the problem of non-comprehension makes things extremely difficult for majority of children The feeling of academic burden arising out of non-comprehension of subject matter included in the syllabus is indeed a serious problem as it is a major hurdle in the achievement of the target of universalisation of elementary education.

After discussing the indicators or manifestations of the problem of curriculum load, the committee identified the following as the roots of the problem:

1. *Knowledge vs. information.* The committee has questioned the assumption underlying most curriculum renewal exercises that some sort of knowledge explosion has taken place, therefore, there is a valid reason to add more and more to the existing syllabi. By equating information with knowledge, more things are added to the syllabus making it heavier for children.
2. *Experts commissioned to write textbooks for school students are isolated from classroom realities.* Since they are not familiar with learning process of children, the textbooks prepared by them prove too difficult for majority of children.
3. *Centralised character of curriculum.* Curriculum development centrally is not relevant to the local needs of different parts of the country. There is need for increasing participation of teachers in the process of curriculum development.

4. *Convention of teaching the 'text'*. Majority of teachers perceive the content of the textbook as a rigid boundary or a definer of their work in the classroom. Boredom is the inevitable outcome when tersely written textbook is taught in a rigid and mechanical manner.
5. *Competition based social ethos.* Our social ethos, particularly in urban areas is now fully entrenched in the competitive spirit which is fast becoming our way of life. Rising aspiration of people in all sections of the society and the growing realisation that education is an important instrument to fulfil their aspirations have resulted in a craze for admission to English medium schools which start imparting formal education too early in the child's life
6. *Absence of academic ethos.* Adequate time, staff, accommodation and its maintenance, funds, pedagogical equipment, playgrounds are essential pre-requisites for effective curriculum transaction but unfortunately, an overwhelming majority of schools do not have even the minimum essential facilities. The method of teaching used in majority of teachers are devoid of any type of challenge for the students. Children are hardly provided ail opportunity to observe and explore natural phenomenon. The concept of library as a readily available source for learning simply does not exist in most schools. Similarly, science laboratories are not equally equipped and are not used for experimentation and discovery.

While forwarding the report of the Committee, Prof. Yash Pal, the chairman of the Committee advised that wide-ranging debates on the report are necessary. In the 49th meeting of the Central Advisory Board of Education (CABE) held on 15.10.1993, both the reports of Yash Pal

Committee and MHRD Group were discussed and the CABE decided to generate a country-wide debate in composite groups of teachers, parents and other interest groups. In December 1993, the State/UT Governments were urged to conduct workshops on these composite groups.

In the 50th meeting of the CABE held on 2.3.1994, the Education Ministers of a number of States/UTs expressed their broad agreement with the recommendations of Yash Pal Committee read with suggestions of MHRD Group and the CABE advised effective dialogue and follow up action with the State/UT Governments in the matter.

Based on the consensus of State/UT views, 2 sets of action- points, one for states/ UTs and other for central agencies like NCERT, CBSE, KVS, NVS were circulated in Juneand July 1994 respectively. The main recommendations of the Committee which have been included in the broad framework suggested to State/UT Governments in June 1994 are,

i) Greater involvement of teachers in framing curriculum and preparation of textbooks at State/UT level.

ii) Amendment of School Education Acts or Rules of State/UTs for laying down norms for pre-school.

iii) Abolition of tests/interviews for admission in pre-schools and discontinuance of textbooks and homework at pre- school stage.

iv) Abolition of home work and project work at primary stage.

v) Extensive use of audio-visual material and enforcing teacher-pupil ratio of 1:40.

A monitoring Committee for making periodical review of the pace of the implementation process has been set up in the Ministry of Human Resource Development.

The whole question of curriculum load is a complex question and there are no simple solutions. It has to be tackled in a comprehensive way, and not through isolated steps. It may not be possible to enhance overnight the level of competence, motivation and commitment of teachers, provide the facilities required to all the schools, check the growth of commercialisation in education, channelise the parental ambitions and aspirations, and minimise the importance of annual examinations. But this should not mean that we are altogether helpless and can do nothing in this regard. A package of suitable measures, both short term and long term, needs to be initiated urgently to tackle the problem. The measures will naturally include attempts to reform curriculum, raise the level of teachers' competence, motivation and commitment, strengthen the system of supervision to make teachers responsible for nonperformance, provide minimum essential infrastructural facilities to schools and to regulate the system of homework assignment.

## Learning Without Burden

Concern regarding academic burden on students and unsatisfactory quality of learning has been voiced time and again in our country during the past two decades. The question has been discussed extensively by several committee and groups. The Ishwarbhai Patel Review Committee (1977), National Council of Educational Research and Training (NCERT) Working Group (1984) and National Policy on Education (NPE) Review Committees (1990) made several recommendations to reduce the academic burden on students. The curriculum development agencies are generally in agreement with the recommendations of the committee and assure the public that these would be kept in view at the time of the forthcoming revision of curricula. But the problem, instead of being mitigated, becomes more acute when a new curriculum is introduced. This has happened in the case of new curriculum introduced in the wake of implementation of NPE (1986). With a view to have a fresh look on the problems of education, particularly with regard to the problem of academic burden on students, the Ministry of Human Resource Development, Government of India, set up a National Advisory Committee in March 1992 with the following terms of reference

To advise on the ways and means to reduce the load on school students at all levels particularly the young students, while improving quality of learning including capability for life- long self-learning and skill formulation.

Before starting its work, the Committee decided the parameters of its work and also the methodology for completing the task entrusted to it. With a view to keeping a national perspective in view, the Committee decided not to confine its work to the Central Board of Secondary Education (CBSE) or NCERT syllabi and textbooks but to take into account the textbooks used in different states and union territories also. Secondly, the Committee decided to base its recommendations on the data obtained through perception surveys. wide- ranging consultations with teachers and analysis of textbooks and other instructional materials. Thirdly, the Committee decided to look at the work of agencies/organisations doing innovative programmes.

The process of consultation was initiated with a meeting with a few faculty members of NCERT followed by meeting with teachers and principals working in different states at four places in the country, namely Delhi, Thiruvananthapuram, Pune and Calcutta. The consultation meetings were also held with voluntary organisations engaged in innovative programmes, syllabus and textbook writers, private publishers, and Chairpersons of Boards of Secondary Education. Some members of the Committee organised meetings with parents, teachers and students at Bombay, Nasik Baroda and Calcutta. Surveys to ascertain the opinions of teachers and parents were conducted with the help of questionnaires at Bombay and Delhi.

To involve the whole country in this exercise of looking at the problems of school education from the perspective of mechanical load of studies on children, views and suggestions were invited from the students, teachers, parents and general public through advertisements in the newspapers and special announcements by All India Radio and Doordarshan. The Committee received more than 600 memoranda, letters and write-ups from students, teachers, parents and professionals interested in children's educations.

The wide-ranging consultations with knowledgeable people, analysis of the existing instructional materials and reactions of the teachers and students have enabled the Committee to understand the functioning of the present educational system which forms the basis of its recommendations.

In its work, the committee received cooperation from a large number of teachers, principals, syllabus and textbook writers, organisations, associations and departments. We gratefully acknowledge their contribution in our work. Particularly, we are grateful acknowledge their contribution in our work. Particularly, we are grateful to the State Council of Educational Research and Training (SCERT), Delhi, where the Committee's office was located, for providing all types of administrative support which tremendously facilitated our work. We are also thankful to NCERT and its Department of Social Sciences and Humanities for providing finances and other facilities for holding meetings of the Committee. The education departments of the states of Kerala, Maharashtra and West Bengal, and the NCERT Field Advisors in these states deserve appreciation for hosting the regional consultation meetings held at Thiruvananthapuram, Pune and Calcutta. Special thanks are due to voluntary organisations, Alla Rippu, Digantar and Eklavya for sharing their experiences with the members of the Committee. We express our sense of gratitude to the authorities of Doordarshan and Akashvani for making special announcement requesting the audience to send their views and suggestions to the Committee. Above all, we are extremely grateful to hundreds of parents, students and teachers who responded to our invitation and sent their views in writing, in many a times after holding meetings/workshops at their places.

The weight of the school bag represents one dimension of the problem; another dimension can be seen in the child's daily routine. Right from early childhood, many children specially those belonging to middle classes, are made to slog through home work, tuitions and coaching classes of different kinds. Leisure has become a highly scarce commodity in the child's, especially the urban child's life. The child's innate nature and capacities have no opportunity to find expression in a daily routine which permits no time to play, to enjoy simple pleasures, and to explore the world.

It is hard to reconcile the rigorous 'academic' regime that is imposed on children from an early age with the widespread complaint made about the declining norms and performance of the formal system of education. Teachers routinely complain that they do not have enough time to explain anything in detail, or to organise activities in the classroom. 'Covering' the syllabus seems to have become an end in itself, unrelated to the philosophical and social aims of education. The manner in which the syllabus is 'covered' in the average classroom is by means of reading the prescribed textbook aloud, with occasional noting of salient points on the blackboard. Opportunities for children to carry out experiments, excursions, or any kind of observations are scarce even in the best of schools. In the average schools especially the school located in a rural area, even routine teaching of the kind described above does not take place in many cases. In several states, school teachers encourage children to attend after-school tuition given for a fee while regular classroom teaching has become a tenuous ritual.

One message of this situation is that both the teacher and the child have lost the sense of joy in being involved in an educational process. Teaching and learning have both become a chore for a great number-of teachers and children. Barring those studying in reputed or exceptional institutions, the majority of our school-going children are made to view learning at school as a boring, even unpleasant and bitter experience. They are daily socialised to look upon education as mainly a process of preparing for examinations. No other motivation seems to have any legitimacy.

The contribution that teachers make towards this kind of socialisation is especially worrisome. Trained teachers are expected to be aware of the wider aims of education; indeed, aims like development of the "child's total personality" are the shibboleths of teacher training institutions everywhere in the country. It appears that teachers feel they can do little to pursue such lofty aims in any realistic sense under the harsh circumstances created by factors like excessively large classes, a heavy syllabus, difficult textbooks, and so on. Moreover, majority of them neither know nor have the necessary skills to realise the goals of education. The recommended pupil- teacher ratio of forty to one is now more an exception than a norm, and in many parts of the country it is customary to have sixty to eighty students in one class. The Committee learnt that in many states senior secondary classes often have one hundred or more students, many of them spilling into the corridor. In the national capital, many 'model' secondary schools, Central Schools, and several elite public' schools have classes, including primary classes, with more than sixty students.

This kind of class-size understandably generates a feeling of helplessness among teachers, but why must teachers feel helpless in the face of curriculum-related problems such as heavy syllabi, poorly produced textbooks, etc.? Why don't they act in more vocal ways and involve themselves in curriculum reform? Apart from the fact that there are very few forums encouraging curriculum inquiry and reform in any systematic manner, it seems to be an entrenched attitude among teachers to regard all decisions about curriculum and textbooks as the responsibility of 'authorities'. The fact is that while the teachers' involvement in the preparation of syllabi and textbooks is verbalised as a matter of principle, in practice it takes the shape of token involvement of a handful of teachers. Most teachers have reason. therefore, to think that they have little to say about the changes made from time to time in syllabi and textbooks. Even in such extreme cases where a textbook has a factual mistake, no complaints are made by teachers asking for correction of error. There is no established procedure or official forum to mobilise teacher vigilance and participation in curriculum improvement. On the contrary, there are cases where an individual teacher who complained about an error in a State-published textbook, was taken to task. Even if such cases can be described as rare or exceptionally unfortunate, they explain why the majority of teachers intuitively feel that it is not their business to critically examine the syllabus and texts they teach.

**Examination System**

Much has been written by various official committees on the ills of our examination system. The major, well-understood defect of the examination system is that it focuses on children's ability to reproduce information to the exclusion of the ability to apply concepts and information on unfamiliar, new problems, or simply to think. The public examinations taken after Classes X and XII have assumed the importance of major events which have a set character or culture of their own. The awe they generate, the responses they trigger, and the kind of preparation they demand have all got so entrenched into the social lore that minor improvements in the style of question papers do not make difference to the dominant influence that the examination system has on the processes of learning and teaching. The influence is so strong that schools start holding a formal written examination several years prior to Class X indeed, in the primary classes in many parts of the country, And children receive the message almost as soon as they start attending school that the only thing which matters here is one's performance in the examination.

Both the teacher and the parents constantly reinforce the fear of examination and the need to prepare for it in the only manner that seems practical, namely, by memorising a whole lot of information from the textbooks and guidebooks. Educated parents, who have themselves gone through examinations, and the uneducated parents, whose knowledge of the examination system is based on social lore, share the belief that what really matters in education is the score one gets in the final examination. This belief is undoubtedly rooted in social or market reality. Percentage of marks obtained in the high school, higher secondary, or BA/B.Sc examinations is what ultimately matters in determining a student's chance of being called for an interview for admission to a university or for employment. Since the examination store is what a candidate carries with him or her as the key authoritative record of school or college performance, higher level institutions or employing agencies understandable rely on it. It is a process in which no beginning or end can be meaningfully established. Changing the system of examination in a structural or even in a merely procedural sense does not require that a source outcome or cause-effect relationship be established; yet, the examination system goes on, apparently with the help of energies or rationales located in the system of education itself.

**Load of Textbook**

The pervasive effects of the examination system can be seen in the style and content of textbooks and not just guidebooks which are specifically manufactured to help children pass an examination. If 'facts' or 'information' constitute the main burden of an examination, the same is true of textbooks. Barring exceptions, our textbooks appear to have been written primarily to convey information or 'facts', rather than to make children think and explore, Over the years some attempts have been made to incorporate a certain amount of reflective writing in textbooks. Such writing is so exceptional that its examples can be spotted and named without difficulty. 'How leaves are designed' in a Class VIII textbook is one such piece of writing*. It stands out from among the thousands of pages of textbooks in different subjects that our teachers and children have to go through painstakingly so that they can retain the information recorded in those pages in a highly compressed, usually abstruse manner. The more common style used in the textbooks is exemplified by passages of the following kind:

— The term pH is defined as the negative logarithm to the base 10 of the hydrogen ion concentration expressed in gram ions per litre or moles per litre. (Class X)

— Fatty acids are slowly hydrolysed during digestion in the small intestine to form glycero and fatty acids through the enzyme action of lipase which is secreted by the pancreas, (Class X)

—We find that while dividing a decimal by a multiple of 10,000 or 1,000, we first move the decimal point to the left as many places as there are zeros in the number and then divide the resulting decimal by the second factor of the divisor. (Class V)

The problem of readability in textbooks becomes grim in the context of a system which often leaves the child with no resource other than the prescribed textbook. The extent to which the child can rely on a teacher to elucidate tersely written text material is dependent on the quality of teachers, their training, and their accountability. From what impression the Committee could form about these aspects of the system, it seems valid to say that the child is very often helpless in the face of a style of teaching that is far from being interactive, let alone the absence or irregular presence of teachers.Under the circumstances that are widely prevalent in our country, a child is more likely than not to mug up the definition of 'pH'quoted above without grasping it. And mugging does get the child through the examination!

Textbooks and guidebooks form a tight nexus. In some parts of the country children are compelled to buy the guidebook (or 'key') along with the textbook. The economic and business aspects of this pairing apart, the academic function of the textbook has become quite dubious indeed. It is not perceived as one of the resources for learning about a subject, but as the only authoritative resource. This kind of sanctity distorts what useful purpose the textbook could serve Teachers see it as a body of 'truths' which children must learn by heart. This perception and urge to 'cover' the chapters of the prescribed textbook. turn all knowledge into a load to be borne by the child's memory.

The distance between the child's everyday life and the content of the textbook further accentuates the transformation of knowledge into a load. We are not talking here about advanced science or mathematics, but about elementary science, social studies, language and arithmetic. Textbooks treat these subjects in a manner that leads to alienation of knowledge from the child's world. This tragic phenomenon takes different forms in different subjects in natural sciences, it takes the form of esotericisation of the subject, In the social sciences it becomes manifest in the coating of every inquiry in didacticism. suggestive of one preferred answer to every question.

A common source of alienation of subject-matter from the children's perspective and life is the presentation of the life-style and world view of the urban well-off class. This life-style is characterised by access to concrete housing, modern kitchens, electrical gadgets, and so on. Of course there is nothing 'wrong' with this life-style; but the symbolisation of this life-style in every illustration and description that concerns a child's home life alienates millions of children who live in houses with traditional kitchens, or with no separate kitchens. Objects of daily use in common Indian homes, such as a broom or clay pitcher, are seldom seen in textbooks.

One wonders whether the common Indian broom, which could be a versatile resource for learning about the social and physical environment, is perceived by our textbook writers and illustrators with a sense of stigma or as a symbol of backwardness. Or could it be' that it is simply too common to be seen as being of any use in an educational material? Neither of the two guesses is totally irrelevant in view of the complete absence of common objects of ordinary Indian life in the world depicted in textbooks.

The most common message that children get from the textbooks is that the life ordinary people live is 'wrong' or irrational. And this kind of didactic rejection does not apply to non-middle class life alone. All simple joys of childhood are also criticised. No better example of this can be given than the message conveyed in a Class V exercise which asks children to decide whether the statement 'Road is also a playground' is correct or wrong. The right response is that this statement is 'wrong', the message of the lesson being that playing on the street can be dangerous.

This message is of course true in a normative sense, but it ignores the reality of the overwhelming majority of urban children who have no other space except the street to play. The moot point is not the scarcity of space, but rather the need to accept the universally valid fact that children enjoy playing on the street. This joy must be respected in a text written from a child-centred point of view. To argue that a respectful acknowledgment of this joy will amount to sanctioning carelessness. or to say that children must be warned about the risks of playing on the street is to trivialise the issue. Every child who plays on the street fully knows the dangers involved in it. Science textbooks need not waste valuable pages on such trivial preaching which is precisely what they do throughout the elementary classes in place of using these golden Years of childhood to arouse curiosity about things and ideas.

We hardly need to assert that our textbooks are not written from the child's viewpoint Neither the mode of communication, nor the selection of objects depicted, nor the language conveys the centrality of the child in the world constructed by the text. This last dimension of language deserves some elaboration. The vocabulary and syntax used in the textbooks in the Hindi region were critically referred to by a number of individuals and groups whom the Committee met during the course of its deliberations. Not just the textbooks used for the teaching of the natural and the social sciences, but even the textbook used for the teaching of the mother tongue are written in such stylised diction and sentence-structure, that children cannot be expected to see the language used in them in their own. Words, expressions and nuances commonly used by children and others in their milieu are all absent from textbooks. So is humour. An artificial, sophisticated style dominates textbook lessons, reinforcing the tradition of distancing knowledge from life. The language used in textbooks, thus, deepens the sense of 'burden' attached to all school-related knowledge.

A highly disturbing tendency we discovered in text writing, which exacerbates the problem we are discussing, is that of treating pictures as substitutes for experience. We found textbooks asking children to observe a picture of the object under study rather than asking children and the teacher to go out and observe the object itself in nature. For example, a Class V science text says : 'Look at the picture of a cactus plant. Observe the thick green structure..... Such an instruction preempts what motivation there may be in a teacher or child to bring an actual cactus plant to the class or to grow one. The most painful example of this phenomenon brought to our attention was one in which a private publisher claimed that he had made the teacher's task 'easier' by turning an official 'Teacher's Guide', which suggests that the teacher should take children outside the school and identify some common birds, into a text where the pictures of all the common birds with with their names were provided for ready use. This case is especially painful as it shows how even a specific instruction given in a Teacher's Guide (Teacher's Guides are themselves rare; and in subjects in which they have been prepared in certain states, circulation has not been satisfactorily looked after) to encourage teachers to extend the lesson beyond the four walls of the classroom is co-opted within the dominant, traditional approach of teaching everything verbally from a textbook. Over the recent years, some textbooks have adopted the vocabulary of observation and exploration or discovery as a necessary part of science teaching, but even here, virtually all commands for observation conclude with statements about what will be seen if an observation is actually made, thereby making it unnecessary for the teacher and children to find an object and actually observe it.

**Structure of Syllabus**

The absence of the child's viewpoint is also reflected in the organisation of syllabi in different subjects. We received a large number of complaints from parents as well as teachers that the content of syllabi lacks an overall organisation or coherence. Gaps in the syllabi between the lower and the Higher Secondary stages are as common as repetitions of the same content. These weaknesses of organisation apparently lead to memorisation and poor comprehension, both exacerbating the sense of curriculum load. Gaps between the secondary and the senior secondary stages seem to be glaring in the science syllabi. When students come to Class XI, they often find themselves without a clue even if they have done well in Class X. The level of abstraction attempted in the senior secondary stage science syllabi and textbooks, especially the physics textbooks, represents a jump in many topics. Apparently, those preparing the senior secondary syllabi and texts lacked adequate familiarity with the syllabi and text used in the earlier classes. In fact, they had no occasion to interact with the persons involved in the preparation of syllabi and textbooks for secondary classes OX and X.

Repetitions of concepts and information also leads to boredom and a sense of load. The need to repeat is rooted in the flawed structure of syllabi. In the primary classes, ideas and information are presented in a synoptic manner, making the text look deceptively simple. In the later classes, the same ideas are repeated, with some elaboration which does not prevent the child from viewing the ideas as trivialised by repetition. In the study of nutrition and health, for example, virtually the same ideas and information are given in the syllabi and texts of Classes III, IV, V, VII and X. Even the questions given at the end of the lessons in the texts are almost of the same kind. Apparently, the structure of syllabi is not carefully thought out. Indeed, our Committee was told by senior experts, who have been involved in syllabus and textbook preparation, that experts working on the syllabus of different levels (secondary and senior secondary) had no contact with each other. Reference to such procedural lapses, however, is not necessary to explain the tendency towards repetition that is embedded in the structure of the syllabus and has been reinforced by tradition.

History is the most clear case in point. Although it forms one part of the subject called social sciences, it offers a prime example of curriculum load. Despite many changes that have come about in the style of history texts, the history syllabus continues to be a frustrating and meaningless experience for children. The aim of teaching history is defeated because children are not enabled to relate to their own heritage. Traditionally, it requires children to form an overall picture of the 'whole' if India's known history, from ancient to modern times, during the three years from Classes VI to VIII. Since the texts for these classes are required to cover such a vast span, the density of these texts becomes extremely high which means that historical time is greatly compressed, i.e. a few sentences are deemed to 'cover' several decades. The synoptic style forces the child into 'accepting' whatever is narrated. There aren't enough details that a child could use to work out some kind of argument or interpretation, but the sheer volume of text (which is suppose to 'cover' 'all' of India's history in three years) forces the child (and the teacher) to 'take in' as much text as possible without 'wasting' time in studying or constructing an argument.

This common problem of the history syllabus apart, we found that the content of the history syllabus in certain states was conceived as a densely packed box of informations. The syllabus of history in West Bengal illustrates this tendency in tragically exaggerated proportions. For example in Class VIII, children are required to learn 17 topics in all which are : 1. Modern age; 2. Renaissance in Europe; 3. Europeans widen the world; 4. Reformation in Europe; 5. The English Revolution in the 17th century; 6. India; 7. Foundation and growth of the British power in India till 1857 in short narrative form; 8. World in the 18th century; 9. Europe since 1815; 10. (a) Developments in China till 1911; (b) Rise of Japan as a great power till 1914; 1 1. India under the crown 1858-1914; 12. The First World War; 13. The Bolshevik Revolution; 14. Europe 1919-1939; 15. The Second World War; 16. India 1919-1947; 17. (a) Revolution in China 1911-1949 (b) Revolution in South East Asia after 1945; (c) Spread of nationalism and unrest in subject countries during the Second World War.

The entire syllabus is to be covered in 135 pages of a text, according to the instruction given in the syllabus itself. Apparently, the syllabus makers believe that compression of information in terms of page-space does not affect the readability, let alone comprehensibility of a text.

The problem of densely packed syllabi like this one cuts across disciplines. In geography, it takes the form of all the continents being 'covered' under regional geography between Classes VI and VIII. In mathematics and the natural sciences, the packing of details makes any kind of learning with understanding, leave alone enjoyment, virtually impossible Numerous examples could be given from these disciplines to illustrate the problem. In one page of a Class VII science textbook we find all these items 'covered' : definition of time period, how to find the number of oscillations per second, definition of frequency, 'Hertz unit of frequency, the ideas that vibrations have amplitude and frequency, definitions of these, the concept of sound as vibration, loudness and pitch. and finally frequency/pitch and its relation to speed of rotation and tension. We are not citing this example as a specific case to be looked into, but as evidence of a deeply rooted tendency, rather all ideology, which impels syllabus and textbook planners to include 'everything' without ally regard for children's ability at different ages to learn and the time available in an average school for teaching a subject. Class XI and XII textbooks of science, prepared recently with a view apparently to implement the National Education Policy, have been widely criticised on these scores. Children studying science subjects have been asked by their teachers to look for private tutors, the rationale being that there may not be enough time in the class to cover the syllabus, and some of the syllabus being beyond the capacities of the teacher. The terse content of these texts was apparently edited and reviewed in some haste, we were informed, due to constraints of time while sending the manuscripts for publication. Perhaps it can be argued that these textbooks are liked by the highly motivated and the brightest among the students and teachers. If this indeed in the case, it gives all the more reason to worry about the fate of the overwhelming majority of children studying in ordinary schools.

In mathematics, the situation seems to be grim right from the start of the child's school carrier. Far too many abstractions are introduced all at once with scant attention paid to well-known facts about development of mathematical thinking in children. To begin with, children are expected to handle arithmetical operations on a very large numbers early. In Class I, they are supposed to go up to 100 (compared to this a British child in this class spends the whole year working with numbers up to 20), in Class II up to 1000. in Class III, up to 10,000, in Class IV up to a million, and in class V up to a crore. Even though the conservation of volume and weight are known to emerge in the child's mind after the conservation of length is fully established, all three are introduced simultaneously (usually in one unit of study) at the young, age of seven or eight years, with the expectation that children will compute with standard units. Concrete operational thought, which is characteristic of elementary school children, demands manipulation of objects and activities using a variety of materials (to enable 'elaboration' of a concept, i.e. its dislocation from any one material or object). Such activities become impossible to organise under a curriculum which 'progresses' so swiftly from concept to concept. Also, children of this stage find proportional reasoning difficult yet percentage and ratio are introduced in Classes IV and In the middle and higher classes, the tendency to follow the logic of the discipline of mathematics rather than psychology of learning as the basic of the curriculum becomes even more dominant. Mathematics, thus, acquires the image of an esoteric discipline which has little application in the real life of the child.

The general problems of curriculum conceptualisation that we have discussed in this part of our report can all be seen reflected in the emerging pre-school sector of the education system. Despite official stipulations that no textbooks be used at this stage, preschool teachers and parents in the urban centre are feeling 'compelled' to burden the young child with textbooks and the formal learning they represent. The sense of compulsion comes from a widespread feeling that unless academic training of a child starts early, he or she cannot cope with the fast-paced pedagogy and the competitive ethos of the later school years. The pernicious grip of this false argument manifests itself in absurd, and of course deeply harmful, practices in pre-schools and primary schools, such as early emphasis on shapely drawing, writing, and memorising information. Intrinsic motivation and the child's natural abilities are being smothered at a scale so vast that it cannot be correctly estimated. Our national commitment to the development of human resource is daily challenged in our nurseries and primary schools.

The problem we have tried to identify in this part of the report is not confined to urban areas as some people think. It is deeply relevant to children's education in rural India although their, more basic problems - such as abysmally pure condition of schools, absenteeism among teachers etc. may cloud the problem curriculum load. In our view, the problem of high drop-out rate, which has rightly pre- occupied our policy-makers for a long time, has one of its origins in the curriculum scenario we have portrayed. A curriculum policy that takes away the elements of joy and inquiry from learning obviously contributes to the rate at which children leave school in early years, undoubtedly under the force of economic and social circumstances. As we have indicated earlier, symbolic tilt towards an urban, middle class way of life in text books can also be expected to make the rural Child's association with his or her experience at school thin and brittle. Quality of teachers and the equipment available to them also make an impact on the tenuous and fragile links that the first- generation learner in many parts of rural India tries to establish with the system of education.

## Knowledge vs. Information

India has to catch up with the developed countries where an explosion of knowledge has occurred; therefore, our children must learn a lot more than they used to, which means that new topics, new concepts and information have to be added to the syllabi and textbooks. This argument seems to be so widespread and tenacious that those who believe in it use it as an undebatable 'given'. When it is pointed out to them that children of the so-called developed countries learn certain concepts a lot later than our children do, supporters of the 'explosion of knowledge' argument simply say that the European societies are already way ahead of us, so they can afford to instruct their children at a relaxed pace. In geography, when it is pointed out that European and North American children do not have to study every continent, the answer given is that in Western societies children have access to many resources of learning outside the school whereas the majority of 'Our children are dependent on the school for getting to know about the world. The idea entrenched in the 'explosion of knowledge' theory finds similar justifications for the present state of syllabi and texts in other school subjects.

The notion that there has been an explosion of knowledge apparently treats knowledge and information as synonymous. It is true that the twentieth century has been a period of massive expansion in human capacity to find new facts and to store them, but the concepts and theories that assist in the generation and organisation of information call hardly be said to have multiplied at an 'explosive' rate. Also, the important thing in children's education ought to be concept-formation and growth of capacity for theorybuilding, rather than possession of vast amounts of information. The 'explosion of knowledge' idea prevents us from appreciating that learning in childhood is not the same thing as storing information about different subjects. If we say that a child has knowledge of phenomenon 'X' we can anticipate three possible ways in which this statement will be interpreted:

i) the child has been given information about phenomenon 'x';

ii) the child can reproduce information about phenomenon 'x';

iii) the child has understood phenomenon 'X' and he or she can apply this understanding on other phenomena.

It is mostly the first two meanings that hold in the context of formal education in our country, the first being used as a basis for the second. 'Understanding' is often confused with 'acquisition of facts'.

Such a confusion leads to the neglect of 'understanding' as an aim of education. It would be correct to say that this neglect of understanding has gone so far and deep in our education system that a child can pass almost any examination without any understanding of the phenomena he or she has been told about in books or in the classroom. To a great extend, this paradoxical situation can be attributed to the excessive emphasis placed in our syllabi and textbooks on information or 'names' of things. Children have no choice but to memorise all 'names' in order to 'prove' at an examination that they have 'understood' a phenomenon. Despite all kinds of claims that examinations have been reformed, they continue to focus on testing the possession of 'correct information' (i.e. the names of things, definitions, examples etc.). Recall-type questions outnumber the questions that test the child's capacity to speculate, evaluate or judge, and to apply all idea in an unfamiliar context. Board examinations, taken at the end of Class X and Class XII have remained rigid, bureaucratic and essentially uneducative (as the child never sees why he or she was marked in a certain way), and mainly a sources of awe because of the amount of information they demand in a manner ready for instant recall. Such a system obviously influences the test and annual examinations taken by schools in earlier classes as well as the daily pedagogy practiced in classrooms. The fact that entrance test of prestigious institutions like Indian Institute of Technology have less focus on recall (although they put a premium on speed) is ignored, and even these tests are cited for justifying the excessively large syllabi in certain subjects in the senior secondary classes.

## Classroom Realities

The new topics and information put into the syllabus and textbooks at the time of each successive revisions are usually added at the behest of experts of different subjects. These experts are university-level teachers sometimes including individuals of high stature in the research world. Their involvement in the writing or revision of textbooks is indeed appreciable but they have little exposure to children in classroom situations. Their exposure to school teachers is also confined to interaction with the few teachers who are selected as members of syllabus and textbook committees. Several factors, such as the difference of social and official status, make it difficult for school teachers serving on these committees to freely put across their feelings and experiences regarding the teachability of a syllabus or the style of a textbook.

Teachability can be defined as the quotient of content that an average teacher can put across at a comfortable pace in a thirty five minute school period. If our textbooks were to be judged in the light of this criterion, most of them, espectially in the sciences, mathematics, and the social sciences, would appear as unreachable. The amount of information and concept-load they present are far in excess of the amount that can be put across in any meaningful way in thirty-five minute period allotted for a school subject in one academic session. It appears that no rigorous count, using the thirty-five minute as a unit, of the total teaching time available for a subject in any year is used as a basis for determining syllabus and text content. Indeed, the syllabi and textbooks are evidence to say that the experts involved in preparing them have little knowledge of school and classroom realities. This limitation of the experts extends to their possible ignorance of children and of the processes that children use for learning new ideas. Textbooks simply do not reflect the versatile search of the ordinary child for clues to make sense of natural or social phenomena. Typically school texts proceed in a linear fashion, adding bits of information in, and concepts as they go along. The linear fashion they follow often spill across school years, i.e. something left of in Class VII is picked up again in Class IX, and so on. Very seldom is an effort made to construct knowledge-patterns in a non-linear ways.

We feel that if experts involve in the preparation of syllabi and textbooks have the opportunity to work with children and their teachers, they would have a chance to develop some insight into children's learning strategies. This would have helped them to develop the ability to emulate such strategies in script-writing for textbooks. Interaction with children might enable experts to develop a certain amount of sensitivity towards the living and versatile approaches used by children. Also, in the course of such interaction, the experts might also perceive the need to equip themselves with knowledge of children's psychology, particularly the psychology of learning, before venturing out on the task of textbook preparation. This, of course, implies that the job of syllabus and textbook preparation be perceived as a serious professional activity, not as a part-time obligation.

In the specific context of the curriculum planning and textbook production, we feel, the system invites a number of problems upon itself on account of being unnecessarily centralised. It seems there is a widespread misconception which justifies centralisation in these matters. This misconception treats the content of syllabuys and textbook as synonymous with learning and testing norms. On the basis of this confusion, it is argued that syllabi and textbooks should be the same all over a state, even all over the country, in order to ensure uniformity of standards. This kind of argument completely overlooks the lopsided manner in which standards are set under the present system by an examination system which focuses on information rather than on skills and capacity to apply skills. Indeed, there is a 'catch 22' situation; the examination system ignores skills, concentrating on memorised information, definitions and descriptions; therefore, syllabus and textbooks, which cannot do justice to diversify milieux, varying needs and facilities, become necessary to ensure that all children 'know' the same 'facts'.

The circular argument has created a situation in which curriculum and textbook preparation is confined to the state capitals and New Delhi. At regional and local levels, teachers do not perceive curriculum development and preparation of educational materials as part of their job. And indeed, the way these tasks have been defined and traditionally carried out in our country, they are not the teacher's job. The teacher sees his or her role as one of elucidating whatever content of knowledge is prescribed in the syllabus. At the primary and lower and secondary stages, teachers come to know the syllabus through the textbooks which acts as the de facto syllabus. 'Covering' the syllabus means 'covering' or finishing the textbook. This kind of perception results in the confinement of classroom life a narrow orbit. Classroom knowledge assumes total independence from the child's own experience and knowledge of the world. As a consequence of this decoupling, children begin to compartmentalise knowledge into two categories; that which has currency in school and classroom, and the other which has uses and relevance outside the school. Necessarily, the knowledge in the first category ceases to have any 'life' and becomes increasingly ritualistic and burdensome. Teachers also carry the same kind of categorisation in their mind; very few of them are able to help the child make bridges between what is learnt at school and what is required to face real-life situations. One reacher who tried to make such a bridge in a lesson about letter-writing was asked by a Class VI child: "Madam, shall we write it the way we write at home or in the school way?"

While several factors, including those related to the training of teachers, call be held responsible for this. aspect of situation, we feel that the centralised structures of syllabus and textbook preparation set the tone. Howsoever 'good' a textbook produced at central level may be of professional standard, it can not reflect the subtler nuances of life in a village of Kashmir or Assam. Adaptation to local conditions is indeed officially carried out to match the content of textbooks with local conditions, but it does not change the basic character of a textbook. Adaptation of syllabi to local conditions is even less effectively possible.

### Teaching the Text

Lack of adequate opportunities for teachers to participate in the prcesses of syllabus and textbook preparation is a major factor indirectly responsible for the problem of unrealistic syllabi or curriculum load. Teachers perform a more direct role in the context of this problem by perceiving the context of the textbook as a rigid boundary or definer of their work in the classroom. Boredom is the inevitable outcome when a tersely written textbook is taught in a rigid, mechanical manner. Poor grasp among teachers of their role as translators of the curriculum into classroom activity is a widely prevalent characteristic of our system. We are citing this as a relevant aspect of the phenomenon of curriculum load without suggesting that there is a vicious circle here, i.e. teaching cannot improve unless there are better textbooks, etc. We feel that strategies to improve textbook writing and production must work parallel to strategies for improvement in teacher training and for creating an ethos in which teachers would feel motivated to take an academic interest in their work. The perception that a teacher can do little in the classroom that is different from what the textbook says is part of historical legacy. This legacy must be transcended and the self-perception rooted in it must be changed. Teacher training institutions and the mass media, both can assist in making this change possible.

In the context of constructing a new self-image of the teacher pre-service training is a key but elusive area of reform. Past attempts to improve teacher training programmes and institutions have met with rather limited success. By and large, teacher training continues to be isolated from mainstream academic areas related to education. In service training too in most places, has assumed the character of a ritual devoid of academic substance or the capacity to stimulate. The current effort to provide statutory status to the National Council for Teacher Education (NCTE) (As envisaged in the National Education Policy) may perhaps make some impact on the weak training that is generally available in the country to people who want to work with children especially young children.

Administrative and legal concern needs to be applied to several training programmes running as commercial success stories, such as those offering a degree by correspondence. Similarly, there is need to examine existing policies with regard to nursery teacher training courses and institutions. Indeed, what is required is a review of the overall training policy which permits the traditional bifurcation of degree programme from non-degree programmes and their application to different stages of school education. We hope that after acquiring statutory status, the NCTE will work out a comprehensive training programme to cover all stages of schooling, ending the bifurcation we have mentioned above. Such a programme will have to be radically different from the present one which are anchored in the culture of late nineteenth century normal schools, and are sadly lacking both in perspective and means to equip teachers with the capacity to understand children and their learning processes in a professional manner.

### Competition-based Social Ethos

Our social ethos, particularly in the urban areas, are now fully entrenched in the competitive spirit which is fast becoming our way of life. The desire to catch up with the industrially developed countries has given it further impetus. Rising aspirations of people in all sections of the society and the growing realisation that education is an important instrument to fulfil their aspirations have resulted in a craze for admission to Englishmedium schools which start imparting formal education too early in the child's life.

The educated sections of the society believe that command over English is the key to upward mobility in social life. This has led to unprecedented growth in the number of private schools where English is not only taught as a subject but is also used as a medium of education in all subjects right from Class I. It is a well-known fact that young children studying in English-medium schools mug up the content of science and social sciences without understanding. It is an accepted principle or pedagogy that whatever is memorised without understanding proves burdensome for children. Any language other than the mother tongue of the child, if used as medium of instruction, is a big source of academic burden on children. Most of the parents in urban and semi-urban areas do not realise it, in fact they try to promote the use of English as medium of education. Unfortunately, instead of resisting pressure of the competitive spirit prevalent in the society or directing in appropriate channels, our educational system has succumbed to it. The most conspicious manifestations of this phenomenon in education area upgradation of content of syllabus by advancing introduction of many topics and subjects in utter disregard of the process of maturation. The entrance test for admission to professional courses like engineering and medicine have influence in the objectives, content and methodology of education in many ways. The 'quiz culture' which has taken roots in education, can be attributed to these tests.

With a view to provide incentives to 'high achievers' and 'talented'in different fields, high profile competitions are organised by different departments and institutions in the name of 'talent search', which at the most provide moments of brief glory to the winners but damage the 'ego-strength' of numerous others who participate in the contests at the cost of lesuirely pursuit of knowledge at their own pace and in their own ways. The experience of the ignominy of failure on the part of millions of children have long term deleterious effect on the personality of the individual and the matrix of society. It would be better to reward group performance so as to convey the message to everyone that excellence in group work rather than individual effort should be the target.

Adequate time, staff, accommodation, and its maintenance funds, pedagogical equipment, playground are essential pre-requisites for effective curriculum transactions but, unfortunately, an overwhelming majority of schools do not have even the minimum essential facilities. It is a matter of great concern that the number of teachers with a sense of commitment is gradually shrinking while cynicism, feelings of helplessness and hopelessness are on the rise. Lack of adequate infrastructural facilities, rigid administrative structures and growing cynicism are responsible for the absence of academic ethos in majority of schools.

The methods of teaching used by majority of teachers are devoid of any type of challenge for the students. Transmission of information rather than experimentation or exploration or observation characterises the teaching-learning process in most of the classrooms. We have no reason to believe that there is something wrong with our children, rural or urban. Luckily they have not compartmentalised knowledge; they are interested in seeking understanding rather than mere information. As they are educated by us while they grow older, freshness goes away as does romance and curiosity. Before anything is learnt they want to find out why they need to know. Must we, in the name of so-called 'proper education' go on committing the murder of their innate desire to discover to learn on their own?

Children are not allowed to observe and explore natural phenomena, but at the same time they are also not provided opportunity to explore the world of books. The concept of a library as a readily available resource for learning simply does not exist in most schools. Even those rare schools that do happen to have a library stock little more than copies of prescribed textbooks, often stored behind locked doors. If children are to be prepared for experiencing the beauty and nature and the fascination of ideas without feeling the curricular load, priority has to be given to developing school libraries and their adequate and appropriate utilisation.

Similarly science laboratory even in the few cases where they are adequately equipped are not used for experimentation and discovery. A laboratory is not perceived as a place where children can conduct even those experiments which are not prescribed in their syllabi and come out with novel observations that need exploratory fameworks. The main purpose of a laboratory programme is to visualise children's natual talents and develop their ability to learn to observation and exploration. Over-regimentation of prescribed experiments with the entire emphasis on getting the final result, is contrary to this spirit. Laboratories should be conceived as exploratories and school should have the freedom to structure experiments to suit the needs of their children.

We have come tlo the conclusion that the problem of the load on school children does not arise only from over-enthusiastic curriculum designers, or poorly equipped teachers, or school administators, or book publishers, or district, state or central educational authorities. Yes, what all these groups, agencies and administrators do can exacerbate or alleviate the problem. But, there is a deeper malaise in our society, which impacts our young children. If we continue to value a few elite qualifications far more than real competence for doing useful things in life, and if the economic distance, between those who can manage to cross some academic hurdles and those who can't, continues to widen, we will probably continue to spend our effort in designing hurdles instead of opportunities for children to learn with joy. As the body of the Report analyses, a major problem is connected with the notions of 'knowledge explosion' and the' catching up' syndrome. We believe that these problems cannot be fully addressed through easily manageable administrative actions. They need wider discussions because they are centrally connected with images of our civilization self-esteem and societal goals. Such a wide discussion can come about through publication of this Report, and through a set of seminars, meetings and media discussions. Academics, thinkers, need to pour over this basic problem.

The question of medium of instruction, particularly in early life, will not be fully resolved till the time our dominant and externally connected sections of society continue to give more importance to elementary graces in a foreign language, than to intimate connections with the 'vernacular' knowledge which our children gain during every week of their growing up before they go to school. It is because of this reason that we have restrained ourselves from repeating the recommendation that mother tongue alone should be the medium of instruction at the primary stage.

1. A number of organisations and departments organise competitions at district, state and national level for students in various fields such as school subjects, exhibitions, essay writing, elocution, etc.

Perhaps the spirit behind these activities is to recognise and reward the talent in diverse fields. But, unfortunately this tends to produce somewhat unhealthy singling out of people for their brief moment of glory. Competitions where individual achievement is rewarded need to be discouraged since they deprive children of joyful learning. However, group activities and group achievements must be encouraged and rewarded to give a boost to cooperative learning in schools.

2.

(a) The process of curriculum-framing and preparation of textbooks of decentralised so as to increase teachers' involvement in these tasks. Decentralisation should mean greater autonomy, within state- level apparatus, to district-level boards or other relevant authority, and to heads of schools and classroom teachers to develop curricular materials on their own, best suited to the needs of local environment. All the schools be encouraged to innovate in all aspects of curriculum, including choice of textbooks and other materials.

(b) Voluntary organisations with a specific commitment to pedagogical innovations within the formal or non-formal system be provided greater freedom and support in development of curriculum, textbooks and teacher training. A suitable and adequate mechanism be evolved for wider dissemination of the experiences of such organisations.

(c) We endorse the idea of setting up education committees at village, block and district level to undertake kplanning and supervision of schools under their jurisdiction.

(d) Sufficient contingency amount (not less than 10 per cent of the total salary bill of the school) be placed at the disposal of heads of schools for purchase, repair and replacement of pedagogical equipment.

3. The culture of writing textbooks be changed so as to involve a much large number of teachers in the preparation of textbooks. The scientists and experts in various disciplines may be associated with the preparation of textboooks as consulstants and not as writers of the books. Initiative in this regard should rest with groups of enlightened and innovative teachers who should be provided training in book writing.

4. At least three parallel systems of school education (syllabus, textbooks and examination) are running concurrently in different states. In each state majority of schools are affiliated to the State Board of Education while a few are affiliated to either CBSE or Council for the Indian School Certificate Examination (CISCE). The schools affiliated to CBSE in the states other than Delhi enjoy the prestige of being elite schools. The CBSE curriculum becomes a trend-setter for the State Boards leading to heavier curriculum for majority of children. Therefore, the committee recommends that jurisdiction of CBSE be restricted to Kendriya and Navodaya Vidyalayas and all other schools be affiliated to the respective State Boards.

5.

(a) Appropriate legislative and administrative measures be adopted to regulate the opening and functioning of early childhood education institutions (pre-schools). Norms regarding accommodation, staff, apparatuses, play material be laid down for the recognitioin of these schools. It should be ensured that these institutions do not perpetrate violence on young children by inflicting a heavy dose of 'over-education' in the form of formal teaching of Reading, Writing and Numbers. The practice of holding tests and interviews for admission to nursery class be abolished.

(b) Norms for granting recognition to private schools be made more stringent. This will prove conducive for improving the quality of learning on the one hand and arrest growing commercialisation on the other. The norms, thus developed, be made uniformly applicable to all schools including the state-run institutions.

6. There is no jurisdiction for torturing the young children by compelling them to carry very heavy bags of books everyday to schools. Textbooks should be treated as school property and thus, there should be no need for children to purchase the books individually and carry them daily to homes. A separate time-table for the assignment of home work and for the use of textbooks and notebooks be prepared by the school and be made known to the children in advance.

7. The nature and character of homework needs a radical change. In the primary classes, children should not be given by homework, save for extensioin of explorations in the home environment. In the upper primary and secondary classes, homework, where necessary, should be non-textual, and textbooks, when needed for work at home should be made available on a rotation basis.

8. The existing norm for teacher-pupil ratio (i.e. 1:40) should be enforced and all attempt should be made

to reduce this to 1:30, at least in the primary classes, as a basis for future educational planning.

9. Greater use of the electronic media be made for the creation of a child-centred social ethos in the country. A regular television programme addressed to students, teachers and parents and possibly called 'Shiksha Darshan' be launched, along the lines of the 'Krishi Darshan' programme.

10.

   (a) Inadequate programme of teacher preparation leads to unsatisfactory quality of learning in schools. The B.Ed. programme should offer the possibility of specialisation in secondary or elementary or nursery education. The duration of the programme should either be one year after graduation or three-four years after higher secondary. The content of the programme should be restructured to ensure its relevance to the changing needs of school education and to make it more practicum-centred. The emphasis in these programmes should be on enabling the trainees to acquire the ability for self learning and independent thinking. Pre-service teacher education programme, being a professional course, has to be a rigorous, thorough and intensive programme. Therefore, B.Ed. degree courses by correspondence be derecognised.

   (b) The continuing education of teachers must be institutionalised. The organisation of inservice education programmes and other activities aimed at professional growth of teachers be systematically designed and conducted imaginatively.

11. The public examinations taken at the end of Class X and XII be reviewed with a view to ensure

replacement of thew prevailing text- based and 'quiz type' questioning by the concept-based questioning. This single reform is sufficient to improve the quality of learning and save the children from the tyranny of memorisation.

12.

(a) A project team with a number of sub-groups be set up in each state to examine the syllabi and textbooks for all school classes. The sub-groups be required to decide the following:

i) The minimum number of topics required to be taught.

ii) The minimum number of concepts to be introduced within each topic.

iii) The total time needed for teaching this minimum number of concepts corn fortably by a teacher in the total working days realistically available in a year.

(b) Mathematics curriculum for primary classes in all parts of the country be reviewed with a view to slowing down the pace at which children are required to learn basic mathematical, concepts, and broadening the scope of primary mathematics to include areas other than number work (e.g. space and shape-related concepts and problem solving). the tendency embedded in the syllabi and textbooks of primary mathematics to accelerate children's mathematical skills by teaching them mechanical rules at the expense of understanding and intelligent application ought to be discouraged in future syllabi and texts.

(c) Language textbooks should adequately reflect the spoken idiom. An attempt should be made in future textbooks to give adequate representation to children's life experiences, imaginary stories and poems, and stories reflecting the lives of ordinary people in different parts of the country. Pedantic language and excessive didacticism ought to be avoided.

(d) Science syllabi and textbooks in the primary classes should provide greater room and necessity for experimentation than they do at present. In place of didacticism in areas like health and sanitation, the texts should emphasise analytical reflection on real-life situations. A great deal of trivial materials included in primary- level science texts should be dropped.

(e) The syllabi of natural sciences throughout the secondary and senior secondary classes be revised in a manner so as to ensure that most of the topics included are actively linked to experiments or activities that can be performed by children and teachers.

(f) Besides imparting knowledge of history and geography, the social sciences curriculum for Classes VI-VIII and IX-X should convey the philosophy and methodology of the functions of our socio-political and economic system enable the students to analyse, understand and reflect on the problems and the priorities of socioeconomic development. The repetitions nature of history syllabus should be changed. The history of ancient times should be introduced for systematic study in secondary classes OX and X). The history syllabus lot classes VI-VIII should focus on the freedom struggle and post-independence developments The civics, as it is taught today, puts a great load on children's capacity to memorise Therefore, it may be dropped in its present form and be replaced by contemporary studies'. The study of geography be related to contemporary reality.

# 9

# Financial Problems in Higher Education

The University Grants Commission (UGC) Act, 1956 empowers the Commission to allocate and disburse grants to central universities and institution deemed to be universities for their maintenance and development and for any other general and specific purpose.

There are 10 central universities but one of them, i.e. the Indira Gandhi National Open University (IGNOU) is regulated directly from the Ministry and is, therefore, not under the purview of the UGC. The other nine, viz. Delhi University, Jawaharlal Nehru University, Jamia Millia Islamia, Aligarh Muslim University, Banaras Hindu University, Visva Bharati, Hyderabad University, North Eastern Hill University, and Pondicherry University are under the UGC umbrella. UGC is, therefore, responsible for maintenance and development support (financial) to these nine central universities. The Committee is informed that. four more new central universities, two in Assam, one each in Nagaland and U.P. are being established. These would be due for development grants immediately and maintenance grants in due course.

Section 3 of the UGC Act defines an institution deemed to be university' It lays down that Government of India may confer the status of Deemed to be University on an institution which is not a university. The Government does so on the recommendation of UGC. So far 34 institutions have been conferred institutions deemed to be university status. This is an ongoing process and there are always 10-20 applications with UGC seeking institutions to be deemed university status. For historical reasons UGC provides eight of these full maintenance and development grants while others get

The colleges affiliated to Delhi and Banaras Hindu Universities which were originally assisted directly by the Government, later came under direct UGC assistance. As a result, UGC took over the responsibility to provide maintenance and development grants to these colleges.

Thus nine central universities, 57 Delhi colleges, and 8 institutions deemed to be universities depend fully on UGC for their maintenance and development expenditure. UGC has no source of income other than what is allocated to it. by the Government of India through the Ministry of Human Resource Development. Therefore, the capability of UGC to provide grants to the universities /institutions is dependent on the resources made available to it by the Government of India.

## Maintenance of Grant

The exact amount of maintenance grant payable to central universities, institutions deemed to the universities and Delhi colleges for any year is determined on "covering the deficit " basis, i.e., the internal receipt is deducted out of the actual expenditure incurred in any year. The general financial principles also require that public funds should not be allowed to accumulate as reserves. Accordingly, no institution can build up any reserve out of the maintenance grant paid to it. Because of wide variations in costs and needs in different parts of the country and also due to largeness of the institutions, norms for expenditure for different. variables under maintenance grant have not been introduced. Therefore, in assessing the reasonableness of next years' requirement there is considerable subjectivity. The maintenance grant increases incrementally for each institution every year, with the size of increment varying from institution to institution.

Till 1988-89, however, it was possible for UGC, by and large, to provide grants to these institutions on the basis of the recommendations of their respective Finance Committees. Since then the increasing strain on the financial resources of Government has resulted in reduced levels of grant to UGC which in turn adversely affected the size of the maintenance grants sanctioned to these institutions.

In 1990-91, as a result of financial crisis, due to the Gulf war, a 10% cut was imposed by the government in the non-plan expenditure of all government departments and autonomous bodies in receipt of government grant. Accordingly, in 1990-91, though at the beginning of the year the non plan budget of UGC was kept at Rs.238.20 crores, due to the economy cut it was reduced by Rs. 17 crores. This made it impossible for the UGC to provide maintenance grant. to cover the full deficit as recommended by Finance Committees of the respective universities/institutions.

In 1991-92, the budget provision for the UGC remained at the same level as initially provided for in 1990-91. However, realising that universities, institutions deemed to be universities and Delhi colleges could not possibly manage with the maintenance grant at 1990- 91 level, the UGC provided 5% increase in salary component and 10% in non-salary component over the 1990-91 disbursement. This caused an additional liability to UGC which it met by diverting Plan funds.

During 1992-93, UGC was provided with a non-plan grant of Rs.247.09 crores in the budget as against the total expenditure of Rs.266.27 crores incurred by it during 1991-92. In order to apprise the Institutions of the impending crisis and to enable them to make necessary financial adjustments well in time for the financial year, the Chairman, UGC, addressed the Vice Chancellors of central universities, Vice-Chancellors/Directors of institutions deemed to be universities and Principals of Delhi colleges on 1.4.1992, informing them that UGC could pay them only as much maintenance grant as was paid to them in 1991-92. The Chair-man also suggested that these institutions might economise and augment their income to the extent possible, keeping in view the specific situation in each individual institution.

## Meeting with Vice Chancellors

The Commission organised a series of consultations with the Vice Chancellors, directors of institutions and Principals of colleges who are in receipt of non-plan grant. As per the consensus arrived at these meetings, a Committee was constituted comprising representatives from these institutions to suggest specific measures for economy as well as for augmenting income. The report of this Committee was considered at a meeting of the Vice-Chancellors of central universities and institutions deemed to be universities. At this meeting, the Heads of the institutions felt that since the situation in regard to each institution is different, a common pattern for measures of economy or for augmenting income was not feasible and therefore this should be decided by the institutions themselves. The Vice-Chancellors/Directors also emphasised the following three major issues:

(i) Since the UGC Act specifically provides for "maintenance of such institutions", UGC and Government should provide sufficient funds required for the purpose. UGC and the Government should not make partial-funding for maintenance.

(ii) As the scope for economy and augmenting of income is limited, this would only be a short term remedy and it will not be possible for the universities to manage with inadequate maintenance grants for a long period of time.

(iii) The present formula of deducting income for providing maintenance grant should be changed, in which case the augmentation of income will be meaningful and, similarly, no itemwise limits within the maintenance grant be enforced.

Keeping in view the seriousness of the matter, the Minister of Human Resource Development had a meeting with the Chairman, UGC and the ViceChancellors of central universities on 7-8 July, 1992. At this meeting the Minister pointed out that in the present financial situation no institution could keep itself totally insulated from its effect. Each university and college has to make necessary structural adjustment to cope with the situation. The Minister, however, announced "de-freezing" of the maintenance grant which was conveyed to all institutions in July, 1992. In pursuance of this announcement the Government provided an extra amount of Rs.39 crores to UGC to meet its non-plan requirements for the year 1992-93.

In fact, this extra allocation amounted to only Rs.19 crores over and above the actual grant disbursed. Keeping this in view the Commission advised the institutions that the extra amount provided should cover 7.5% more for salary component compared to 1991-92 and 5% for non-salary components. The pensionary benefits would be supported in full, as per actuals. The requirement of the universities, however was much more because:

a) the annual increment on salary is about 3-4% every year;
b) the increments and two DA instalments for January and July, 1992 announced by the government in July 1992, equalled to about. 14% of the salary component. This was much more than what UGC had projected earlier on the basis of the size of earlier DA instalments;
c) in addition to the salary component, the maintenance grant includes provision for non-salary components like maintenance of buildings, roads, water and electricity charges, subscription to journals, consumables and chemicals in laboratories. Inflationary expenditure on these items increased by almost 10-15% every year and in fact, in respect of imported equipment and journals the increase was as high as 100-200% compared to 1989-90 figures. The increase of 5% provided by UGC was inadequate to meet the expenditure of these items.

## Problems and Issues

The present system of financial assistance to the universities is decades old. While there has been profound changes in recent times with regard to various aspects of management and financial environment, assistance to universities and their internal management have so far not undergone any substantial structural reform or change.

For instance, the fee structure in most of the universities has not changed during the last 40-50 years. Though reliable data is not readily available, during the 1950s the tuition fees accounted for about 15-20% of the total expenditure of a higher educational institution. But today, tuition fees amount to only 2-3% of the total recurring expenditure.

Similarly, no uniform norms have beenevolved about the ratio which should be maintained between the teachers and students and between teachers and non-teaching staff. Different viewpoints are expressed by different universities and colleges for the maintenance of ratio of students to teachers and teachers to non-teaching staff.

Development grants (Plan grants) are intended to facilitate expansion and diversification of activities in the universities. They are not intended to supplement the requirements under maintenance (non-plan) grant. Considering the restrictive nature of maintenance grants, the universities have depended mainly on plan grants for their development. In the nature of' things, the Plan grants have not been designed to partly absorb the cuts in the non plan grants. Nor are these grants large enough to provide relief for the impact caused by cuts in the non plan grants.

Under these circumstances the question of adequacy of maintenance grant has become critical. At the same time the entire approach to the sanction of maintenance and development grants merits reconsideration in the light. of developments narrated above.

The whole question of funding Central Universities requires a fresh look. It has to be a comprehensive review. The funding of a university must have a direct relationship to its objectives and should be designed to promote quality, efficiency, autonomy, accountability and relevance. The Committee endeavours to propose measures to facilitate the fulfillment of these objectives.

## Role of Government in Financing Higher Education

It is necessary to have a clear perception of the role of the state in financing higher education in our country as a whole and financing of the central universities, in particular.

There is a popular impression that in many countries higher education sector is relatively self-sufficient, that is, it does not have to depend on either the state support or support from outside funding agencies. This, however, is not borne out, by actual situation as prevailing in various parts of the world today. Table- III.1 shows that higher education institutions depend on public funds and other outside incomes to a much large extent. Even in the well known private universities and institutions in the United States, the share of fees is less than 40% and in public institutions it is around 15%. In British universities it is less than 14% and in France the corresponding figure is less than 5% of the total income of the institutions. However, global trend is increasingly to make institutions of higher education be dependent on a larger share from fees and sales of services both to students and to other users, such as industry and government.

All over the world the state makes substantial funding for higher education. But the states increasingly feel that equity and social justice can be ensured better through direct support of students through scholarships and grants. Similarly, accountability and pursuit of national priorities in higher education and research are seen to be secured more through contractual agreements with institutions and through selected programmes and specific projects rather than through open-ended subsidies to institutions.

The Indian attitude towards educational development has been influenced by our perception of the role of higher education. The establishment of the Banaras Hindu and Aligarh Muslim Universities has a national significance which has been influenced by our freedom struggle to establish an Indian identity in the sphere of higher education. The establishment of the central universities is unique Indian experiment influenced by the federal character of the state polity emphasising regional linkages, the need to preserve and promote national integration and achievement of quality performance comparable to international standards.

In the past, we viewed the development of each sector of education in parts, but after the Education Commission (1964-66) we began to view education in totality, the different sectors fitting into a common pattern. This holistic view is duly reflected in the National Policy on Education (1986).

The growth and development of higher education sector has been viewed by Indian policy makers and planners from the very early times as not merely an effort to establish India's cultural identity on the international scene but also as a means to enhance the quality and productive capacity of our manpower. It is perceived also as a crucial input in our efforts to achieve self reliance and autonomy in many frontal areas of strategic activity.

The success of these are seen to-day in the advancements made in many areas, such as: Food and Agriculture, Nuclear Science, Space Science and Technology, Computer Development, etc., which are of vital importance for the scientific and technological development of the country. It would be unfortunate if in the present debate on allocation of resources between sectors of education, this perception of the crucial role and importance of higher education is lost sight of.

There is no denying, that while primary education is fundamental to the nation, higher education determines its economic and technological progress. While it is mandatory that the nation achieves universal elementary education and total literacy, at the same time it cannot afford to neglect and relegate to a neglected position our quest to achieve global standards in higher education. The Committee deprecates the tendency which views education in a truncated fashion and sets one sector against another. The advancement of quality primary and secondary education itself depends upon the quality of higher education. Equity and social justice demand that the newly emerging beneficiaries from the secondary education sector, who increasingly represent vulnerable groups, are able to afford an access to higher education. In a democracy broad based education will promote expectations and ambitions which must be supported by access to higher education.

Broadly putting it, the Committee has viewed the role of higher education :

i. as an essential input- for meeting the manpower requirement for important and crucial areas of national development and for the integral pail of national effort at human resources development;

ii. as a critical input to ensure social justice and equity for providing upward mobility and access to higher levels of economic and social activities fortune weaker sections; and

iii. as an important input for improving the quality of life by making higher levels of knowledge available to a wider base of population and for preserving our cultural heritage.

Viewed in this context the role of higher education will continue to be a very important element of national endeavour and will fully justify support, and intervention by the State.

## Role of Central Universities

We will now consider the role of central universities against this background. The central universities are a special feature of our federal system and represent the response of that, system on a national level to many different, cultural and intellectual aspirations of Indian society. Not all our central universities fit into a common pattern. For example, the Banaras Hindu and Aligarh Muslim Universities have strong foundations rooted in our national and cultural traditions and represent a particular stage of development, in our national aspiration. The Delhi University was largely designed to cater to the needs of a capital region with its cosmopolitan character. And it was chosen to fulfil the twin role of providing higher education as per the model and demands of the state policy and, at the same time, develop high traditions of scholarship at the national and international levels. Jawaharlal Nehru University was aimed at promoting the ideals for which Nehru stood for and was designed as a unitary university to promote national integration, social justice, secularism, democratic way of life, international understanding and scientific approach to the problems of society. Visva Bharati was to attain the objectives set out by the institution founded by Rabindranath Tagore. The North Eastern Hill University aimed to pay special attention for the improvement of the social and economic conditions and welfare of the people of hill areas of the North Eastern region, and for the promotion of their intellectual, academic and cultural advancement. The objectives of the University of Hyderabad lay in the circumstances of its creation at the time of' the formation of the State of Andhra Pradesh. The Pondicherry University has been setup very recently fort tie intellectual and cultural development of the region with particular reference to the French language and culture of the area.

All central universities have certain common features of being centres of excellence and promoters of national integration- They all strive to maintain an all-India character in regard to recruitment of' staff and admission of students. They are all expected to function as centres of innovation for programmes and courses which may be beyond the reach of state universities. The Committee would like to refer to the reports of the various committees in the past in regard to the central universities, but restrict to giving only the following extract from the Report of Banaras Hindu University Enquiry Committee, 1969.

Central universities should not be regarded as central Merely because the Central Government finance them. They should have distinguished character of their own. They should seek to supplement and not always duplicate the facilities and achievement of the state universities. In the case of central universities, their role and responsibility is clear-it is to function effectively and vigorously on an all India basis to help build up a corporate intellectual life in the country to further national integration. Broadly speaking the central universities should provide courses which need facilities on demands beyond the reach of the state universities or for which the demands would be too small if limited only to the requirement. of an individual state. The central universities should regard it as a part of their special function to contribute towards the removal of imbalances from the academic life of our country, and take suitable action to help deserving students from the educationally backward areas. In order to achieve this object. such facilities as may be necessary should be made available to the central universities." The Committee feels that in determining grants to central universities one must- bear in mind the specific goals assigned to them by their founders or by historical circumstances, of their national character and of being the pioneering and model institutions for the whole country.

## Present Pattern of Funding Universities

Budgeting in India distinguishes two sets of activities, one as non-plan or non development or maintenance budget, and the other as plan or development budget. In actual practice, the difference is more procedural than real, although conceptually the plan budget provides for growth, diversification and innovation while the non-plan takes care of sustenance of the ongoing system. All activities of recurring nature taken up during a five year plan period are classified as non plan or maintenance activities after the plan is over. Thus the non plan or maintenance budgets grow in size after successive five year plans are completed the commitment is transferred to non plan part of the budget. The funding of central universities also reflects this practice. Support to the universities is classified separately as maintenance or non plan, and development or plan grants.

**Authority**

Section 12(b) of the UGC Act authorises the UGC to allocate and disburse out of the fund of the Commission, grants to universities, established or incorporated by or under a Central Act, for the maintenance and development of such Universities. This authorises the Commission to allocate and disburse maintenance grants to the central universities.

**Policy**

Eac[illegible] [illegible]ntral university and institution deemed to be u[illegible] has a Finance Committee comprising [illegible]s of the university, local educationists and a [illegible]rom UGC and the Ministry of Human [illegible]ment, (usually the Financial Adviser). [illegible]ttee is a statutory authority in the [illegible]ded by the Vice Chancellor, which [illegible]ncerns, is responsible for the [illegible]oth for its maintenance and [illegible] ongoing activities of the [illegible]es covered under the current five year plan and projects funded from sources outside the development plan, come under the maintenance expenditure. This is also termed as the non plan budget which includes salary and allowances of teaching and non teaching staff, and expenditure on libraries, laboratories, workshops, services, estate and general infrastructural maintenance.

The prevailing practice is that all items of recurring expenditure incurred during a current plan period and sanctioned by the UGC on the basis of approved norms is included at the end of the plan period in the maintenance or non plan sector on the same norms and patterns. The non plan expenditure, therefore, evolves out of the pattern and system which is based on the plan programmes approved for the university. There are no separate norms and patterns of providing maintenance grants apart from this accepted practice. The maintenance grant budget for every year provides for an increased outlay on the various items which takes into consideration the annual incremental impact of salaries, DA and wage increases and any increase in tariff rates relating to other service charges and a general provision for inflation.

We quote from the Report of the Committee to Enquire into the Working of the Central Universities (Madhuri Shah Committee) the exact position.

"Maintenance Grants 5.207 For quite a long time the maintenance grants to central universities had been paid on the basis of the Block Grant System fixed for a specified period. With the rapid development of the central universities, and in the absence of well defined norms for proper assessments and fixation of levels of expenditure for different items, it had been decided that the block grant for the year be determined by the UGC on the basis of an examination of the Budget Estimates received from the universities. This had become all the more necessary because of several additional Dearness Allowance instalments announced by the Government, and the steep increase in prices of books, journals and other items. While fixing the annual Block grant for particular year, the following conditions were also prescribed:

(a) The opening balance of a university out of the block grant fixed for a particular year would be carried forward to the succeeding year, which would however be adjusted by the end of the third year.

(b) To ensure that expenditure is incurred within the total resources available, in the best interest of its academic function, the following guidelines were prescribed for reappropriation within the Budget Estimates prepared on the basis of the grant payable and the resources generated from its own income:

   (i) No appropriations may be made which would have the effect of augmenting the provision for salaries and allowances.

   (ii) The provision made in the estimates for scholarships and fellowships should not be reapropriated to any other head, and

   (iii) If there are any savings in Non-Plan recurring budget, they could be utilised for meeting critical academic non- recurring requirements.

The above guidelines were prescribed in addition to the following instructions issued earlier in relation to the payment of Block grants for which prior approval of the UGC was a condition.

(i) Creation of posts with a maximum of the scale of pay beyond Rs. 1000.00 per month,

(ii) Revision of existing scales of pay,

(iii) Upgrading of posts,

(iv) Granting of more than five increments above the initial salary at the time of appointment, and

(v) Sanctioning/payment of unusual allowances other than those approved by the Commission."

The presence in the Finance Committee of the university of a UGC representative and the representative of Department of Education who is usually the Financial Adviser (who also has a link with the Ministry of Finance), is crucial for the deliberations. They ensure that the proposals included in a budget are in accordance with the guidelines on the subject. The proposals are usually finalised after detailed and extensive discussions which are then forwarded to the UGC. As the representative of UGC sits on the Finance Committee, UGC does not go into further detailed scrutiny. The proposals received from the university are consolidated and presented to the government for sanction of appropriate funds for the maintenance grant in the budget. Usually, the requirements of maintenance grants are subject to negotiations between the UGC and the Ministry of Human Resource Development and also Planning Commission. It has been the experience of UGC that excepting in cases where steep rises are noticed in respect of individual items, the government accepts the proposals of UGC with little modifications.

In 1991, as a result of budgetary crisis, a IO% cut was imposed on the departments of government and autonomous institutions. This resulted in a cut in the maintenance grant, sanctioned to UGC for 1991 and UGC had therefore to excercise cuts in the then non plan grants to the universities. In 1991-92, maintenance grant was sanctioned at 1990-91 level because of continuing difficult resource position, with there suit that normal incremental expenditures involved in the maintenance costs could not be sanctioned. The UGC, however, had to provide partial relief to the universities by diverting plan funds. While the Government ultimately provided some relief, there had to be diversion of plan funds to meet the crisis. During the financial year 1992-93, the reduction in the maintenance grant resulted in financial hardship for the universities. The Government decided that the half-yearly increase of DA, increase in conveyance, overtime allowances. daily wages, bonus and other benefits extended to Central Government employees which are applicable to autonomous institutions would not. be supported by supplementary grants and would have to be managed from within the maintenance. grant. The fixation of the maintenance grant at levels lower than the predicted levels and the discontinuance of support for the periodical increase in DA and other benefits resulted in heavy deficits in the non plan funds of the universities. The net impact of these cuts in the maintenance grants resulted in diversion of very slender resources, available with the universities in, the form of maintenance grant for support to libraries, equipment and essential academic activities, to meet the commitments on payments such as salaries, remuneration and service charges etc. This resulted in adverse impact on the quality of the academic programmes.

Since a large portion of maintenance grant covers salary and allowances of the staff a ten per cent cut on the maintenance grants, results in large cuts on the academic items which constitute a relatively smaller proportion of the maintenance grant.

The pattern of maintenance expenditure in central universities has become complex because of the nature and development of these universities. In their earlier stages only basic infrastructural expenditures incurred by the universities during a plan period were reflected in the maintenance budget, but with the development of universities' academic, research and other programmes, many of their other activities also came under maintenance expenditure.

Universities under-take research and constancy projects for various agencies,departments and organisations of the government. These projects demand employment of staff, purchase of equipment and in many cases construction of buildings. When these projects are completed, the equipment is taken over by the universities. Some of these are costly equipments and require maintenance for subsequent use. While the staff employed on the project is usually retrenched, core staff required for maintenance and functioning of the equipment is retained. Similarly buildings require maintenance costs for their upkeep and utilisation. Sometimes projects offered by sister organisations and departments of government to the universities are terminated midway and the control of the projects transferred to the universities with the liabilities for maintaining the equipment ,and core staff. This again leads to additional burden on the maintenance budget of the universities.

It has been reported that for many plan programmes approved by the University Grants Commission, even minimum staff required is not provided and in some cases programmes are sanctioned on the undertaking that universities would manage them with their own resources. The universities in these cases have no alternative but to create positions within their power of delegation and operate these programmes with the support of maintenance grant.

The nature of the system of appointment of staff in the universities and conditions regarding job security in regard to the academic and non academic staff in various departments, make it difficult for universities to dispense with their services when not required or shift them to new set of activities. The net, result has been that the staff is retained causing heavy burden on the maintenance expenditure. In many cases staff on research projects retained on humanitarian grounds or on court orders becomes an additional load on the university budget.

The effect of all this has resulted in steep increase in the maintenance grants of the universities year after year. The increase in salary, DA and other allowances results in an increase by 14% to 15% annually in the maintenance grant. Besides these, increase in tariffs, costs and prices is estimated at about 10%. The increase in the cost of maintenance of equipment, particularly imported equipment, and purchase of journals is very high. The maintenance expenditure has gone up further at comparatively high rates in recent years. To understand maintenance grant, the special problems affecting different universities has to be kept in mind. In the case of many universities, maintenance of buildings more than ten years old and replacement of equipment which has out-lasted its normal life require special support.

The internal administrative and financial management of the university systems has undergone little change to adapt itself to the challenges offered by changes externally. The fee structure in most universities has not changed in the last 40 to 50 years. The practice of adjusting income generated internally by the university against the non plan grant due to them and also setting off the savings towards grants has resulted in discouraging the universities from generating additional resources and promoting internal efficiency. In fact the existing system has led to practices in which an inefficient institution secures greater support. And because of wide variations in the costs and in the nature of the institutions, it has not been possible to evolve common norms for expenditure for the various activities in the maintenance grant. Considering the incremental nature of the grant, there has been no effort to link activities to financial norms. The result has been the presence of considerable measure of subjectivity in the determination and operation of maintenance grant.

It is clear from above that maintenance grants by their very nature increase annually and are negotiated by the universities with the UGC and UGC in turn negotiates the same with the Government. As in the case of all incremental grants, there were no problems till the recent crisis in the budget allocations. In the nature of things, the procedure and method of sanctioning maintenance grants has provided little scope for exercising economy, promotion of efficiency and developing savings. As the pattern of grants sanctioned to each university is based on negotiations, common pattern of sanction has not been evolved. It has not been possible to compare per student, per department, per activity, outlays within the universities and among the central universities in absence of application of unit cost system.

### Utilisation of the Maintenance Grants

The utilisation of the maintenance grants has not posed problems to the universities. While there may have been individual cases of failure to utilise the grants in certain activities, by and large, maintenance grants have been fully utilised as they generally cover ongoing activities. The procedure for grants also provides for adjustment of unutilised grant in the grant for the succeeding year.

Development grants, also called plan grants, are sanctioned to universities for expansion of their activities and for developing new programmes. The support covers expenditure on staff, buildings, equipment, libraries and other related activities. As the universities develop, the size of their maintenance grants becomes larger and larger but the size of development grant does not grow proportionately. The development grants have comparatively less recurring items of expenditure than non plan grants.

In the case of development grants, UGC formulates its proposals for the plan period which includes plan programmes of central universities and presents them to government. These programmes are based on UGC's analysis of past performance of central universities, their lines of development and needs. UGC also estimates the availability of resources based on allocation made in the past. These proposals are then finalised after detailed discussions between UGC and Government. They then go before the Planning Commission for final allocation. The experience of UGC has been that the plans formulated by them are considerably trimmed by the Planning

Commission. After the allocation of plan funds, the UGC tentatively apportions the funds among central universities and between the various other schemes of the Commission. After indicating the provisional allocation of funds to each of the central university, UGC calls for detailed proposals. The earlier practice was to send visiting Committees to these universities for finalization of the Five Year Plan of universities. This procedure was time consuming and resulted in delayed formulation of plans. Later the system was changed. Now the plans are scrutinised by expert committees at the Head Quarters after holding discussions with universities. While initially indicated allocations could be modified in this process; changes are marginal.

It can be seen that the development grant is essentially in the nature of ad-hoc grant provided once in five years by UGC to the central universities on the basis of negotiations. Undoubtedly, there would be elements in these programmes which are based on standard costs and pattern. The UGC while providing grants to individual central universities takes into consideration their special needs and circumstances. These do not constitute any common pattern and this remains largely an ad-hoc exercise.

After approval of the five year plans of the universities the UGC determines their annual plan programmes and the releases of funds.

We find that the grants for central universities are considered under the following broad heads: general development, medical colleges and hospitals, campus development, Delhi college buildings and new central universities. Apart from this the central universities having engineering/ technology departments receive separate grant available to UGC from AICTE. The categorisation has perhaps been necessitated by developments in the central universities and pressures which have emanated from different sectors. It appears that this will require revision in future so that there is a measure of uniformity in regard to the pattern of assistance to be provided to the central universities.

We would like to quote from the report of the Madhuri Shah Committee regarding the mode of preparation of development plans of central universities.

### Income Generation by Universities

While UGC provides overwhelming support to the universities, income from fees and other sources is very limited. The Committee is of the view that while government /UGC may continue to be the major funding agency, the universities must generate internal resources which should be sizeable in course of time.

#### Fees

As there has been no increase in the fees for decades, income from fees has now become an insignificant part of the total income as well as expenditure of the universities. There is also a historical background to this issue. The universities are regarded in India largely as noble and charitable ventures, as an essential part of the welfare programme, with little concern for cost effectiveness and income generation. Consequently, over a period of time, universities are regarded as cost free activities. Most of university services are provided free and in many cases even the costs are not recovered. The beneficiaries, apart from the students include a wide variety of users including the public. They have also view the universities in this light.

The fees for prospectus, admission, magazine, examination and such other activities hardly recover their costs. The fees for library, laboratories, games and similar other activities have been designed in a manner that they are not self-supportive or support the activities in any significant manner. The hostels have been subsidised to an extent that even charges on consumables like electricity and water are not recovered. While electricity charges are going up, there is no monitoring of its use in most of the universities. The consumers are not identified nor billed, where necessary. Electrical appliances including heaters, often unauthorised, are in extensive use but electricity utilised to operate these are not paid for by a large number of consumers. The municipal services extended to the universities are also not paid for. There are many other aspects of university activities where subsidy have been built in, which has made permanent inroads into the budgets of universities. Universities, in many cases, are in a position to let out their facilities and services and generate income and they can design and operate courses of studies to mobilise additional resources. But, over a period of time, the need to generate their own income seems to have lost its emphasis.

One of the major deterrent, universities encounter in their efforts to generate income is the practice that any earnings so mobilised is adjusted against payable maintenance grants. This also retards universities' measures to effect savings. Resources saved are also adjusted against the maintenance grants, thus robbing these efforts of any impact. The Committee strongly recommends that universities must be allowed to retain additional earnings and savings raised by their own efforts and these should not be adjusted against their maintenance grants. The income so generated may be kept in a separate fund and utilised by the universities for furtherance of the objectives of the universities. By savings, the Committee imply resources economised by efficient management. UGC should also develop a mechanism of providing an appropriate incentive grant in the nature of a matching grant to encourage universities to explore and mobilise additional resources.

**Tuition Fees**

Tuition fees have not been revised for a very long time in spite of the costs of all services going up. Tuition fees may be revised upwards with immediate effect and may be periodically adjusted, keeping in view the rate of inflation. A mechanism must also be evolved by universities where by these fees are regularly and periodically adjusted to the rise in the costs. The revised fees should be made applicable to the new entrants to a course of study. The revision of fees must be related in a meaningful manner to the recurring cost of the course of study and employment opportunities offered by the course, that is, that the tuition fees will be different within an university for different courses of study.

**Other Fees**

The universities must also review all other fee structures.

Fees for admission, examination etc. must be so charged as to recover the recurring costs on the operations. Fees for library, laboratory, sports and similar other facilities must be revised upwards to recover a significant part of the recurring cost.

*Hostel and Mess fees:* These are not only heavily subsidised but some of the items of subsidy, such as use of electricity, water, etc. are often not even quantified. These fees should be revised with immediate effect to meet all the actual recurring costs and in due course of time part of the capital cost as well. The Committee recognises that this is a sensitive issue and recommends that the student community should be involved in the discussions to raise resources where their interests are affected.

*Municipal, Civil and other Services*: The universities must review all their municipal, civil and other services extended to individual members of the university in their personal capacity and charge appropriately to recover costs. These may include cost of transport, phone, postage and stationery, typing, computing, photocopying, etc.

**Student Support**

There is a genuine apprehension that raising of fees and removal of subsidies may result in denial of access to sections of students who are not in a position to meet the increased rates.

**Other Sources of Incomes**

The universities may initiate measures to rent out their facilities such as auditoria, class rooms, computer services, playgrounds, guest houses, hostels, lawns, messes, etc. This should be, done judiciously and without any detriment to the academic interest and atmosphere of the institution.

Universities should encourage individual departments to design programmes and short-term courses of study, etc. to generate resources without any adverse impact on their main academic activities. These units should be allowed to retain a substantial portion of the income so earned for supporting their main academic activities.

The universities may accept endowments, contributions. large investments, etc. to support and promote their academic activities and infrastructural development.

The universities should take concrete steps to seek support for research programmes and offer constancy services to a wide spectrum of sponsors, including departments of central and state governments, public and private sectors, industries and other bodies. These project proposals should always incorporate specific allocations for reimbursement for staff, facilities and infrastructure support. This must be used to strengthen the basic infrastructure of the universities.

The universities may constitute appropriate consultative mechanisms within the system to plan and operationalise measures for mobilising resources. This must be viewed as an effort by the institution and its members as a whole and not a function of the management alone and hence should include representatives of faculty, students, alumni, and nonteaching staff.

The UGC may constitute in consultation with the Government appropriate organisational mechanism to facilitate this and must extend full support to the universities. Universities which initiate and implement these measures must be given not only support and encouragement but positive incentives in the form of supporting grants, etc.

Each university should take the initiative to organise and set up an effective Alumni Association with a view to mobilising resources from a over the country and abroad. An Advisory Body consisting of the well wishers of the university may be set up to pursue action in this regard.

Section 12 A of the UGC Act 1956, empowers UGC to prescribe fees and indicate the scale of fees also. This power has never been excercised. Discussions with Vice-Chancellors, and other authorities showed that they are receptive to these proposals. However, keeping in view the background and responses in the past towards efforts to raise fees, they have indicated that the initiative and approval should come from UGC and higher authorities.

# 10

# Policy and Legalisation for Educational Development

The Indian Constitution which came into force on 26 January, 1950 provides the basic legal framework for governance. India, a union of states, is a parliamentary democracy with a federal structure. It comprises 25 states and 7 union territories. The Constitution makes an elaborate distribution of governmental powers-legislative, administrative and financial-between the Union and the states. The seventh schedule to the Constitution has three lists: the Union List with 97 entries in respect of which the Parliament has exclusive powers to legislate; the State List with 66 entries in respect of which the state legislatures have similar powers and the Concurrent List with 47 entries where the Parliament as well as state legislatures have concurrent legislative powers. Should there be a state as well as a central legislation on a matter enumerated in the Concurrent List, the central legislation would prevail unless the state legislation was reserved for the prior consideration of the President and had received such an assent.

Normally the executive powers of the Union* and the states are co-extensive with their legislative powers. However, in respect of matters in the Concurrent List the executive powers remain with the states, unless the

Constitution or Parliament, by law, expressly provides otherwise. Though the Constitution creates a dual polity based on divided governmental powers, the division is not water tight; it is flexible. Apart from the large concurrent sphere several entries in the State List have interface with the Union List. Adequate mechanisms exist for sharing of resources and responsibilities, between the Union and the states, for harmonious exercise of their powers in the larger national interest.

Substantial resources devolve from the Centre to the states through institutional mechanisms like the Finance Commission and the Planning Commission, about 60 per cent of the state budgets as a whole are financed by central devolution. Since the first five year plan, which was launched in 1951, planning has emerged as a vital function of the government. The salience of Indian planning lies in that it operates in a democratic polity and within a mixed economy. The states have considerable freedom for planning. Therefore a major challenge in national planning is to reconcile the planning priorities of states with the national plan frame. The National Development Council (NDC), set up in April 1952, imparts a national character to the entire process of planning. The NDC consists of the Prime Minister, all ministers of the Union cabinet, the chief ministers of states and members of the Planning Commission. It is assigned the three important functions of reviewing the working of the national plan from time to time, of considering important questions of social and economic policy affecting national development, and recommending measures for the achievement of aims and targets set out in the national plan.

In individual sectors similar bodies exist in which a national consensus is forged and emerging frictions resolved through an interactive and interaction process involving the Centre and the states. Thus, the Central

Advisory Board of Education (CABE), set up in 1935, has been playing a lead role in the evolution and monitoring of educational policies and programmes, the most notable of which are the "Plan of Post-War Educational Development in India" (1944), popularly known as the Sargent Report, the National Policy on Education 1968, National Policy on Education (NPE) 1986, Programme of Action (POA) 1986, the revision in 1992 of NPE and POA. It would, therefore, be a truism to say that if one abstracts the din and bustle that is a concomitant of a vibrant democracy the Indian polity is best characterised as one of co-operative federalism.

Within a state there is generally a four-tier structure of administration: region/zone/range, district, taluka/block/mandal, and villages. Urban areas have local bodies such as municipalities and municipal corporations. Traditionally, the district has been the most important unit of administration and planning. Many states had introduced the system of Panchayati raj, generally a three-tier structure of local self government in rural areas at the village, block and district levels. These structures are creatures of state legislations; their patterns, powers and functions vary widely. Two landmark constitutional amendments were recently enacted which bestowed on the local bodies in rural and urban areas constitutional status and specific functions including primary education. These amendments are expected to promote decentralised management of primary education.

## EDUCATION IN INDIAN CONSTITUTION

Several articles in the Constitution of India bring into focus the general principles governing educational development in the country. These articles are rooted in India's struggle for independence. Basic education was one of the important goals of the freedom struggle and Mahatma Gandhi, even while leading the epic struggle against colonial power, evolved an alternative education system. The Directive Principle contained in Article 45 of the Constitution enjoins that "the State shall endeavour to provide, within a period of -ten years from the commencement of this Constitution, for free and compulsory education for all children until they complete the age of fourteen years." The expression "the State" which occurs in this Article is defined in Article 112 to include the government and parliament of India, the government and the legislature of each of the states and all local or other authorities within the territory of India or under the control of the government of India.

Article 29(1) of the Constitution provides that "any section of the citizens residing in the territory of India or any part thereof having a distinct language, script or culture of its own shall have the right to conserve the same." Article 29(2) lays down that "no citizen shall be denied admission into any educational, institution maintained by the State or receiving aid out of State funds on grounds only of religion, race, caste, language or any of them."

Article 30(1) enjoins that "all minorities, whether based on religion or language, shall have the right to establish and administer educational institutions of their choice," while Article 30(2) lays down that "the State shall not, in granting aid to educational institutions, discriminate against any educational institution on the ground that it is under the management of a minority, whether based on religion or language." Article 350-A lays down that "it shall be the endeavour of every State and of every local authority within the State to provide adequate facilities for instruction in the mother-tongue at the primary stage of education to children belonging to linguistic minority groups."

Special care of the economic and educational interests of the under-privileged sections of the population is laid down as ail obligation for the State under Article 46. As per this Article, "the State shall promote with special care the educational and economic interests of the weaker sections of the people, and, in particular, of the Scheduled Castes and the Scheduled Tribes. and shall protect them from social injustice and all forms of exploitation."

Till the 42nd amendment of the Constitutional education was in the State List except for certain specified items in the Union List like determination of standards in institutions for higher education or research, establishment and maintenance of central universities as well as specified institutions for scientific or technical education and research. The objective of incorporating education in the Concurrent List was to facilitate evolution of all-India policies in the field of education. Though the parliament was thereby empowered with the authority to legislate on education the Centre has been relying on a consensual process to promote educational development. The concept of concurrency was given an operational meaning by the National Policy on Education (NPE) 1986. This policy envisages concurrency as a "meaningful partnership between the Centre and the States" and placed on the Union Government a larger responsibility in regard to the national and integrative character of education, quality and standards, manpower planning, research and advanced study, and international aspect of education, culture and human resource development.

The Union government has also set up a number of resource institutions at the national level. The National Council of Educational Research and Training (NCERT) has been assisting and advising the Union and state governments in the formulation and implementation of policies and programmes in the fields of school and teacher education. It maintains a national network of field advisors and four Regional Colleges of Education. The National Institute of Educational Planning and Administration (NIEPA) assists and advises the Union and states in the areas of educational planning and administration in the country. Apart from research, it is also engaged in training senior education officials of the Centre and the states.

The Central Institute of Indian Languages (CIIL), Central Institute of English and Foreign Languages (CIEFL), the Rashtriya Sanskrit Sansthan (National Institute of Sanskrit) and the Kendriya Hindi Sansthan (Central Institute of Hindi) are resource institutions for promoting the development of languages in the country.

## Organisation of Education System

Decisions regarding the organisation and structure of education are largely the concern of the states. Within the overall policy framework, each state independently determines the educational structures to be adopted.

As envisaged by NPE 1968, a broadly uniform educational pattern has emerged all over the country comprising ten years of school education followed by two years of higher secondary education and three years of education for obtaining the first degree. A child is normally admitted to class I at the age of six and is expected to complete class V at the age of +11 years, class VIII at the age of +14 years, class X at the age of +16 years and class XII at the age of +18 years.

Some variations can, however, still be found in the educational structure within the school stage. The primary and upper primary or middle stage together constitute the elementary stage. It has been envisaged that there should be a common structure for the elementary stage consisting of five years of primary schooling followed by three years of upper primary/

middle school education. However, in a few states the primary stage comprises classes I-IV followed by the upper primary stage comprising classes V-VII. The upper primary stage may be an independent unit or combined with primary or secondary stages of learning or both. Given the large number of children who do not participate in schools, non-formal education assumes significance. Non-formal education (NFE) focuses on out-of school children in the age group 9-14 years; two important components of NFE design are inbuilt flexibility and equivalence.

## EFA in the Indian Context

In the Indian context, Education for All (EFA) would imply:

(i) Expansion of early childhood care and development activities including family and communities, especially for poor, disadvantaged and children.

(ii) Universalisation of Elementary Education (UEE), viewed as a composite programme of access to elementary education for all children up to 14 years of age; universal participation fill they complete the elementary stage through formal or non-formal education programmes; and universal achievement at least of minimum levels of learning.

(iii) Drastic reduction in illiteracy, particularly in the 15-35 age group, bringing the literacy level in this age group at least to 80 per cent in each gender and for every identified disadvantaged group, ensuring that the levels of three R's are relevant to the living and working conditions of the people.

(iv) Provision of opportunities to maintain, use and upgrade their education, and provision of facilities for development of skills, to all persons who are functionally literate and those who have received primary education through formal and non-formal channels.

(v) Creation of necessary structure and setting in motion processes which would empower women and make education an instrument of women's equality.

(vi) Improving the content and process of education to better relate it to the environment, people's culture and with their living and 'working conditions, thereby enhancing their ability to learn and cope with problems of livelihood and environment.

## National Policy on Education (NPE), 1986

The NPE, 1986 is a land mark in the Indian education. Based on an in-depth review of the Indian educational system and evolved through a consensual process it provides a comprehensive framework to guide the development of education. The NPE was distinct in that it was followed by a detailed strategy of implementation, accompanied by the assignment of specific responsibilities and financial and organisational support, in the form of a Programme of Action (POA). The Policy and its POA were updated in 1992 through a similar consensual process involving all state governments, resource organisations and educationists.

The extant policy and its POA give unqualified priority to UEE, adult literacy and education for women's equality; this priority is reflected in the budget allocations during the current five year plan (1992-97). What the policy posits is a 'dual track' approach, desired to promote simultaneously adult literacy and primary education, with focus on girls, and disadvantaged groups. In the extant policy, there are several points of departure in the pursuit of EFA:

(i) The emphasis has shifted from enrolment per se to enrolment as well as retention and achievement. As the POA, 1986 put a crisply "enrolment by itself is of little importance if children do not continue beyond one year, many of them not seeing the school for more than a few days."

(ii) Taking a realistic view of the enormous task of achieving UEE in its entirety (access, retention as well as achievement), the NPE envisages that free and compulsory education of satisfactory quality should be provided to all children up to 14 years of age before the commencement of the twenty-first century.

(iii) The policy seeks to address the more difficult aspects of access. It was for the first time, in 1986, that an educational policy had admitted that the school would not reach all children, particularly millions of girls and working children whose participation in school system is thwarted by socioeconomic parameters. The policy called for a large and systematic programme of Non-Formal Education (NFE) as an integral component of the strategy to achieve UEE. NFE should have enough flexibility to enable the learners to learn at their own pace and at the same time would have quality comparable with formal education.

(iv) The policy postulates integration of the gender perspective in all aspects of the planning. There is a pronounced policy shift from an equalisation of educational opportunity to education for women's equality. The policy enjoins that the national education system should play a positive, interventionist role in the empowerment of women, foster the development of new values through redesigned curricula, textbooks, the training and orientation of teachers, decision-makers and administrators, and the active involvement of educational institutions. The removal of women's illiteracy and obstacles inhibiting their access to, and retention in, elementary education are given an overriding priority.

(v) UEE is contextual; contextuality entails -local area planning with disaggregated target-setting and decentralised participative planning. The focus has shifted from educationally backward states to educationally backward districts.

(vi) While financial resources are important and necessary they are not sufficient for achieving EFA. A host of measures, both on the supply side and the demand side, mobilisation of community support and enlisting NGOs need to supplement higher financial outlay.

(vii) The policy recognises that unattractive school environment, unsatisfactory condition. of buildings and insufficiency of instructional material function as demotivating factors for children and their parents. The policy, therefore, called for a drive for a substantial improvement of primary schools and provision of support services.

(viii) The NPE, 1986 commended the adoption at the primary stage of a child-centred and activity-based process of learning.

(ix) The NPE, 1986 and its POA postulate a large programme of restructuring of teacher education, pre-service as well as in-service.

(x) The total literacy campaigns with their unique social mobilisation, forging of a broad based alliance between the district administration, NGOs and social activists, and the innovative use of the confluence of culture and communication and the new pedagogy of improved pace and content of learning (PCL) with its inbuilt mechanism for evaluation of learning outcomes, are to be the main vehicle for promoting adult literacy.

(xi) The policy shifts from sectoral to a multisectoral approach with convergence of all developmental inputs; the resultant synergy is expected to improve the delivery of services and enhance the efficiency of resource utilisation. Thus in primary education convergence is sought between schooling, child services, nutrition and primary health care and other basic services. In non-formal education and adult literacy, convergence is sought between education and development, themes like population education, immunisation, nutrition and afforestation.

### STATE POLICIES

State policies closely follow the national policies as the states have been closely associated with the formulation of the NPE and its POA significant development of the 1992 review NPE and POA has been that states have undertaken to formulate state POAs harmonising the situational imperatives with the national policy framework. Several states have already come up with their own POAs. In the spirit of concurrency, states have been associated in tilt, formulation and implementation of national programmes like total literacy campaigns, operation blackboard, teacher education and the new district primary education programme. All the five year and annual plans of states have minimum needs component which includes adult literacy and elementary education. The release of central assistance to state plans is linked with the performance in the minimum needs component.

Incentive schemes of different kinds are already a well established feature of elementary school system. These are almost entirely in the state sector. The coverage as revealed by the Fifth All India Educational Survey (1986) indicated that of about 0.53 million primary schools, no less than about 0.15 million schools were providing mid-day meals of some sort to about 13.6 million children. About 0.25 million schools were providing free uniforms to 11 million children and about 20.2 million children were getting free textbooks in 0.35 million schools. At the upper primary level, as many as about 10.3 million children were getting free books, 4.3 million were getting free uniforms and 7.1 million some sort of mid-day meal. Education is free for girls up to class XII. Other incentives, including scholarships, also exist in different places.

## STATUS OF EFA

At the time of Independence, India inherited a system of education which was not only quantitatively small but also characterised by the persistence of large intraand inter-regional as well as structural imbalances. Only 14 per cent of the population was literate and only one child out of three had been enrolled in primary school. The low levels of participation and literacy were aggravated by acute regional and gender disparities. As education is vitally linked with the totality of the development processeducation being "the basic tool for the development of consciousness and reconstitution of society," in the words of Mahatma Gandhi-the reform and restructuring of educational system was recognised as an important area of state intervention.

The need for a literate population and universal education for all children in the age group of 6-14 was recognised as a crucial input for nation building and was given due consideration in the Constitution as well as in successive five year plans. This has resulted in a manifold increase of spatial spread, infrastructural facilities, increased coverage of various social groups; but the goal of providing basic education to all continues to be elusive.

**Demographic Composition**

India is the second most populous country in the world with a population of 846.3 million in 1991, accounting for 16 per cent of the world population and just 2.4 per cent of the total land area of earth. Its share in total world population has increased from 15.2 per cent in 1981 to 16 per cent in 1991.

The year 1921 is a year of the great divide in the demographic history of India when mortality started to decline leading to acceleration in the rate of population growth. During the next three decades (1921-51) the rate of population growth continued at a level of over one per cent per annum. The slight dip in the growth rate in 1941-51 partly reflects the Bengal famine of 1942-43 and dislocation,-, due to the partition of India in 1947. After independence the rate of population growth accelerated considerably because of extension of public health services. The growth rate was at its peak in the period 1961-81 with the population growing at a rate of 2.2 per cent per annum. The decade 1971-81 is a turning point in that fertility started declining and continued to decline every year thereafter. during the decade 1981-91 the rate of population growth declined from 2.2 per cent per annum to 2.1 per cent.

Though the decline is a welcome sign the pace of decline is not enough to ease the relent less pressure on social services. The population is expected to cross the one billion mark, by 2001. There are sharp regional variations. Another feature of the growth of population in India is the absolute size of its increase in the decade of 1981-91 India added 163 million people: an incremental population almost equal to the population of Indonesia, the fifth most populous country of the world. India adds every year a population almost equal to that of Australia. Given a population increase of this magnitude it would be difficult to provide even rudimentary social services despite best efforts.

The projected population in the age group Of 6-14 years, the target group for universal elementary education, as on 1st March 1991 was 153 million constituting about 18 per cent of the total population. Of this 51 per cent were boys and 49 per cent were girls. The projected population in the age group of 15-35 years, the target group of adult literacy programmes, is 254 million, constituting about 30 per cent of population in 1991. Empirical evidence establishes a strong negative correlation between female literacy on the one hand, and fertility and infant mortality rates on the other.

About one-third of the population in the age group of 0-6 years is concentrated in 125 districts which have only 13.5 per cent of the female literates in India. The higher the educational level of women, the lower is the total fertility rate and the lower the number of death by age 2 per 100 live births, Analysis of data for 15 major states accounting for 96 per cent of the total population of the country shows that female literacy and education are positively associated with population growth rates. Given this correlation, the National Family Welfare Programme as well as the total literacy campaign incorporate the cardinal principle that fertility regulation cannot be a matter of mere promotion of contraception but has to strongly promote the socio-economic factors which strongly influence fertility behaviour such as female literacy and education.

**Literacy**

In the post-Independent period literacy rate has shown substantial increase from about 18.33 per cent (of population aged 5 and above) in. 1951 to 52.19 per cent (of population aged seven and above) in 1991. The female literacy has also increased substantially from 8.86 per cent (of population aged 5 and above) in 1951 to 39.19 per cent (of population aged 7 and above) in 1991. The decennial census of 1991 had augured well on many accounts. For the first time the number of literate persons was higher than the number of illiterates. During the decade 1981-91 female literacy increased at a faster pace (9.6 per cent) than the male literacy (7.5 per cent).

The index of gender equality, i.e., the proportion of ratio of female literates to total literates ratio of female population to total population which ideally should be 1.00, improved from 68.31 in 1981 to 75.61 in 1991. The rural-urban differential in male literacy has declined from 27.1 per cent in 1981 to 26.3 per cent 1991. However, it is a matter of concern that the rural-urban difference in female literacy has increased from 34.6 per cent in 1981 to 35.1 per cent in 1991. Roughly, the literacy rate for women is at the same level as that of men three decades ago. There are wide regional variations ranging from near universal literacy in Kerala to 20.84 per cent female literacy in Rajasthan. At a more disaggregated level, the female literacy varies from 7.68 per cent in Barmer district of Rajasthan to 94.00 per cent in Kottayam district of Kerala.

The regional concentration of female illiteracy is highlighted by the fact that 155 of the 247 districts whose female literacy rates art, lower than the national average, are situated in the four states of Uttar Pradesh (with 51 Such districts), Madhya Pradesh (38), Rajasthan (27) and Bihar (39). Removal of gender and regional disparities is central to the efforts to achieve universal literacy.

The literacy rate among SCs has increased from 21.38 per cent in 1981 to 37.41 per cent in 1991; correspondingly' the literacy rate among ST's has increased from 16.35 per cent in 1981 to 29.60 per cent in 1991. In spite of these increases the levels of literacy among SCs and ST's are distinctly lower than that of the population as a whole (52.19 per cent). The gender disparity is conspicous among SCs and STs also.

**Access and Participation Facilities**

There has been a spectacular increase in elementary education during the post-Independence period. The elementary education system of India has expanded to be one of the largest in the world. The number of primary schools increased from 209,671 in 1950-51 to 565,786 in 1991-92; the corresponding increase in upper primary schools was from 13,596 to 152,077 These 717,863 schools together with 270,000 nonformal education centers enrol 136 million children as compared to 22.3 million in 1951. Universal provision of education has been substantially achieved at the primary stage (classes I-V). According to the Fifth All India Education Survey (1986), 94.5 per cent of the rural population had schools within a walking distance of 1 km. and 83.98% of the rural population have an upper primary school within a walking distance of 3 km; The survey estimated that there were 31,815 habitations in the country which had a population of 300 or more but did not have a primary school within the walking distance of one kilometre. Most of these habitations are situated in educationally backward states like uttar Pradesh, Madhya Pradesh, states like Uttar Pradesh, Madhya Pradesh, Bihar, Jammu and Kashmir, Assam and Arunachal Pradesh. The Sixth All India Education Survey, whose concise report is expected by 30 November, 1994, would throw light on the further spread of institutions since 1986.

## Goals of Elementary Education

About 19 to 24 million children in the age group 6-14 of whom about 60 per cent are girls, and about 121.3 million adult illiterates in the age group 15-35 of whom 62 per cent are women, constitute the target group of the endeavour to achieve EFA. As it is, India has the dubious distinction of having the largest number of adult illiterates and out-of-school children in the world-30 per cent of the world's adult illiterates and, 50.22 per cent of out-of-school children. Given the demographic pressure the numbers are likely to increase further.

NPE, 1986 imparted a sense of urgency to the long-cherished but elusive goals of UEE, and universal literacy, particularly in the age group 15-35. It also promoted a weltanschaung which:

(i) transcends institutional preoccupations and exclusive concern for the school system, and

(ii) instead adopts a broader functional view of education, as a wide diversity of learning opportunities, as a dynamic, cumulative lifelong process, applying to all people, but laying special stress on girl children and youth, particularly of the disadvantaged sections of society.

It is this conceptualisation of education that underlays its strong emphasis on:

(i) a large, systematic programme of NonFormal Education with quality comparable with formal education,

(ii) linkages between ECCE, primary education, adult literacy and post-literacy and continuing education,

(iii) professional upgradation of teachers, and

(iv) forging an alliance of teachers, NGOs, volantary agencies and community to further the cause of elementary education. important strategical developments in recent years include: (i) the shift to district as the unit of planning for implementation of adult literacy and elementary education, (ii) the increasing resort to social mobilisation to further basic education, and (iii) integration of adult literacy and non-formal programmes with the development themes like small population norms, health care, environment and nutrition.

The objective of Early Childhood Care and Education (ECCE), as stated in the NPE, 1986, is the total development of the young child in the age group 0-6, with special emphasis on children belonging to underprivileged groups and first generation learners. The NPE views ECCE as an important programme in its own right. The role of ECCE is also envisaged in the context of

preparation of children for primary school support service for girls in UPE, and support service for working women in low-income groups.

Being holistic in approach, ECCE Should attend to all aspects of the child's development. The content of ECCE, in addition to the vital and central inputs of health care and nutrition, is a programme of structured and unstructured play activities, play materials and learning experiences which promote the social, emotional, mental, physical and aesthetic development of the child. The entire effort is directed towards providing a natural, enjoyable and joyful environment to the child taking care of providing all necessary inputs for their proper development and growth without in any way putting any restraints on them.

**Target Froups**

The POA has defined some of the target groups as follows:

— very poor urban slum communities;
— ecologically deprived areas where children are required to fetch fuel, fodder, water and do other household chores;

- — family labour and household chores in rural areas and artisan households;
- — working children in the unorganised sector;
- — inherent, or seasonal labour, who have a mobile and transient life-style, like road workers;
- — construction workers in urban and rural areas;
- — landless agricultural labour;
- — forest dwellers and tribals in remote areas;
- — residents of remote, isolated hamlets.

The main vehicle for ECCE is the ICDS, which has the largest outreach and which, with planned expansion, will be able to reach 80 per cent of the vulnerable population by the end of the eighth plan.

Strengthening the pre-school education component of ICDS. adapting. its location, duration and other elements in order to serve as a support service for enrolment, particularly of girls in elementary education; and adapting its location, duration an other elements in order to serve as a support service for low income working mothers.

Strategies to achieve the objectives are of two types-one is concerned with the development of specific ECCE structures and programmes, and the other with approaches that cut across all programmes and seek to achieve a convergence of services. The various models suggested below describe structures and organisational approaches for the delivery of ECCE. With additional inputs and adaptation of the existing programmes for the young child the following models emerge:

(i) ECCE model (0-6 years) attached either to a primary school or to an NFE centre. In most cases this is, in fact, an ICDS centre.

(ii) ECE models (3-6 years). This model is mostly found attached to a primary school, using the infrastructure of the school system.

(iii) Primary school preparation model. This model is an application of ECE to the existing primary school programme either through a summer school readiness programme or a "first month project" covering the new entrants in class I.

An important step towards strengthening the ECCE component of the on-going schemes has been to achieve a convergence of services between various government departments. Apart from the ICDS programme, there are also Balwadis and day-care schemes managed by Departments of Women and Child Development/Social Welfare and voluntary organisations, as well as pre-primary schools run by local bodies and state governments. With a view to achieving synergies from this convergence the state governments have been requested to take the following steps:

a) Coordination of timings between primary schools and Anganwadis/Balwadis centres;

b) Primary school buildings may be used for Anganwadis/Balwadis activities wherever possible;

c) Primary school teachers to visit Anganwdis/ Balwadis centres to ensure better enrolment at primary school level;

d) Organisations such as SCERT to be identified to draw-up pre-school materials and curriculam in local languages and locally acceptable techniques which could be used in ECCE activities;

e) Personnel imparting early childhood education to be trained specifically in ECCE component by SCERT and other organisations;

f) To identify institutions which could run ECCE training courses and to provide recognition to these courses; and

g) To impress upon all employers to open ECCE centres at work sites wherever women are employed.

Some of the broad approaches being implemented through diverse institutions and services to enhance emphasis on ECCE:

(i) The use of mass media to create awareness about the significance of ECCE and ways of promoting child development.

(ii) The involvement of older children in health care and education of younger children through child-to-child activities, including making of toys, participating in creative activities for mental stimulation, promoting healthy habits, cleanliness and nutritional awareness. These activities are taken up in primary schools, health centres, NFE centres, Bal Bhavans, voluntary agencies and community centres.

(iii) The involvement of mother/other family adults through home-based activities for children's development.

**Universalisation of Elementary Education (UEE)**

There is now total appreciation and understanding that:

(i) target setting needs to be comprehensively specified in terms of access, participation and learner's achievements.

(ii) national and state targets are not specific enough, and that disaggregated targets need to be set for each district, block and village.

(iii) within each area specific unit of planning targets should be set separately for girls and disadvantaged groups.

(iv) ideally the targets should emanate from the grassroots.

The national targets for the eighth plan have been identified as:

*Access*

(i) Universal enrolment of all children, including girls and persons belonging to SC/ST;

(ii) Provision of primary school for all children within one kilometre of walking distance and of facility of non-formal education for school drop-outs, working children mid girls who cannot attend schools;

(iii) Improvement of ratio of primary school to upper primary school from the existing 1:4 to 1:2, this being a pre-condition for larger opportunity for widening girls' participation at upper primary stage;

*Retention*

(iv) Reduction of drop-out rates between classes I to V and I to VIII from the existing 45 per cent and 60 per cent to 20 per cent and 40 per cent respectively.

(v) Improvement of school facilities by revamped Operation Blackboard, to be extended to upper primary level also;

*Attainment*

(vi) Achievement of minimum levels of learning by approximately all children at the primary level, and introduction of this concept at the upper primary stage on a large scale;

*Monitoring*

(vii) Local level committee, with due representation to women and teachers, to assist in the working of primary education to oversee its functioning; (viii) Improvement of the monitoring system for UEE to see to the achievement of the above-mentioned goals.

National experience with the pursuit of UEE had established the following:

(i) UEE is contextual. The contextuality various widely across the country. Even in states like Kerala where participation is nearuniversal much requires to be done in respect of quality and achievement. In such states the pursuit of UEE would be mainly in the areas of quality, facilities and achievement. In other states participation and demand aspecfs need more attention.

(ii) Contextuality entails local area-planning with disaggregated targets and decentralised planning and management. Planning for UEE had hitherto been mainly at the national and state-level. Barring some states and union territories, these entities are too large and heterogenous for effective planning; they cannot provide contextuality. Ideally the planning should be from below, right from the village upwards but given the objective conditions, a beginning has to be made with district as the unit of planning. The district plans are to be prepared through an intensive process of interaction with the local bodies, teachers and NGOs so that it is "owned" by all who are to be associated in implementation and it refelects the ground-level realities.

(iii) Resources are an important but not sufficient condition for achieving UEE. A host of measures, both financial and non-financial, both on the supply side and on the demand side, need to complement higher allocation of resources.

(iv) The strategies for UEE have hitherto emphasised, mainly access in terms of construction of classrooms and appointment of teachers. This has been inadequate and needs to be augmented by:

a. a holistic planning and management approach which goes beyond implementation of a disjointed set of individual schemes, perceives the task of UEE in its totality, integrates all the measures needed to achieving UEE in the specific context of the district;

b. this holistic planning should incorporate a gender perspective in all aspects of the planning and implementation process and be an integral part of all measures needed to achieve UEE.

c. addressing the more difficult aspects of access, particularly access to girls, disadvantaged groups and out-of-school children;

d. improving school effectiveness;

e. strengthening the alternatives to schooling, particularly the non-formal education system;

f. stressing the participative processes whereby the local community facilitates participation, achievement and school effectiveness;

g. toning up teacher competence, training and motivation;

h. stressing learning competence and achievement;

i. stressing need for improved teaching/ learning materials;

j. overhauling of planning and management in respect of both routine and innovative areas.

k. convergence between elementary education and related services like ECCE and school health.

Consequently, the strategies for the eighth plan adopt a disaggregated approach, with focus on preparation of district-specific, populationspecific plans for UEE within the broad strategy frame of micro-planning through people's participation and introduction of MLLs in schools to improve learner achievement. Micro-planning will provide the framework of universal access and universal participation while MLLs would be the strategy frame for universal achievement.

## MICRO-PLANNING

Acknowledging that programme specific approach towards UEE planning has led in the past to a situation in which individual programme targets have taken precedence over the basic goals of EFA, micro-planning aims at "a family-wise and child-wise design of action" by which "every child regularly attends school or NFE centre, continues his/her education at a pace suitable to him/her, and completes at least five years of schooling or its equivalent at the non-formal centre." Basic to such an intensive programme strategy is

(i) the concept of participative planning, in which the community is mobilised to take responsibility for identifying its own needs and is given an assertive role in ensuring the successful implementation of programmes, and

(ii) a decentralisation of administrative functions to enable local educational personnel to take decisions in respect of their areas and respond with flexibility to the demands of the community.

Micro-planning necessarily implies area-specific planning, in which the area is ideally a revenue village, but practically a block, taluk or district. Within this area, the steps by which micro-planning will be operationalised are:

(i) mobilising community participation through environment building activities,

(ii) decentralising educational administration so that it is accountable to the local community,

(iii) re-orienting and strengthening local level administrative and resource support systems,

(iv) ascertaining educational requirements of the area,

(v) bringing to school all children who can be enrolled and providing NFE programmes or other innovative and supportive measures for those who cannot,

(vi) seeing that all children, particularly girls and those belonging to disadvantaged group, regularly and actually participate in primary education, and

(vii) planning for the improvement of schools or NFE centres so that effective learning can take place.

The primary instrument of organising micro-level planning at the village level would be the Village Education Committee (VEC). In states like Maharashtra where the Panchayati Raj system has taken root the VEC has been functioning as a committee of the Panchayat and could potentially take on the tasks of micro-planning. The 73rd and 74th Constitutional Amendments hold out the possibility of similar institutional arrangements evolving in rural and urban areas in all the states of the country. It needs to be ensured that these structures are not legalistic but participative, and that they genuinely provide 'voice' to women, persons belonging to SC and ST, and educational functionaries. Similar village participation structures at the block/ taluk level, and at the district level would be the instruments of planning at higher levels of aggregation. The report of CABE Committee on Decentralised Management of Education (1993) has suggested guidelines to the states on the constitution of participative structures.

Decentralisation of education system holds out the possibility of introducing great flexibility in the school system through measures such as, shifting of school timings and adjusting the school timing to suit the local socioeconomic conditions and of improving school effectiveness through community support.

## Minimum Levels of Learning

The strategy to improve learning acquisition in school focuses attention on what is happening in the classroom, and seeks to bring the principles of equity and quality to bear upon it. The strategy aims to lay down learning outcomes expected from basic education at a realistic, relevant and functional level, prescribes the adoption of measures that would ensure that all children who complete a stage of schooling achieve these outcomes. These outcomes define the Minimum Levels of Learning common to both school and equivalent NFE programme.

The main steps by which MLLs are being introduced in schools are:

(i) an assessment of the existing level of learning achievement;

(ii) a definition of the MLLs for the area and the time-frame within which it will be achieved;

(iii) reorientation of teaching practices to Competency-based teaching;

(iv) an introduction of continuous comprehensive evaluation of student learning;

(v) review of the textbooks and their revision, if required;

(vi) the provision of inputs as necessary including provision of physical facilities, teacher training, supervision and evaluation, etc., to improve learning acquisition to the MLLs.

The endeavour is to monitor learning achievement to direct greater resources where levels of learning are lower, and to consciously accelerate the pace of development in the needy areas, thereby to reduce disparities, equalise standards and govern inputs for quality improvement by the performance of the system.

## Planning at District Level

The eighth five year plan (1992-97) departs from the earlier plans in that the district would be the unit of planning for UEE instead of the state. District specific plans would be developed by the state governments as projects with specific activities, clearly defined responsibilities, definite time-schedule and specific targets. Each district project would be prepared within the major strategy framework and would be tailored to the specific needs and possibilities in the district. Apart from effective UEE, the goals of each project includes the reduction of existing disparities in educational access, the provision of alternative systems of comparable standards to the disadvantaged groups, a substantial improvement in the quality of schooling facilities, obtaining a genuine community involvement in the running of schools, and building up local level capacity to ensure effective decentralisation of educational planning. That is to say, the overall goal of the project is reconstruction of primary education as a whole in selected districts instead of a piecemeal implementation of schemes. Such an integrated approach is expected to achieve synergies among different programme components.

Broadly, districts are categorised into three categories:

(i) High literacy districts, in which access and enrolment are almost universal and community awareness of the need for education is already high;

(ii) Districts in which total literacy campaigns have been successful leading to an enhanced demand for elementary education; and

(iii) Low literacy districts in which the provision of education facilities is unsatisfactory, the delivery system inadeqaauate and community awareness low.

The strategies with regard to access, participation, achievement, environment building, and community participation are different for the three categories of districts. In the high literacy districts the emphasis is on mopping up the residual unenrolled children and on quality and achievement. In districts where TLCs are successful the strategies to achieve UEE would build upon the community awareness generated in the districts. In low literacy districts the strategies would% cover environment building also. The District Primary Education Programme (DPEP) launched in 1993-94 seeks to operationalise the strategy of district level planning. The Programme also builds upon the experience gained in:

(i) the implementation of the Bihar Education Project (with UNICEF assistance) and the Lok Jumbish Project (with SIDA assistance);

(ii) the planning of Basic Education Project in Uttar Pradesh (with IDA assistance);

(iii) the implementation of the Andhra Pradesh Primary Education Project (with ODA assistance), Shiksha Karmi Project (with SIDA assistance) and Mahila Samakhya (with Dutch assistance).

In BEP and UP projects too, investment is concentrated in the chosen districts and district specific investment is complemented by a few state level interventions such as strengthening of state level institutions. Where the Programme goes beyond the UP and Bihar projects, is its:

(i) emphasis on local area planning with the district plans being formulated in their own right rather than being derived from a state plan project document;

(ii) greater rigour and infusion of professional inputs in planning and appraisal;

(iii) more focused targetting in that the districts selected would be: a. the 247 educationally backward districts with female literacy below the national average; and b. districts where TLCs have been successful leading to enhanced demand for elementary education;

(iv) more focused coverage in that the Programme would initially focus oil primary stage (classes I-V and its NFE equivalent), with stress on education for girls, and for socially disadvantaged groups; and

(v) emphasis on capacity building and networking of district, state and national level institutes in the fields of education, management and social sciences to provide the resource support for the programme.

To begin with, projects are now being formulated in 43 districts in the eight states of Madhya Pradesh, Orissa, Assam, Haryana, Maharashtra, Karnataka, Tamil Nadu and Kerala. The objective is to gradually extend the coverage to all the districts which satisfy one of the twin criteria for coverage. The attempt would be to start the Programme in at least 110 districts in the eighth plan with an estimated outlay of Rs. 195 million of which Rs. 172 million are proposed to be drawn from external sources.

## Expansion og Facilities

The extant planning norms envisage provision of a primary school within one kilometer's walking distance of habitations with a population of 300; in remote, hilly and desert areas the population norm is lowered to 200. It is estimated that according to these norms 35,000 new schools need to be established in unserved habitations during the eighth plan.

Populations in very small habitations where schools would not be viable would be reached by alternative channels such as NFE centres, voluntary schools operated by NGOs, parateachers as in the Shiksha Karmi scheme and provision of residential schools facilities. Opening of residential school is an important strategy in tribal tracts with scattered miniscule habitations.

In order to increase enrolments at the upper primary stage, the infrastructure at this stage will be expanded. The existing norm of providing an upper primary school within 3 kms of walking distance is generally inconvenient for girls. This norm will be progressively relaxed so that the ratio between primary and upper primary schools will be 2:1.

A major initiative by the central government for upgradation of facilities in primary schools was the scheme of Operation Blackboard launched in 1987. The scheme has three interdependent components, namely, provision of

(i) a building comprising at least two reasonably large all-weather rooms with a deep verandah and separate toilet facilities for boys and girls;

(ii) at least two teachers in every school, as far as possible one of them a woman; and

(iii) essential teaching-learning material including blackboards, maps, charts, toys and equipment for work experience

The scheme has so far covered 469 thousand schools comprising 91 per cent of the primary schools in the country.

Taking into account the evaluation studies the scheme was recently revised so as to:

(i) provide flexibility to schools in providing teaching-learning materials relevant to their curriculum and local needs;

(ii) dovetail the scheme with microplanning wherever undertaken, so that supply of inputs is matched by demand side interventions to promote participation;

(iii) intensify training in the use of teachinglearning equipments,

(iv) extend the scheme to upper primary schools.

## Teacher Training

Teacher performance is the most crucial input in the field of education. Whatever policies may be laid down, in the ultimate analysis, these have to be interpreted and implemented by teachers, as much through their personal example as through teaching-learning processes. Teacher selection and training, competence motivation and the conditions of work impinge directly on teachers' performance. The NPE, 1986 calls for a substantial improvement in the. conditions of work and the quality of teachers' education. The policy also emphasizes the teachers' accountability to the pupils, their parents, the community and to their own profession.

A major institutional intervention, after NPE, 1986 was the setting up of District Institutes of Education and Training (DIETS) to provide quality pre-service and in-service education to elementary teachers and functionaries engaged in adult education and NFE. Eventually DIETs are expected, in their jurisdiction, to provide academic and resource support to basic education and also to engage in action research and innovation. As of now, DIETS are being Set up in 346 districts out of the 462 districts in the country; in 190 districts DIETS are already conducting training programmes. It is proposed to set up 450 DIETs by the end of the eighth plan (1997-98). Efforts are afoot to strengthen the SCERTs so that they can provide the resource back up.

A bill is under consideration of the Parliament to vest the National Council of TeacherEducation (NCTE) with statutory powers for determination and maintenance of standards of teacher education. This measure is expected to improve the quality of pre-service training, and upgrade the syllabi and curricula of teacher training programmes.

## NFE Programmes

NFE programmes, as a major government sponsored effort, are comparatively new to elementary education, having started in the sixth plan (1980-85). Following the NPE, 1986 the scheme of non-formal education was revised; NFE has been visualised as a child-centred and environment-oriented system to meet the diverse educational needs of the comparatively deprived geographical areas and socioeconomic sections of society; it also seeks to provide for organisational flexibility, relevance of curriculum, diversity in learning activities to relate them to the learners' needs and de-centralised management. The programme is being implemented on a project basis, generally co-extensive with the community development block, each project having about 100 NFE centres.

This scheme is, as of now, the main vechicle for the NFE programme. In order to further strengthen this Scheme many measures are being adopted. These include:

(i) linking the setting up of NFE with microplanning excercises;

(ii) involvement of the community in the setting-up and supervision of NFE centres, in the identification of the NFE instructors within the community, with preference being given to women instructors;

(iii) strengthening training component and creation of a training infrastructure through networking (training responsibility will be shared by NFE project, district level institutions like DIETs and DRUs, state level institutions like SCERT, and National Institutes like NCERT and NIEPA);

(iv) effective decentralisation of project management;

(v) relating pupil evaluation to MLLs;

(vi) facilitating lateral entry for students of the NFE stream into the formal stream;

(vii) linkages between non-formal courses with open schools;

(viii) providing avenues of continuing education through linkages with the public libraries and Jana Shiksha Nilayams.

The emergence of Total Literacy Campaign has provided an important alternative avenue of non-formal education for children in the age group 9-14; the efficacy of this avenue can be related to the intense social mobilisations. Thirtynine NGOs are engaged in experimental and innovative projects of NFE. Two innovative projects of NFE stand out: the Shiksha Karmi and the PROPEL project.

**Shiksha Karmi Project**

This project seeks to tackle the problem of teacher absenteeism in remote villages of Rajasthan. The crucial innovation in this project assisted by the Swedish International Development Agency (SIDA) is a substitution of the primary school teacher by a team of voluntary education workers-Shiksha Karmis-who would be selected by the local community and imparted intensive training. The project has a strong component of training inputs. It aims to cover in a phased manner about 1050 remote villages in 70 blocks of Rajasthan by 1994. The total outlay on the project for the period June 1991 to June 1996 is Rs.412.3 million. Independent evaluation had shown that the levels of attainments are comparable with those of equivalent levels of the formal system.

**"PROPEL" Project**

"PROPEL" Project is an experiment to liberate the creative energies of the rural masses for ail integrated local effort towards development. The cherished goal of "education for all" call be reached faster if rural communities are mobilized for self-reliance in promoting and managing local education through systematic microplanning. PROPEL (Promoting Primary and Elementary Education) is an interdisciplinary, action-research project conducted by the Indian Institute of Education, Pune. The project covers 137 contiguous villages, about 18,000 households and 110,000 population, In PROPEL, Village Education Committees and Village Councils help streamline Panchayat action for conducting pre-school, non-formal education of different kinds, literacy activities and women's development groups. Exploration is undertaken by the villagers for collaborative and convergent development. Community participation instills relevance into curricula, materials, teacher-orientation, testing and evaluation, supervision and management. Innovative ways are found to raise social finance for local education effort. Transparency of all educational operations is the core of this community mobilization project which has been selected by UNESCO as a 'show-case' project for Asia.

**"GYANA JYOTI"**

A Movement by Teachers for Universalization of Primary Education in Orissa

"GYANA JYOTI", the 'flame of knowledge', the 'torch of wisdom' was a statewide movement spearheaded by the teachers' associations aimed towards creating awareness among the Teachers Community and the people of Orissa dn mobilizing them to contribute towards the attainment of the goals of Universalization of Primary Education in the State of Orissa.

After a series of discussions, the office-bearers of sixteen Teachers' Organisations committed themselves to work together for Universalization of Primary Education in the State. As a first step, a State-level convention was organized by them oil the Teachers Day, the 5th September 1992. Five thousand teachers from all over the State attended the convention and they took a pledge to work unitedly to universalize primary education by 2000 AD, and to enrol an additional five lakh children in the primary schools by the end of 1993. At the meeting the Gyana Jyoti, was lit which was carried through out the State. The torch covered five thousand kms. covering seventeen districts in the State; enroute more than five hundred public meetings were conducted. The Gyana Jyoti received warni and cheerful welcome from hundreds and thousands of people including teachers, children and local public who participated in the meetings wherever Gyana Jyoti travelled. In the public meetings, the leaders of the Teachers' Organizations appealed to the people to enrol their children in the primary school and to ensure their regular attendance and completion of atleast primary school level education. They also called upon everyone to participate actively in the environment building activities and support the attainment of the EFA/UPE goals. The media extensively covered the Gyana Jyoti movement in the State. The government had extended full support and encouraged the children and the teachers to participate in the Gyana Jyoti movement; the most striking feature was the fact that Gyana Jyoti movement received active support from the industrial as well as political sector.

The movement has been considered to be a historical one in many ways. After travelling seventy days between the 5 September to 14 November 1992, it reached Bhubaneswar, the capital of Orissa where a I massive function was organized on 14 November 1992. This function was attended by over fifty thousand school teachers and female health workers. For the first time both the health workers and the teachers joined their hands and expressed their desire to work closely and unitedly for achieving the goals of Universalization of Primary Education and Health For All by 2000 AD. As a follow up, the teachers' organisations worked out a detailed future action plan. The plan indicates their decision to organize block-level conventions involving primary school teachers, health workers and panchayat leaders to create awareness about Universalization of Primary Education; to conduct house-to-house survey to enumerate the number of children of the school going age group and to enrol them in the school by next academic year. The action plan also talks about how to arrest teachers' absenteeism, students' drop-out rate, achieving minimum level' of learning, creating appropriate learning environment in primary schools. Tile plan also covers issues such as strategies/intervention required for improved enrolment, retention and learning amongst the scheduled castes, scheduled tribes and girl children in the primary schools.

## Programmes for Women Education

The gap between boys' and girls' participation in elementary education is the biggest single gap to be filled for universalisation. The problem of UEE is, in essence, the problem of the girl child. The gender disparity, particularly in the rural areas, reflects the social attitude to the girl child. While the solution for this problem does not lie entirely in the educational system, education can and should play a positive interventionist role in the improvement of women's status. Both demand and supply side interventions are called for to improve girls' participation. The interventions have to be attitudinal as well as monetary. The main demand side interventions have been:

(i) programmes for awareness generation among women, amongst which the most successful and reputed is the Mahila Samakhya;

(ii) incentive schemes which reduce the direct costs of education. Incentive schemes of different kinds are already a wellestablished feature of the elementary school system. These are almost wholly funded by the states. The coverage and extent vary widely. In all states, education is free up to class XII for girls. Many states also provide incentives by way of uniforms, free textbooks and stationery, attendance allowance. A remarkable scheme mobilising community support is the Savitri Bhai Phule Foster Child Scheme in Maharashtra;

(iii) linkages between schools with ECCE centres and creches. The main supply side interventions have been:

(i) Gender sensitisation of the education system and its functionaries so that gender concern is reflected across the board in all educational programmes, more particularly in the area of basic education. The Department of Women's Studies of the NCERT has been playing a commendable role in gender sensitization; it is actively associated with the revision of school textbooks for elimination of gender bias.

(ii) Recruitment of more female teachers: The proportions of women teachers have been increasing gradually. In 1986-87, 40.2 per cent of the primary school teachers were women as compared to 15 per cent in 1950-51. The corresponding proportions for the upper primary stage were 30.92 and 15 per cent respectively. Under the Operation Blackboard, 59 per cent of the teachers appointed were women. There is, however, a concentration of women teachers in urban areas and inter-state disparities are conspicuous. In 1986-87 the proportion of women elementary teachers was about 21 per cent in rural areas as compared to about 56 per cent in urban areas. At the primary stage the percentage of female teachers in rural areas ranged from 9.81 per cent in Madhya Pradesh to 61 per cent in Kerala among major states. At the upper primary stage, the corresponding range was 8.38 per cent in Orissa to 58.36 per cent in Kerala. The problem is more basic as rural girls do not get as far as secondary education to become eligible for entry into primary teachers training institutions. In 1986-87, for every 100 rural girls in class I only one was in class XII. Appropriate policies should be put in place to increase secondary education and teachertraining opportunities for rural girls.

(iii) Effective NFE programmes.

**Mahila Samakhya**

A Dutch-assisted project, Mahila Samakhya, Which literally means women's equality through education, is a women's empowerment project which does not aim at service delivery but seeks to bring about a change in women's perception about themselves and that of society in regard to women's 'traditional roles'. It endeavours to create an environment for women to seek knowledge and information in order to make informed choices and create circumstances in which women can learn at their own pace and rhythm. The centrality of education in the struggle to achieve (-quality is an important focus of Mahila Samakhya.

The nodal point around which the programme devolves is the village level "Mahila Sangha" or women's collective, which constitutes an easily accessible forum for women to discuss problems relating to their daily routine such as child care, health, fuel, fodder, drinking water, education; problems related to their status, role within the society and in the family; and problems related to their self-image as women. These village women's groups Set out their own agenda for education and collective action. They try to seek solutions to their problems by initiating action and pressurising the block and district structures to respond.

At least two women from each village work as activators with the women's collective, and help to catalyse discussion and action. The process is helped along by a Sahayogini who is a local woman trained by the programme to facilitate and coordinate the activities of about 10 Sanghas.

Their primary functions are tuned to the needs of these collectives by way of providing information, support and guidance when required, and to act as a link between village level activities and the district implementation unit of the programme. The district unit shoulders the overall responsi

**A Mahila Samooh (Women's Collective)**

"Gagarpur" is a village with about 200 households (population 12,000). At the outskirts of the village there are two hamlets. In one of them lives a community of tribals, who were nomadic and in the old days known for their dare-devilry. In another hamlet live 20 families of deprived and disadvantaged communities. There is no water well or hand-pump in this hamlet. There is an old primary school with two dilapidated rooms and two teachers. Only one teacher comes to the school everyday. Seventy-five children (10 girls) are enrolled; but only 25 children come everyday. One adult education centre was started two years ago, but the instructor is not enthusiastic.

Dhanno is an illiterate woman, like 98 per cent of women of the village. A social worker spotted her for her zest for life, lively nature and capacity to break out into a song. The social worker was familiar with the Mahila Samakhya programme and thus sent her for an intensive three week training programme, after pleading with her family who were opposed to her going out of the village.

During the training, Dhanno became aware of the plight of her fellow trainees, their individual plight, their 'personal shame', frequent wife beating, backbreaking work; recurrent child birth; health problems, especially gynaecological ones, morbidity; and above all her feeling of being unwanted had become the common problem of "womanhood", of poverty and of the social structure. After almost 20 years she rediscovered her childhood. She played games and laughed loudly. Tile group sang, enacted plays and skits, and was excited about holding a pencil to draw on paper. They talked a lot, shared and asked themselves, "why does society always say put three women together, and they will invariably fight?" She came back to the village, with a twinkle in her eyes. The women were curious; they asked her about the training. Dhanno sang the song and showed the posters. She made them sit on chairs and gave them tea. She told them about drought relief work, about other schemes, and she got talking. The women enjoyed meeting and talking about the "outside world"; "tell us more", they said, the Mahila Samooh started becoming a reality. Then the supervisor visited the village, told them about Mahila Samakhya; how they could ask for non-formal centres for learning ... A new world was unfolding before their eyes. The school teacher was angry about these "interfering" women, but he soon realised that the District Education Officer had been getting regular reports about his school. He asked the supervisor what brought her to the village every fortnight, and why could she not be like other inspectors. She then replied, "I work for the women; I am responsible to them; and above all enjoy coming here." Gagarpur women are excited, full of plans; they now want to organise a health camp, to learn, to understand, and to act. When the social worker asked them how it all happened, they said, "In the past we were always told what to do and what we should demand but in Mahila Samakhya they asked us first and let us do it ourselves."

A State Project Director oversees the programme at the state level. The state level office provides a facilitative atmosphere for the conduct of the programme, the necessary resource support for the functional areas, of the project and arranges for the interdistrict linkages of the programme so as to create a wider network for the women's movement. At the national level the programme is coordinated by the Project Director with guidance from a national resource group of eminent women.

Some of the key principles of the Mahila Samakhya programme are that:

a) project functionaries and officials are facilitative and not directive;

b) planning, decision-making and evaluative processes are accountable to the collective of village women;

c) women participants determine the form, nature, content and timing of all activities in their village, and that staff selection processes are participatory; and

d) the programme is not hurried and does not have 'targets', but is a self-paced process, built on existing knowledge and women's own priorities for learning.

As of now the programme is being implemented in 14 districts, spread over the four states of Uttar Pradesh, Karnataka, Gujarat and Andhra Pradesh. Mahila Samakhya has played a lead role in the total literacy campaign in the districts of Gujarat and Karnataka and is engaged in providing alternative avenues of education like NFE in Uttar Pradesh.

## Educational Development of SC/ST Students

The central focus in the SCs' educational development is their equalisation with the non-SC population at all stages and levels of education, in all areas and in all the four dimensions—rural male, rural female, urban male and urban female.

The measures contemplated for this purpose include:

(i) Incentives to indigent families to send their children to school regularly till they reach the age of 14;

(ii) Pre-matric scholarship scheme for children of families engaged in occupations such as scavenging, flaying and tanning to be made applicable from class I onwards. All children of such families, regardless of incomes, will be covered by this scheme and time-bound programmes targetted on them will be undertaken;

(iii) Constant micro-planning and verification to ensure that the enrolment, retention and successful completion of courses by SC students do not fall at any stage, and provision of remedial courses to improve their prospects for further education and employment.

(iv) Recruitment of teachers from Scheduled Castes;

(v) Provision of facilities for SC students in students' hostels at district headquarters, according to a phased programme;

(vi) Location of school buildings, Balwadis and adult education centres in such a way as to facilitate full participation of the Scheduled Castes;

(vii) Constant innovation in finding new methods to increase the participation of the Scheduled Castes in the educational process.

The following measures would be taken urgently to bring the Scheduled Tribes on par with others:

(i) The socio-cultural milieu of the STs has its distinctive characteristics including, in many cases, their own spoken languages. This underlines the need to develop the curricula and devise instructional materials in tribal languages at the initial stages, with arrangements for switching over to the regional language. The Central Institute of Indian Languages, Mysore and the Tribal Research Institutes in many states have been playing an important role in this area.

(ii) Educated and promising Scheduled Tribe youths will be encouraged and trained to take up teaching in tribal areas.

(iii) Residential schools, including Ashram schools, will be established on a large scale as their effectiveness has been demonstrated in many states.

(iv) Incentive schemes are being formulated for the Scheduled Tribes, keeping in view their special needs and life styles. Scholarships for higher education will emphasise technical, professional and paraprofessional courses. Special remedial courses and other programmes to remove psycho-social impediments will be provided to improve their performance in various courses.

(v) Anganwadis, non-formal and adult education centres are being opened on priority basis in areas predominantly inhabited by the Scheduled Tribes.

(vi) The curriculum at all stages of education is being designed to create an awareness of the rich cultural identity of the tribal people as also of their enormous creative talent.

## Educational Development of Handicapped Children

POA, 1992 seeks to achieve universal enrolment of these children by the end of the ninth plan, in general schools wherever possible and in special schools and in special sections of general schools of children who require such special education. It also envisages reduction of dropout rates on par with other children, by adjustment and adaptation of curriculum and teaching to the said needs of the children as well as reorienting pre-service and in-service teachers training programmes.

The strategy of area-specific and populationspecific micro-planning for UEE is equally relevant for this disadvantaged group. Planning for UEE and adult literacy at all levels-centre, state, district, block and project-should provide for the educational needs of this category of children.

Education of children with disability is a component in the training of educational planners and administrators as well as pre-service and in-service teachers. DIETs, CTEs and IASEs, which have been provided facilities for this component, pay particular attention to this aspect of teacher training. While drawing up schemes for strengthening SCERTs, constitution of cells for education of the handicapped will be considered as envisaged in IEDC.

All the DIETs to be established by the end of the eighth plan are to have resource rooms and trained faculty to teach the essential component of education of children with disability. They would also run orientation programmes for teachers at least from lab areas and practising schools to establish field demonstration of IEDC programme. The SCERTs would support field demonstrations under the scheme of IEDC.

Similar action is suggested for the 250 CTEs and 50 IASEs. The budget provision is available in the scheme itself. The pre-service training curriculum would induct essential components in these areas, wherever it has not been done so far.

All in-service teachers should receive awareness input on education of children with disability in orientation programmes. In each area I institution where IEDC is implemented all teachers receive orientation as envisaged in the scheme of IEDC. The heads of institutions and educational administrators would also receive training. Considering the large numbers to be covered, the Indira Gandhi National Open University and NCERT should plan credit courses on special education to equip general teachers to meet special needs. The NCERT will provide training to the IEDC cell staff. Multicategory training of resource teachers would be encouraged in UGC supported programmes.

Curriculum flexibility is of special significance for these children. Special needs of these children will be met, if child-centred education is practised. The curriculum adjustment and adaptation of teaching methods and material would be worked out, field-tied and provided to the users. The following actions are to be taken:

(i) Guidelines for child-centred education, including special needs in the class room, are being developed at the NCERT.

(ii) Guidelines for adjustment of curriculum and instructional material and methods for visually and hearing handicapped at primary level have been developed. These would be made available to teachers. Work for upper primary and secondary school level will be started and completed by the end of 1994.

(iii) The achievement of minimum levels of learning by children with mild disabilities are being ensured through resource support and alternative learning material, wherever needed.

(iv) The Boards of Examination would make adjustment and adaptations in examination for the handicapped children.

(v) Study of more than one language should not be compulsory for deaf children.

(vi) Teaching of Science and Mathematics is either not available to handicapped children or they opt for an easier substitute. Special efforts are being made by the NIH and the NCERT to develop an action programme to improve access of disabled children to these important areas.

(vii) Child-to-child help in education of children with disability is an effective resource in view of large classes and multigrade teaching. NCERT would develop a package and make it available to teachers by the end of 1993.

(viii) The special learning aids and equipment like braille books, braille kit and audiovisual material are being developed and made available to schools by NIHs and NCERT.

## Use of Mass Media

Radio and television are being used in a limited way both for advocacy as well as educational purposes. The CIET, SIETs, NIHs and other organisations would develop a variety of programmes so that they can be regularly telecast/broadcast. The MHRD would approach the Ministry of Information and Broadcasting for providing adequate time for this purpose.

The CIET, SIETs; and NIHs would also develop software in non-telecast mode and make it available to DIETs, other training centres and NGOs working with disabled persons.

Field publicity units would be utilised by states for advocacy programmes. Newspapers and magazines have started popular advocacy and educational writing in this area. The NCERT and the NIHs would develop packages and hand them over to journalists in workshops.

Integrated Education for Disabled Children (IEDC) IEDC is the main scheme for promoting work of handicapped children in selected schools. The POA, 1986 target of increasing enrolment of children by 25 per cent per year was achieved as enrolment of disabled children in general schools increased from 15,000 to 30,000. Subject to availability of resources, the cumulative enrolment would reach 50,000 by the end of the eighth plan. However, an additional 100,000 children with mild disabilities are being provided resource support from teachers and learning aids and equipment.

## National Curricular Framework

The NPE, 1986 envisaged a national system of education based on a national curricular framework containing a common core along with the academic components. The NPE/POA envisaged a child-centred approach to education to promote universal enrolment and universal retention of children up to 14 years of age and substantial improvement in the quality of education in the school. In pursuance of NPE/ POA, the NCERT brought out in 1988 a National Curricular Framework for all stages of school education. The revised curriculum took into account the need for reduction of curriculum load, keeping in view the requirements for modernisation and relevance.

Following the guidelines in the National Curricular Framework, the NCERT revised the entire school syllabi and brought out revised textbooks for classes I to XII. Based on the national curricular framework and the NCERT syllabi/ textbooks, the State and Union Territories have also undertaken measures of curriculum renewal and development of new textbooks for different stages of school education for their introduction into the school system in a phased manner. Curriculum transaction uses child-centred approach using play material. Science and mathematics kits have been developed and are supplied to schools. These, along with locally available learning material, form teaching resource in schools.

An innovative project for meeting educational needs of all children in the class room has been evolved as a design model of in-service training with in-built transfer of training effects to classroom practice and the effective use of action research as means of institutionalization of an innovation. The Multisite Action Research Project (MARP) evolved the concept of inclusive school, the school which effectively responds to the educational needs of all children. The project was conducted in 22 locations involving 338 experienced teachers, 248 preservice teachers and 9896 pupils in 115 schools. The experience gained from this project is being incorporated in the basic education projects. These are also finding a place in the teacher training programmes.

For the first five years of schooling, comprising primary education, a specific subject of environmental studies has been introduced in the national curriculum framework. This subject includes rudiments of Geography, Science and other natural phenomena relevant to the surroundings of the child. From the sixth to the eighth year of schooling (upper primary category), environment is taught as a distinct subject in some states while in most other states teaching of the subject is an integrated enterprise with environmental concerns infused in various subjects. This 'orientation' approach is invariably in vogue at the higher stages of schooling and college and university sectors.

In the field of adult and non-formal education, in preparation of reading and learning materials, special emphasis is laid on including environmental information.

## Multisite Action Research Project

The teacher educators and selected school principals were provided five-day training in active learning approaches using the material developed for the teacher education resource pack. It was followed by one day practice with new material. On the seventh day action research projects were planned in three contexts: (a) Preservice training context (b) Inservice training context (c) Whole school improvement (i) with external intervention (ii) without external intervention.

The teacher educator and principals used active learning approach in training teachers and simultaneous use of the approach in classrooms. The teachers assessed perceptions of children about learning-teaching in the classroom and learning achievements. The action research coordinators assessed learning-teaching attitude of teachers and the transfer of the learnt active-learning-based approach to classroom practice. The significant outcomes of the multisite multilevel action research projects were:

1. The process of teaching can be changed through continuous inservice training accompanied by action research.
2. The active learning approach changes attitude of teachers and pupils to learning and teaching.
3. The pupil's change in perceptions about learning teaching improves learning achievement significantly.
4. Inservice pins and innovative practices can be institutionalized through multilevel action research.

After NLM was established the most significant development was the launching of a mass campaign for total literacy in Ernakulam district of Kerala on 26 January 1989. Spearheaded by the Kerala Sastra Sahitya Parishad, the Ernakulam campaign created a mass upsurge for literacy and brought together the district administration, voluntary agencies and all sections of the society and became a historic trend-setter for total literacy campaigns. Ernakulam district was declared fully literate on 4 February 1990. The Ernakulam success led to the launching of a campaign for total literacy for the whole of Kerala state. Campaigns for total literacy in the union territory of Pondicherry, in Goa, and in the select districts of West Bengal, Karnataka, Maharashtra and Gujarat followed in quick succession. In addition to Kerala and Pondicherry, Burdwan, Midnapore, Hoogly, Birbhum in West Bengal, Dakshin Kannada in Karnataka, Wardha and Sindhudurg in Maharashtra and Gandhinagar, Bhavnagar and Kheda in Gujarat have been declared fully literate. The literacy wave which started from the southern and eastern states is now beginning to extend to practically all parts of the country. As on date, 175 TLC projects have been approved involving 212 districts (either fully or partially) in the states of Andhra Pradesh, Bihar, Gujarat, Haryana, Himachal Pradesh, Karnataka, Maharashtra, Madhya Pradesh, Orissa, Punjab, Rajasthan, Tamil Nadu, Uttar Pradesh and West Bengal. As on date, aproximately, 31 million learners in 9-45 age group are learning with the help of about 4 million volunteers. They are in different stages of learning but it is estimated that about 15 million of them have already acquired the threshold level of literacy and numeracy. Post-literacy and continuing education activities are being launched even as TLCs make significant progress in an area. The objective is to cover 345 districts during the eighth plan and make 100 million people functionally literate. A welcome spin off of the TLCs has been an enhanced demand for elementary education. Linkages between TLC and NFE are consciously being fostered in several districts. Out-of-school children in the 9-14 age group are covered by the TLCs in most districts. To the extent that this target group is effectively reached by TLCs future accretions to adult illiterates are expected to diminish. On the conclusion of TLCs in an area it is proposed to take care of the future learning needs of children of the target group through an expanded NFE programme as well as through post literacy and continuing education centres.

## Characteristic Features of TLCs

There are certain characteristic features of TLCs which make them unique in relation to other programmes. These are as under:

(i) These campaigns are area-specific, timebound, volunteer-based, cost-effective and outcome-oriented.

(ii) These are implemented through the district level committees which are registered under the Societies Registration Act, as independent and autonomous bodies to provide unified umbrella under which a number of individuals and organisations work together. The leadership to this body is provided by the district collector/chief secretary, Zila Parishad (District Council). All sections of society are given due representation in the planning and implementation of programmes.

(iii) No targets are fixed from the top. The targets emanate from the grass-roots level on the basis of a detailed door-to-door survey which is conducted by volunteers. This survey is not only a head-counting exercise, but also a tool of planning, of mobilisation of people and of environment building.

(iv) The success of the campaign rests on mass mobilisation which implies mobilisation of all sections of the society.

(v) The success of the campaign also rests on voluntarism. Voluntarism implies that a large number of functionaries, of their own volition, contribute their time, energy and resources to the campaign without any expectation of award, reward or incentive.

(vi) Communication is yet another important characteristic of the campaign; it is also a pre-condition for its success. Communication has to be open, direct, and credible. Its implications are two-fold. It implies, on the one hand, using the oral culture and tradition to act as an effective vehicle of communication of the message pertaining to gains of literacy and predicament of illiteracy with a view to sensitising the literate and educated and motivating and mobilising potential learners. It is also a two-way flow of information ensuring thereby continuous participation of all layers in the campaign and a process of continuous correction on the basis of information so received.

(vii) The management information system in a campaign is based on the twin principles of participation and correction; it has also to be accountable and credible. A campaign is not enrolment but outcome-oriented. Every learner enrolled in the campaign is expected to achieve certain predetermined measurable levels of literacy and numeracy at the end of the campaign.

(viii) To enable every learner to achieve these levels, a new pedagogy known as "Improved Pace and Content of Learning" (IPCL) has been conceptualised and translated into action in the shape of a set of multi-graded and integrated teaching learning materials and training which places the learner as the focal point in the entire process and which, through reduced duration and continuous ongoing evaluation, helps to heighten learners' motivation and improve the pace of learning.

(ix) Training of all functionaries involved in the campaign is crucial to the success of the campaign. Training has to be primerspecific; it has also to be participative, communicative and a tool of continuous correction, upgradation and human resource development.

(x) Though the TLC is meant to impart functional literacy, it can be at the same time a campaign for universal enrolment and retention of children in schools, immunization, propagation of small family norms, promotion of maternity and child care, women's equality and empowerment, peace and communal harmony, etc.

An objective analysis of the strength, weaknesses and opportunities reveals that the greatest strength of the successful campaigns lies in providing a forum for political parties, representatives of the people and all sections of the, society to come and work together and pledge their unqualified solidarity and support to the campaign despite their ideological differences. The second important strength is that it has proved that learners, despite age and disability, despite social and cultural heterogeneity, despite class, caste and gender divide, can learn with a lot of self-confidence, joy and excitement. They can see for themselves the pace and progress of learning. They can retain and apply the benefits of learning to real life situations.

Campaigns for total literacy have, in this sense, promoted social and emotional integration. They have also promoted linguistic integration and communal harmony. Teaching-learning process in the campaigns has created and reinforced an awareness of the needs, rights and obligations. This awareness has manifested itself in enrolment and retention of children in the school system, immunisation of pregnant mothers and children, health, hygiene, environmental conservation, maternity protection, child care, ORT, small family norms, etc. Yet another strength of the campaign is that women are participating in the teaching-learning process in much larger number and with much greater enthusiasm than men. They have become more vocal, more articulate and more assertive of their needs than ever before. Their self-image and self-confidence have been boosted up beyond measure. Many women have learnt cycling and karate as they learn to read and write.

A number of grassroots level institutions such as village and panchayat level committees are emerging through which the learners can transform themselves from the status of passive beneficiaries to that of active participants in a cumulative proces and manage their own affairs with strength, courage and confidence. Campaigns have produced a unique confluence of creative forces and energies on a large scale. Creative writers, thinkers, artists, environmentalists, educational, social and women activists have come together to write songs, slogans, nukkad nataks and roleplays and to render them soulfully in large parts of the country. Yet another strength is that every activity in the campaign in general and in the learning centres in particular acquires the shape of a festival and every such occasion is fully harnessed to the advantage of literacy. The weaknesses emanate from the fact that factors conducive to the success of the campaign are not uniformly spread across along the districts; in districts where it was difficult to sustain continuity of leadership the campaign faulters and subsequent restoration is rather tough going. All said and done the TLCs have emerged as the most effective model and for the first time universal adult literacy seems to be an achievable objective rather than a hopeless dream.

### Post-literacy and Continuing Education

The strategy of post-literacy and continuing education in this scenario is two-fold. On the one hand, peoples' centres of learning (Jana Shikshan Nilayams) have been opened in several TLC districts and are fully operational. One such centre caters to five villages with a population of about 5,000 and provides for a library, a reading room, a forum for discussion, evening classes for upgradation of skills, simple and short duration training programmes in agriculture, animal husbandry and veterinary, soil management, sericulture, fisheries and other selfemployment programmes, cultural and recreational activities, a single window for information and communication, etc.

With shift in the strategy for imparting literacy from traditional centre-based approach to the mass approach, other modalities are coming to the fore. The most acceptable model which has been accepted by the TLC districts envisaged implementation of the programme with the help of a three legged administrative structure consisting of the people's participatory committees, the district administration, and the full-time functionaries. Learning centres consisting of 30-40 neo-literates are formed under the supervision of 3-5 volunteers. These centres are serviced by rural libraries which will also act as a resource and training support centres. Unlike JSNs these centres are purely volunteerbased. The value of these centres would become increasingly evident to not only the identified neo-literates but also to the community at large. It is for this reason that it is envisaged, and hoped, Out these centres would continue and eventually become community-owned.

The post-literacy campaigns will aim at taking the neo-literates, from dependent to selfguided learning stage and promote development of skills among the neoliterates. The centres will provide a nodal point for convergence of messages and services for all development, health and social welfare departments and schemes. The centres will thus act as an 'information window' to create awareness about the schemes for economic development, environment conservation, social empowerment, health, small-family norms, child care, nutrition and hygiene and legal entitlements. To the extent feasible, it will attempt through convergence of various development schemes like TRYSEM, etc., to provide training for income generation skills.

With a view to securing a transition for neoliterates from guided learning to self-learning and stabilising their literacy levels, a bridge primer (post-literacy 1) has been developed in different regional languages. This would require 30-40 hours of instructor-dependent learning and further lessons for self-learning. The bridge primer would be supplemented by further reading materials-graded books, periodicals, newspapers, etc. suitable to the learning needs and interests of neo-literates. Adequate opportunity would simultaneously be provided for unstructured learning through creation of a learning environment comprising wall-writing, posters, hoardings, etc. as also by opening up avenues of distance learning through open schools, radio/TV programmes, etc.

Some of the districts like Chittoor, Nellore, Burdwan and Midnapore have opened postliteracy (PL) centres and have taken pains to provide specially designed newspapers, supplementary readers (graded materials for neo-literates) and other reading materials (periodicals, neo-literates' newsletter, etc.) the content of which is a mix of functionality, awareness generation, recreation through light fiction/humour, etc. The process has just begun and would require considerable reinforcement and strengthening.

# Bibliography


Chapman, D.W., "Assessing Directions for International Development Assistance in Education", *International Review of Education,* 47(5) 459-476, 2001.

______________ ., "Trends in Educational Administration in Developing Asia", *Educational Administration Quarterly,* 36, 2, 283-308, 2000.

______________ . and Snyder, C.W. Jr., "Can High Stakes National Testing Improve Instruction?: Reexamining Conventional Wisdom", *International Journal of Educational Development,* 20(6), 457-474, 2000.

______________ ., "Trends in Educational Administration in Developing Asia", *Educational Administration Quarterly,* (36)2, 283-308, 2000.

______________ . and Snyder, C.W. Jr., "Can High Stakes National Testing Improve Instruction?: Reexamining Conventional Wisdom", *International Journal of Educational Development,* 20(6), 457-474, 2000.

______________ ., "Trends in Educational Administration in Developing Asia", *Educational Administration Quarterly,* 36, 2, 283-308, 2000.

______________ ., "The management and administration of education across Asia: Changing challenges", *International Journal of Educational Research,* 29(7), 603-626, 1998.

______________ ., & Adams, D., "The quality education in Asia: The perennial priority", *International Journal of Educational Research,* 29(7), 643-665, 1998.

______________ . and Adams, D., "The Quality of Education in Asia: The Perennial Priority", *International Journal of Educational Research,* 29(7), 643-665, 1998.

______________. and Austin, A.E. (Eds.), *Higher Education in the Developing World*, Westport, Conn: Greenwood Publishers, 2002.

Mestenhauser, J., R. Michael Paige, "Internationalizing Educational Administration" in *Educational Administration Quarterly*, Vol. 35, No 4 pp 500-517 Washington, D.C.: The University Council for Educational Administration, October 1999.

Roth, A., & Yang, B., "Theorising intelligence: Western and Eastern educational paradigms", *Educational Practice and Theory*, 19(1), 27-35, 1997.

# Index